International Trade and Transportation Infrastructure Development: Experiences in North America and Europe

International Trade and Transportation Infrastructure Development: Experiences in North America and Europe

Juan Carlos Villa
Research Scientist and Manager Latin America, Texas A&M
Transportation Institute (TTI), Mexico City, Mexico

Maria Boile
Professor, Department of Maritime Studies, University of Piraeus;
Director of Research, Hellenic Institute of Transport, Greece;
Senior Research Scientist, CAIT, Rutgers University, NJ, United States

Sotiris Theofanis
Chairman and Managing Director of ThPA SA, Port of Thessaloniki,
Greece; Senior Research Scientist, CAIT, Rutgers University, NJ,
United States

ELSEVIER

Elsevier
Radarweg 29, PO Box 211, 1000 AE Amsterdam, Netherlands
The Boulevard, Langford Lane, Kidlington, Oxford OX5 1GB, United Kingdom
50 Hampshire Street, 5th Floor, Cambridge, MA 02139, United States

Notices
Knowledge and best practice in this field are constantly changing. As new research and experience
broaden our understanding, changes in research methods, professional practices, or medical
treatment may become necessary.

Practitioners and researchers must always rely on their own experience and knowledge in evaluating
and using any information, methods, compounds, or experiments described herein. In using such
information or methods they should be mindful of their own safety and the safety of others, including
parties for whom they have a professional responsibility.

To the fullest extent of the law, neither the Publisher nor the authors, contributors, or editors, assume
any liability for any injury and/or damage to persons or property as a matter of products liability,
negligence or otherwise, or from any use or operation of any methods, products, instructions, or ideas
contained in the material herein.

British Library Cataloguing-in-Publication Data
A catalogue record for this book is available from the British Library

Library of Congress Cataloging-in-Publication Data
A catalog record for this book is available from the Library of Congress

ISBN: 978-0-12-815741-1

For Information on all Elsevier publications
visit our website at https://www.elsevier.com/books-and-journals

Publisher: Joe Hayton
Acquisitions Editor: Brian Romer
Editorial Project Manager: Michelle Fisher
Production Project Manager: Sujatha Thirugnana
                           Sambandam
Cover Designer: Greg Harris

Typeset by MPS Limited, Chennai, India

Contents

Part III
Trade and Transportation in Europe

5. Trade and transportation evolution in the European Union

Part IV
Trade and Transportation Future Trends

Preface

International trade tripled in the two decades between 1990 and 2010. This expansion is the result of sustained economic growth, as well as a strong increase in economic interdependence among countries, particularly in two trading blocs: North America and the European Union. Consequentially, world trade increased much faster than the transportation infrastructures that handle merchandise trade. Analyzing international trade flows in North America and the European Union, and the related development of transportation infrastructure, I realized that there was no single source of information that has documented how transportation infrastructure is planned, funded, built, and maintained in the three North American countries. This led me to the idea of writing this book with my experience in North America and I invited my colleagues, Maria Boile and Sotiris Theofanis, to enrich the content with European experience. This book also analyzes how supply chains have been evolving to serve trade demand and make better use of existing transportation infrastructure and international regulations.

When I started writing this book, I thought it would be a relatively easy task, given my more than 35 years of experience in the North American transportation sector, having worked in various transportation modes: roadways, rail, maritime, and land ports, as well as in various disciplines including planning, project development, technology implementation, infrastructure privatization, and trade and economic analyses. However, when I started analyzing the details of each topic it was overwhelming. The amount of information I processed and the pace of transformation triggered by recent trade wars, natural disasters, and major infrastructure changes, such as the expansion of the Panama Canal, became a larger task than anticipated.

I was able to conclude this work by defining a cut-off date for data analysis. However, recent events such as Brexit, the new NAFTA, or USMCA, and other events provide ample material for a continuation. I would not have been able to reach this point without the support of my family, particularly my lovely wife Carmen, who has stood by me not only through this endeavor, but also throughout our journey together, moving from country to country and multiple homes. This support has allowed me to participate in multiple transportation and trade-related projects that have contributed to this book. I would also like to thank all my friends and colleagues at the Texas A&M Transportation Institute for their support and the opportunity to share great work experiences that have helped in developing this book. Special thanks are given to Jose Manuel Ancona, who had the patience to work with me gathering and analyzing data, preparing charts and graphs for this book, and to Fernanda Villegas and Gary Amayo, who also helped in preparing charts and checking references. Thanks also to Arturo Becerra, my wife's colleague, who developed the book cover.

Juan Carlos Villa,
January 2020

Global trade has been growing fast during the last several decades, and it is expected to continue to grow, despite the recent slowdown. International and regional advances like those relating to the United States and the European Union have been coupled with other global and regional initiatives, including the recently emerging Chinese Belt and Road Initiative (BRI). These developments have shaped the existing transportation infrastructure and are creating a need for further network development and new transportation services and operations.

We were pleased to join our colleague Juan Carlos Villa in writing this book, providing our perspective and contributing to this tempting initiative. We understand this book and our contribution to be an ongoing and continuing effort in looking at the evolution of global trade and how it influences the development of global transportation infrastructure.

Special thanks go to Eleni Vargianiti and Angelos Aggelakakis for assisting us with the data gathering and analysis.

We would like to dedicate this book to our daughters, Ioanna-Myrto and Maro-Athina, thanking them for being who they are.

Maria Boile and Sotiris Theofanis,
January 2020

Part I

The Link Between Trade and Transportation

Chapter 1

Trade and transportation relationship

1.1 Introduction

International trade is the exchange of products and services between countries. In this book, we are referring to the trade of goods or cargo, which are products conveyed by some sort of transportation mode. Usually, transportation modes for international trade include water, air, or land. Land transport modes used for international trade are road (trucking) or rail. Usually, more than one mode of transport is used to ship freight from the point of origin in one country to the destination in the receiving country. The development of modal and intermodal transportation infrastructure that includes ports, inland terminals, warehousing facilities, and the like increases regional accessibility to global markets. *International multimodal transport* is defined as the carriage of goods by at least two different modes of transport, on the basis of a multimodal transport contract, from a place in one country at which the goods are taken in charge by the multimodal transport operator to a place designated for delivery in a different country. This definition is from the United Nations Convention on International Multimodal Transport of Goods (United Nations, 1980).

International trade has evolved throughout history. When local economies grew to a point that the products or commodities needed to satisfy domestic needs in order to continue its development were not available in the region, they started trading for resources produced outside their communities. Many nations flourished due to their trade capabilities, developing transportation infrastructure and procedures to make the movement of goods more efficient.

A *trade route* is a logistical network identified as a series of pathways and stoppages (links and nodes in a network) used for the commercial transport of cargo, including trade over bodies of water. Allowing goods to reach distant markets, a single trade route contains long-distance arteries, which may further be connected to smaller networks of commercial and noncommercial transportation routes (Burns, 2003).

International Trade and Transportation Infrastructure Development.
DOI: https://doi.org/10.1016/B978-0-12-815741-1.00001-2

Water modes were the first means of transporting goods, as roadway systems were not well developed. Mesopotamia had fertile basins on the borders of the Tigris and Euphrates Rivers that allowed this civilization to flourish and use its "water roadways" to import and export goods.

The most commonly known trade route is the Silk Road that connected the Eastern and Western worlds by land and sea. The name was coined by Ferdinand Freiherr von Richthofen, a German geographer, for the trade of Chinese silk. However, several authors contend that the spice trade with India and Arabia was far more consequential for the economy of the Roman Empire than the silk trade with China.

The Silk Road was not actually a single road, but a network of ancient trade routes across the Afro-Eurasian landmass that connected East, South, and West Asia with the Mediterranean and the European world, even with parts of North and East Africa. The Silk Road was a name applied to all the routes through Syria, Turkey, Iran, Turkmenistan, Uzbekistan, Kyrgyzstan, Pakistan, India and on to China (Fig. 1.1).

One clear example of the importance of trade in economic development comes from Europe around the year 1000, where issues with safety and security on mainland trading routes led to the development of important commercial routes along the coast of the Mediterranean Sea. An important maritime trade network connecting coastal cities in the Mediterranean gave these cities great power and spurred economic development. These so-called Maritime Republics, including Venice, Genoa, Amalfi, Pisa, and Republic of Ragusa,

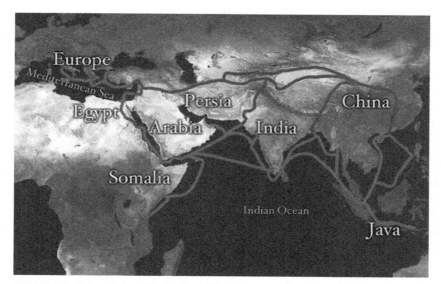

FIGURE 1.1 Map of the Silk Road trading routes. *Cartwright, M.* Globalizaton history. *<https://es.wikipedia.org/wiki/Historia_de_la_globalizaci%C3%B3n>*.

were "empires" along the Mediterranean shores. They monopolized European trade with the Middle East between the 8th and the 15th centuries. The main commodities that were traded included silk and spices, incense, herbs, drugs, and opium. The spice trade was very lucrative as spices were among the most expensive and demanded products of the Middle Ages. Muslim traders dominated the maritime routes throughout the Indian Ocean, sourcing the spices in the Far East and India and shipping them via maritime routes through Ormus in the Persian Gulf and Jeddah in the Red Sea. From there, overland trade was extended to the Mediterranean coast, where Venetian merchants then distributed the goods throughout Europe until the rise of the Ottoman Empire. In 1453 with the fall of Constantinople, Europeans were excluded from this important multimodal trade route (Wikipedia the Free Encyclopedia, 2019).

Another more recent example is the impact of the railroad on the geographic, economic, and political development of the United States. In 1869, the Transcontinental Railroad connected the entire continent east to west and expanded the market availability of goods. Items for sale on the US East Coast could be made available to the population on the West Coast. The railroad made it possible to transport goods in shorter times, increasing the variety of goods for people on the frontier. Railways also offered opportunities for entrepreneurs to start businesses to produce goods and to increase the supply of goods for sale. With the railroad, a product that might not have had enough demand in the local town could be shipped to different markets, increasing demand.

By the end of the 19th century, the United States was becoming an urban nation, and the railroads were supplying these urban areas with food, building materials, fuel, and other commodities. The railroads also allowed those cities to grow, first with steam-driven railroads and later with electric streetcars, moving people longer distances.

These are just a few examples of how trade helped developing cities, regions, and countries. The transportation system is an important element of efficient trade that increases the competitiveness of certain regions. However, freight transportation is demand driven; that is, the demand for the movement of goods will bring about the development of transportation systems.

The remaining of this chapter provides information on the relationship between trade and transportation development in North American and Europe.

1.2 The relationship between trade and the transportation system

The *transportation system* is the channel that handles trade. An efficient transportation system reduces the costs and travel time of goods handling, hence creating jobs not only in the transportation industry but also throughout all the sectors involved in the extraction, production, assembly, distribution, and sale of traded commodities. Exports of commodities create jobs and boost economic growth by forcing local industries to be more efficient and to compete in foreign markets.

The Industrial Revolution was a key turning point in the evolution of world trade. There was some progress in the 17th and 18th centuries, such as advancement in ship design that led to the opening of new markets in the Americas and Asia (Maddison, 2008). However, the new transportation technologies that were developed during the Industrial Revolution, such as steamships and the railways, triggered the expansion of trade around the world.

Steamships were the first revolutionary technology to transform transportation in the 19th century. A *steamship* is a type of steam-powered vessel, which can be ocean faring and seaworthy, that is propelled by one or more steam engines that typically turn propellers or paddlewheels. Initially, steamships carried only high-value freight on inland waterways, but a series of incremental technological improvements led to faster, bigger, and more fuel-efficient ships. This drove transportation costs down and opened the market for the movement of goods along transoceanic trade routes and handling not only high-value commodities but other bulk products as well. By the late 1830s, steamships were regularly crossing the Atlantic; by the 1850s, service to South Africa had begun; and, with the opening of the Suez Canal in 1869, which created an important shortcut to Asia, transoceanic steam shipping took over Far Eastern trade routes as well (World Trade Organization, 2018).

The second important transportation technology breakthrough from the Industrial Revolution was the railroad. Like steamships, the railroad also rapidly reduced trade transportation costs and connected inland regions, complementing the ocean and river connectivity that steamships provided. The Stockton−Darlington Railway (S&DR) route, operational in 1825, was the world's first freight rail line and was replicated in Great Britain and the rest of Europe. A transcontinental line linked the East and West coasts of the United States by 1869 (Findlay & O'Rourke, 2009), the Canadian−Pacific railroad was completed by 1885, and the Trans-Siberian Railway by 1903. By the end of the 19th century, rail lines were moving passengers and freight in Asia and in Latin America. Worldwide railway lines increased from 118,707 miles (191,000 km) in 1870 to nearly 6,325,000 miles (1 million kilometers) in 1913 (Fogel, 1964). Another technological development that increased the potential for distributing products by rail or steamship was the invention of refrigeration after the 1830s, which allowed for the transport of chilled meat and butter over great distances (Mokyr, 1992).

Even though it is not strictly transportation technology, the development of the telegraph in the mid-19th century was a key factor in the expansion of trade and international transportation. By the end of the 19th century, American-, British-, French-, and German-owned cables linked Europe and

North America in a sophisticated network of telegraphic communications. Telegraphs linked financial centers, facilitating world trade and leading to a surge in investment. It is estimated that trade grew approximately 55% and international trade costs for France, Great Britain, the United States and 18 other trading powers, fell 25% in the 1870-1913 period (Jacks, Meissner, & Novy, 2008).

After World War II, there was a second wave of international trade and of growth in economic development. The use of containerization contributed to a substantial decline in ad valorem transport charges—the cost of transport as a share of the value of the traded good—from around 10% in the mid-1970s to around 6% in the mid-1990s (Hummels, 2007). Intermodal rail transportation and the use of double-stack container movements by rail in North America and rail electrification in Europe were other transportation innovations that boosted the efficient movement of trade in the 20th century.

Containerization changed international trade

Containerization was a key factor in the expansion of world trade. The first shipping container was invented and patented in 1956 by an American named Malcolm McLean. McLean's efforts in convincing shippers and port authorities to move toward containerization allowed his trucking company to grow and for him to create SeaLand Industries. Containerization fundamentally transformed the centuries-old ways of the shipping industry to how we do things today. His efforts to increase efficiency resulted in standardized container designs that were awarded patent protection, which he made available by issuing a royalty-free lease to the Industrial Organization for Standardization (ISO). This move led to greater standardization, which helped in expanding the potential for intermodal transportation. In fewer than 15 years, McLean had built the largest cargo-shipping business in the world (Mayo & Nohria, 2005).

The standardized dimensions of containers in the ISO allowed them to be loaded, unloaded, stacked, and transported efficiently over long distances. Transfers among multiple transportation modes (ocean vessels, barges, rail, and truck) enhanced efficiency in the movement of goods. The handling system is mechanized, so handling is done with standardized cranes and forklift trucks (Lewandowski, 2016). All containers are numbered so they that can be easily identified, making inspection and sorting easier, and routing and transportation modes can be planned from the point of origin to the final destination.

Containerization changed the whole transportation industry and international trade. Ports had to be reconfigured to handle containers. However, some of them did not have the land required to expand the holding yards required to store loaded and empty containers. Some ports declined, like San Francisco, and others grew, like Oakland in California. Containerization also impacted the number of longshoremen required to handle cargo at the ports. Similarly, in the United Kingdom, the Port of London and Port of Liverpool declined in importance, while Felixstowe in the UK and Rotterdam in the Netherlands emerged as major container ports.

(Continued)

(Continued)

Containerization also transformed the trucking and rail transportation industries. Railroads developed railcars that allowed stacking containers on top of one another, doubling rail line capacity. The manufacturing industry was also impacted. Small shipments were grouped to fill a container, and pallets were designed to use as much space as possible in a container. The reliability of containerized shipments and the ability to track them also led to just-in-time manufacturing.

US domestic standard containers are generally 48 and 53 feet long for rail and truck transport. The basic dimensions and permissible gross weights of containers are presented in Table 1.1.

TABLE 1.1 Basic dimensions, weight, and load for ISO containers.

Specification		20-ft Container	40-ft Container	40-ft-High cube Container	45-ft-High cube Container
External dimensions	Length	19 ft 10.5 in	40 ft 0 in	40 ft 0 in	45 ft 0 in
		(6.058 m)	(12.192 m)	(12.192 m)	(13.716 m)
	Width	8 ft 0 in	8 ft 0 in	8 ft 0 in	8 ft 0 in
		(2.438 m)	(2.438 m)	(2.438 m)	(2.438 m)
	Height	8 ft 6 in	8 ft 6 in	9 ft 6 in	9 ft 6 in
		(2.591 m)	(2.591 m)	(2.896 m)	(2.896 m)
Internal volume		1169 ft^3	2385 ft^3	2660 ft^3	3040 ft^3
		(33.1 m^3)	(67.5 m^3)	(75.3 m^3)	(86.1 m^3)
Maximum		66,139 lb	66,139 lb	68,008 lb	66,139 lb
Gross weight		(30,000 kg)	(30,000 kg)	(30,848 kg)	(30,000 kg)
Net load		61,289 lb	57,759 lb	58,598 lb	55,559 lb
		(27,800 kg)	(26,199 kg)	(26,580 kg)	(25,201 kg)

Source: International Standard. *Series 1 freight containers—Classification, dimensions and ratings*. ISO 668:2013. <https://www.sis.se/api/document/preview/916460/>. International Standard. *Freight containers—Specification and testing—Part 1: General cargo containers for general purposes*. ISO 1496-1:2013. <https://www.sis.se/api/document/preview/916366/>.

Since Malcolm McLean introduced the idea of containerships in 1956, the shipping industry has been racing to produce the world's largest containerships within the boundaries of physics. As of 2019, the Maersk Madrid is the fourth largest

(Continued)

(Continued)

container vessel, with a 20,568-TEU capacity, a deadweight of 192,672 metric tons, measuring 399 m in length and 58.8 m in breadth (Marine Insight, 2019).

Madrid Maersk *By Kees Torn—SMIT ELBE & MADRID MAERSK, CC BY-SA 2.0. <https:// commons.wikimedia.org/w/index.php?curid = 63512816>.*

Other technological advances that also contributed to the expansion of trade around the world include the development of commercial civil aviation, the improvement of productivity in the merchant marines, and the democratization of the telephone as the main mode of communication. Fig. 1.2 shows costs of

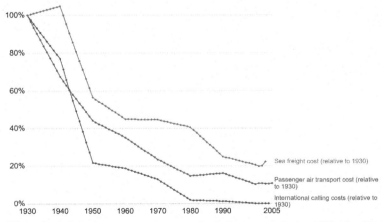

FIGURE 1.2 Decline of transport and communications costs relative to 1930. *Our World in Data.org. (2005). The decline of transport and communication cost relative to 1930. <https:// ourworldindata.org/grapher/real-transport-and-communication-costs?time = 1930>.*

these three variables since 1930 (Ospina-Ortiz, Beltekain, & Roser, 2018). International calling costs had the greatest cost decrease, impacting international trade as it reduces the costs of placing orders and tracking shipments.

Initially, firms sought to locate near their customers in order to reduce shipping costs. However, these transportation and communications improvements and other factors have led to the globalization of manufacturing and production, with the various production stages geographically separated based on identifying locations where labor-intensive segments of production could be performed in low-wage countries. One of the world's best examples of this phenomenon is in East Asia where the geographical distances are short compared to the vast wage differences (Baldwin, 2006). This has led to the expansion of global supply chains (GSCs) or global value chains (GVCs). It is estimated that more than 80% of global trade now takes place within the international production networks of multinational enterprises.

An example of a global supply chain is the production of cotton garments where the cotton is sourced in the United States and shipped to a mill in Japan, which then sends the product to a factory in Malaysia (see Fig. 1.3). A consolidator in Hong Kong sends final product shipments to distribution centers (DCs) all over the world

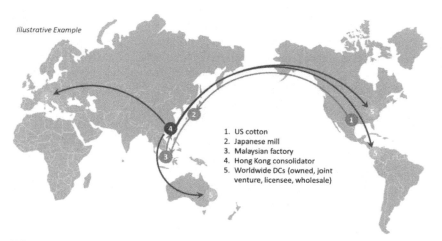

Illustrative Example

1. US cotton
2. Japanese mill
3. Malaysian factory
4. Hong Kong consolidator
5. Worldwide DCs (owned, joint venture, licensee, wholesale)

FIGURE 1.3 Example of a global supply chain. *Laughlin, S.* Transforming the global supply chain. *<https://www.ibm.com/blogs/think/2017/05/41097/>.*

The development and evolution of GSCs have led to a remarkable growth in trade among countries. The chart in Fig. 1.4 shows the value of world exports over the period 1800–2014 in constant prices (i.e., adjusted to account for inflation) and are indexed at 1913 values. Exports today are more than 4000 times larger than in 1913 (Ospina-Ortiz et al., 2018).

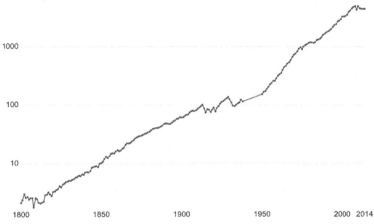

FIGURE 1.4   Value of global exports. *Ortiz-Ospina, E., Beltekian, D., & Roser, M.* Trade and globalization. *<https://ourworldindata.org/trade-and-globalization>.*

Transportation systems facilitate the movement of merchandise within a country and in international trade. A transportation system includes infrastructure, such as roadways, rail lines, maritime ports, land ports of entry, and airports, as well as physical assets, such as trucks, railcars, locomotives, and vessels. These components of the transportation system could be labeled as the *transportation supply*, or *hardware*.

The *software* part of the transportation system handling trade includes procedures and regulations that order the movement of freight internationally and within a country or a region. For example, containers have weight and dimension standards that facilitate handling them with similar equipment around the world. Regional standards and regulations also allow for a more efficient transportation system. In North America, the 53-foot trailer is commonly used in Canada, the United States, and Mexico to handle truck cargo, and equipment is interchanged among the three counties. However, other rules, such as the truck size and weight regulations, are not harmonized among the three North American counties. This lack of consistency introduces inefficiencies when transporting goods between countries. Mexican transportation regulations allow for the use of double trailers or long combination vehicles (LCVs) in high-specification roadways. In Canada, some provinces also allow LCVs, as do a small number of states in the United States.

Mexican regulations also allow for higher gross vehicle weight (GVW) than regulations in the United States or Canada. These differences create inefficiencies in truck-transported trade movement. For example, for shipments from Mexico into the United States that use LCVs, the double trailer has to be separated, requiring a tractor for each trailer, and two trips have to be made, congesting the land border crossings. Table 1.2 shows truck weight and length differences in Mexico, Canada, and the United States.

TABLE 1.2 Comparison of United States, Mexico, and Canada dimensional and weight limits for similar vehicles.

Vehicle		Limit	NOM-012-SCT-2-2017	Comparable US vehicle	Comparable Canadian vehicle[a]
T2-S1-R2		Weight metric tons (lb)	53.5 (117,700)	36.4 (80,000)	41.9 (92,200)
		Length meters (ft)	31.0 (102)	18.7 (61.5)	25.0 (82.0)
T2-S1-R3		Weight	61.5 (135,300)	NA	NA
		Length	31.0 (102)	NA	NA
T2-S2-R2		Weight	61.5 (135,300)	NA	NA
		Length	31.0 (102)	NA	NA
T3-S1-R2		Weight	62.0 (136,400)	NA	NA
		Length	31.0 (102)	NA	NA
T3-S1-R3		Weight	69.0 (151,800)	NA	NA
		Length	31.0 (102)	NA	NA
T3-S2-R2		Weight	69.0 (151,800)	48.0 (105,500) [RMD]	53.5 (117,700) [RMD]
		Length	31.0 (102)	29.0 (95)	31.0 (101.7)
T3-S2-R3		Weight	72.5 (159,500)	NA	NA
		Length	31.0 (102)	NA	NA
T3-S2-R4		Weight	77.0 (169,400)	58.6 (129,000) [TPD]	53.5 (117,700) [TPD]

		31.0 (102)	32.3 (106)	41.0 (134.5)
	Length			
T3-S2-S2	Weight	67.0 (147,400)	NA	NA
	Length	31.0 (102)	NA	NA
T2-S2-S2	Weight	58.5 (128,700)	NA	NA
	Length	31.0 (102)	NA	NA
T3-S3-S2	Weight	69.5 (152,900)	56.8 (125,000) [B-train][b]	62.5 (137,500) [B-train]
	Length	25.0 (82)	33.5 (110)	25.0 (82.0)

Mexican GVW figures correspond to high-specification highway classification limits.

NA, Not applicable.

[a]Limits according to Memorandum of Execution among provinces. Actual provincial limits vary.

[b]Usually operates under permit.

Source: Author with information from SEGOB. *NORMA Oficial Mexicana NOM-012-SCT-2-2017.* <https://www.dof.gob.mx/nota_detalle.php?codigo = 5508944&fecha = 26/12/2017>.

Mexican maximum GVWs are higher than those in the United States and Canada. The most common LCV in Mexico is the T3-S2-R4 with a maximum weight of 77 metric tons, compared to 58.6 for a similar combination in the United States and 53.5 in Canada. The LGVs in the United States and Canada are called turnpike doubles (TPD) and Rocky Mountain doubles (RMD).

The transportation network includes nodes and links that handle freight. *Links* include roadways, rail lines, waterways, and pipelines. *Nodes* include infrastructure such as maritime ports, international ports of entry, inland terminals, distribution centers, and the like. Usually, the nodes in the transportation network are where a transportation mode changes (i.e., vessel to rail or truck) or where a change in regulations take place, as in land border crossings. Fig. 1.5 presents a map of the US highway network with average speeds. Urban areas are the nodes where speed is reduced and cause delays, mainly due to interaction between trucks and passenger vehicles. Speed at the links is relatively good throughout most of the network

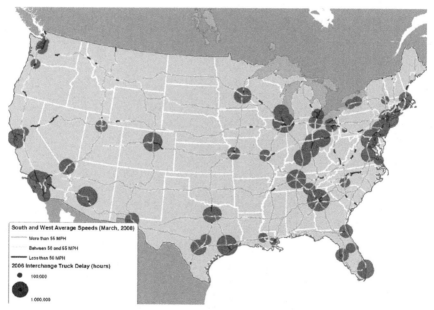

FIGURE 1.5 U.S. Interchange Bottlenecks and National Truck Speeds, 2006. *Federal Highway Administration, Estimated Cost of Freight Involved in Highway Bottlenecks, November 12, 2008. https://www.fhwa.dot.gov/policy/otps/freight.pdf.*

1.3 North American transportation system

The key transportation modes used for trade are waterways, railways, and roadways.

1.3.1 Waterways in North America

The United States has 25,000 miles of inland, intracoastal, and coastal waterways and channels, and approximately 12,000 miles constitute the commercially active inland and intracoastal waterway system maintained by the Corps of Engineers. The Mississippi River and its tributaries and the Gulf Intracoastal Waterway (GIWW) connect the Gulf Coast ports, such as Mobile, New Orleans, Baton Rouge, Houston, and Corpus Christi, with major inland ports, including Memphis, St. Louis, Chicago, Minneapolis, Cincinnati, and Pittsburgh. The Mississippi River from Baton Rouge to the Gulf of Mexico allows ocean shipping to connect with barge traffic, thereby making this segment vital to both the domestic and the foreign trade of the United States (US Army Corps of Engineers, n.d.).

In the Pacific Northwest, the Columbia–Snake River System allows navigation for 465 miles inland to Lewiston, Idaho (see Fig. 1.6). The other West Coast navigable river system in the United States includes the Sacramento and San Joaquin Rivers, the Snake River, and the Umpqua River, which are dredged for navigation. On the border of the United States and Canada, the Great Lakes–St. Lawrence waterways connect the North Atlantic Coast with the heartland and with the upper Mississippi River (Fig. 1.6).

Source: USACE Institute for Water Resources

FIGURE 1.6 Inland waterways of the United States. *IWR Report 2013-R-09, "Value to the Nation of the U.S. Army Corps of Engineers' Civil Works Programs: Estimates of National Economic Development (NED) Benefits and Revenues to the U.S. Treasury for 2010. https://www.iwr.usace.army.mil/Media/Images/igphoto/2000776558/.*

1.3.2 Railways in North America

The North American railway system is well developed and interconnected. All freight railroads have the same standard gauge (1435 mm or 4 ft $8^{1}/_{2}$ in), and none of them are electrified, which makes interconnection very efficient, allowing the interchange of railcars and locomotives. This leads to an integrated system that efficiently handles freight distribution in North America, connecting every major city and every maritime and land port of entry (Fig. 1.7). Just in the United States, the rail network is nearly 140,000 miles (225,000 km).

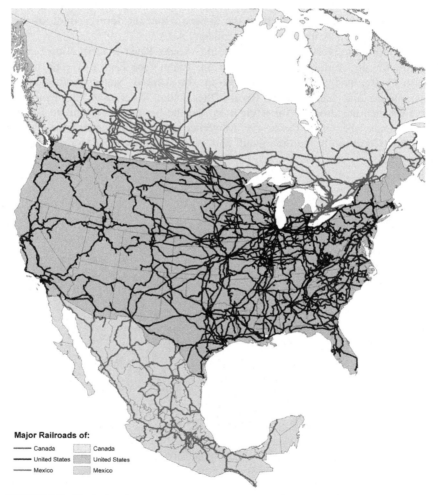

Major Railroads of:

—— Canada		Canada
—— United States		United States
—— Mexico		Mexico

FIGURE 1.7 North American railroad system. *Statistics from North American Transportation Atlas Database (NORTAD).* Texas A&M Transportation Institute with information from the Bureau of Transportation.

1.3.3   Roads in North America

North America's roadway network is very well developed in all three counties. In Canada, the National Highway System (NHS) was established in 1988 by the Council of Ministers Responsible for Transportation and Highway Safety and as of 2016 includes 38,049 km (23,642 miles) of highways, of which 95% is owned and operated by provincial and territorial governments. The provincial highways are the provincial equivalents to the United States' Interstate Highway system (Fig. 1.8).

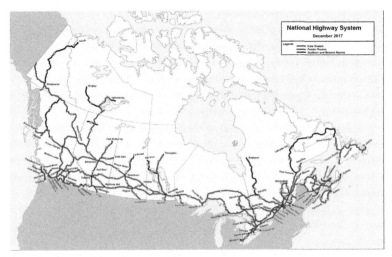

FIGURE 1.8   Canadian National Highway System. *Council of Ministers Responsible for transportation and Highway Safety.* Canada's National Highway System—Annual report 2016. *<https://comt.ca/english/nhs-report-2015.pdf>.*

The United States has the largest system in the world, with 6.4 million kilometers (4 million miles) of roadways, with approximately 75,360 km (46,830 miles) of those Interstate Highways, that is, mostly multilane, dual-carriageway freeways. US routes in the contiguous United States follow a grid pattern, in which odd-numbered routes run generally north to south and even-numbered routes run generally east to west. Usually, one- and two-digit-numbered routes are major routes, and three-digit routes are shorter spur routes from a main route. Odd numbers generally increase from east to west; The Dwight D. Eisenhower National System of Interstate and Defense Highways, commonly known as the Interstate Highway System, is a network of controlled-access highways that forms part of the National Highway System in the United States. Construction of the system was authorized by the Federal Aid Highway Act of 1956. The system extends throughout the contiguous United States and has routes in Hawaii, Alaska, and Puerto Rico.

US Route 1 (US 1) follows the Atlantic Coast, and US 101 follows the Pacific Coast. Even numbers tend to increase from north to south; US 2 closely follows the Canadian border, and US 98 hugs the Gulf Coast. The longest routes connecting major cities are generally numbered to end in a 1 or a 0 (US Department of Transportation, Federal Highway Administration, 2017); however, extensions and truncations have made this distinction largely meaningless (McNichol, 2006) (Fig. 1.9).

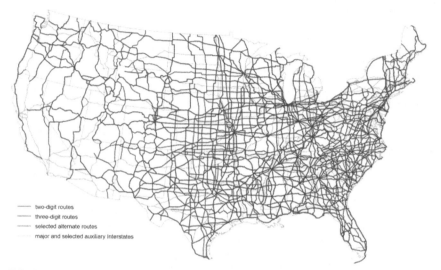

FIGURE 1.9   Map of US highway network. *Wikipedia the Free Encyclopedia.* Map of the current US routes. *<https://upload.wikimedia.org/wikipedia/commons/0/09/Map_of_current_US_Routes.svg>.*

In 2016, the Mexican National Highway Network (NHN) had 393,473 km (244,492 miles) or roadway. Thirteen percent of the NHN is the main Federal Network, 24% are feeder roads, 45% are rural highways, and 18% minor asphalt roads (Secretaría de Comunicaciones y Transportes, 2017). Mexico has an important network of toll roads (9818 km [6102 miles]) that link its major cities. Fig. 1.10 presents the key Mexican road trunk axes, or corridors. The 15 corridors link the Gulf Coast and the Pacific Ocean, as well as the northern and southern borders.

1.3.4   North American gateways

These roadway, railway, and waterway networks facilitate trade among the three North American counties and with other trading blocs. Approximately one-third US American trade takes place within the North American Free Trade Agreement (NAFTA) countries through land ports of entry. US trade

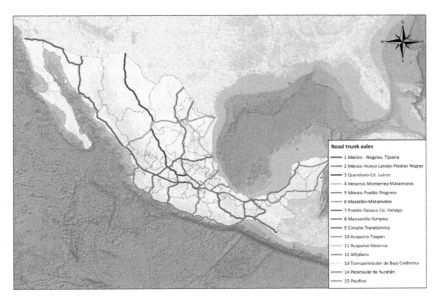

FIGURE 1.10 Mexican National Highway Network. *Statistical Yearbook of the Communications and Transportation Sector. (2016).* Felipe Ochoa y Asociados Consultores with data from Secretaría de Comunicariones y Transportes. <*http://www.sct.gob.mx/fileadmin/ DireccionesGrales/DGP/estadistica/Anuarios/Anuario_2016-old.pdf*>.

with Mexico and Canada by truck, rail, vessel, and air grew by 42% between 2006 and 2018. Trucking is the dominant mode of transport in North America with 71% of the total trade by value in 2018, followed by rail with 16% (Fig. 1.11).

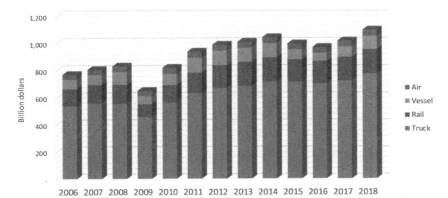

FIGURE 1.11 US trade with Canada and Mexico by mode 2006–18. *US Department of Transportation, Bureau of Transportation Statistics.* North American Transborder Freight Data. <*https://www.bts.gov/transborder*>.

Compared to Europe, trade by vessel among the United States, Mexico, and Canada is low due to regulations governing cabotage (the transport of goods or passengers between two places in the same country by a transport operator from another country). In the United States, maritime cabotage laws govern the transportation of goods and people between two ports, which generally restricts such transportation to US-flagged, US-crewed, US-built, and US-owned vessels. These US laws are commonly referred to as the Jones Act.

Canadian cabotage is ruled by the Coasting Trade Act 1992 (Government of Canada, 2019), which aims at promoting a level playing field by protecting Canadian shipowners from others that benefit from lower wage crews and/or lower safety standards. Foreign and non-duty-paid ships are prevented from operating in the cabotage market unless a license has been granted, which means that only Canadian-flagged and duty-paid vessels are allowed in the cabotage trades, and, on top of this, they must be manned by Canadian crews.

Mexican cabotage is restricted to Mexican shipping companies, which are exempted from licenses issued by the Communications and Transport Secretary and whose vessels are flagged under the Mexican pavilion (Cámara de Diputados del H. Congreso de la Unión de México, 2015). Because of these limitations, the movement of trade by vessel in North America is very low.

Trade by ports of entry (POE) in North America is concentrated in a very few POEs. In 2018, the total US trade with Canada and Mexico was $US1229 billion. Six POE's handled 53% of that trade: three at the US—Mexico border and three at the US—Canada border (Table 1.3).

TABLE 1.3 Value of US—Mexico, US/Canada trade 2018.

Port of entry	US$ million	Proportion (%)
Laredo, Texas	228,773	19
Detroit, Michigan	134,449	11
Port Huron, Michigan	89,325	7
El Paso, Texas	77,321	6
Buffalo, New York	71,090	6
Otay Mesa, California	46,804	4
Other POEs	580,976	47
Total	1,228,738	

Source: US Department of Transportation, Bureau of Transportation Statistics. *North American Transborder Freight Data*. <https://www.bts.gov/transborder>.

Trade figures for 2018 in North America are presented in Fig. 1.12.

POEs present trade imbalances due to import/export flows that can vary by season, as some commodities like fresh produce or grain cannot be stored for long periods. From Fig. 1.12, it is clear that there is a large trade imbalance at the Otay Mesa POE in California, with 63% US imports from Mexico and 37% US exports.

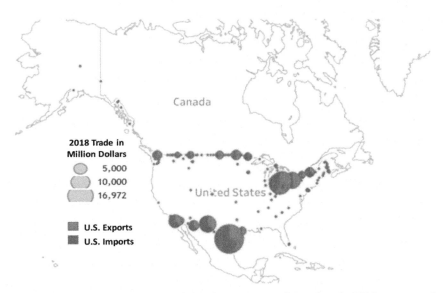

2018 Trade in Million Dollars
- 5,000
- 10,000
- 16,972

- U.S. Exports
- U.S. Imports

FIGURE 1.12 US–North American freight by port, commodity, and mode. *US Department of Transportation, Bureau of Transportation Statistics.* North American Transborder Freight Data. *<https://www.bts.gov/transborder>*.

1.4 European transportation system

Transportation is the basis of the European integration. It allows the free movement of goods, individuals, and services within the internal market. It contributes to the economy, employing around 10.5 million people (European Commission, 2017) and representing over 9% of the EU's gross value added. In the past, the transportation networks in Europe were designed largely from a national point of view. Today, the EU transport policy focuses on bringing member states closer together and on creating a Single European Transport Area comprising all types of transportation: road, rail, waterborne (Furst, 2012). To fulfill its goal, the EU created the Trans-European Transport Network (TEN-T) policy for the development of a Europe-wide network of roads, railways, inland waterways, maritime shipping routes, ports, airports, and railroad terminals. The Trans-European Transport Network consists of two planning layers: the Comprehensive Network, which covers all European regions and is expected to be completed by 2050, and the Core Network, which comprises the highest strategic connections of the most important nodes within the comprehensive network and is expected to be completed by 2030. The core network will connect 94 major ports with rail and road links.

1.4.1 Roads in the European Union

The EU's land transport policy aims to promote an efficient and environmentally friendly mobility and to develop a trans-European road network that guarantees users a high, uniform, and continuous level of services, comfort, and safety. The transport policy legislation establishes common rules among the member states and the harmonization of the maximum weights and dimensions of road vehicles.

The EU-28 has 5 million kilometers of paved road and 76,800 km of motorway network (European Commission, 2018). Fig. 1.13 highlights the Comprehensive and Core network, including roadways completed, scheduled to be upgraded, and new construction.

In a recent report (Pettersson, 2018), the Conference of European Directors of Roads (CEDR) presented statistics from 22 national road authorities, based on data provided on a voluntary basis in 2017. According to these data, of the 84,700 km of roadway network analyzed, approximately 42% are core roads and 58% are non−core roads and comprise approximately 61% of motorways and 39% of nonmotorway roads. Of these TET-T roads, 53%, or about 40,280 km, have more than two and up to four lanes, 20% have more than four and up to six lanes, and only about 3% have more than six lanes. About 18,570 km of these roads have only two lanes or less. Most of the roadways are situated in rural environments, while about 6850 km (about 8.9%) are located in urban areas and carry more traffic than rural roads.

1.4.2 Railways in the European Union

The EU-28 has 217,100 km of railway network, including 116,600 km of electrified rail lines (European Commission, 2018). The Trans-European Rail network comprises the Trans-European conventional rail network and the Trans-European high-speed rail network.

The Trans-European conventional rail network consists of lines intended for passenger services, lines intended for mixed traffic (passengers and freight), lines specially designed or upgraded for freight services, passenger hubs, freight hubs including intermodal terminals, and lines connecting these components.

FIGURE 1.13 Map of the EU roadway network. *European Commission.* Mobility and transport. *<https://ec.europa.eu/transport/themes/infrastructure_en>.*

The Western and Central European part of the railway network is better developed, compared to the Eastern, Northern, and Southern European part of the network. Overall, the nine rail freight corridors have a total length of about 48,900 km.

A schematic of the rail freight corridors in Europe is shown in Fig. 1.14, while a map of the European rail network is shown in Fig. 1.15.

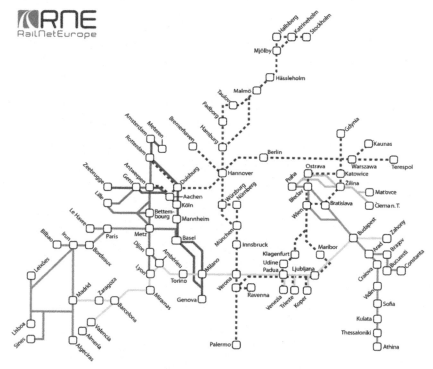

FIGURE 1.14 A schematic of the European rail freight corridors. *Rail NetEurope (RNE). Rail freight corridors general information. <http://rne.eu/rail-freight-corridors/rail-freight-corridors-general-information/>*.

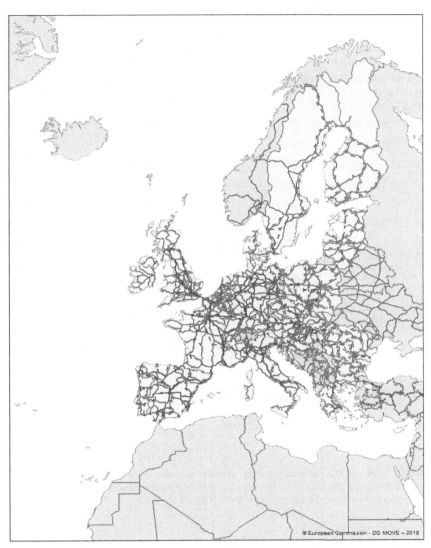

FIGURE 1.15 A map of the European rail network. *European Commission.* Mobility and transport. *<https://ec.europa.eu/transport/themes/infrastructure_en>.*

1.4.3 Inland waterways in the European Union

The European transport network comprises more than 70,000 km of inland waterways (European Commission, 2018), of which over 40,000 km are navigable, and about 20,000 km are accessible to 1000-tonne vessels.

An interconnected waterway network exists in 13 of the EU's member states. Most of Europe's industrial centers can be reached by inland navigation. The most vital inland waterway network is the Rhine−Danube with a length of 14,360 km.

The main types of goods transported on inland waterways are metal ores, coke, and refined petroleum products, as well as agricultural products (Wirtz, 2018) (for 2018). The share, in tonne-kilometers of various types of goods transported via the inland waterway freight system in Europe, is shown in Fig. 1.16.

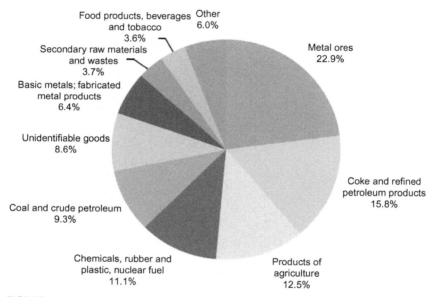

FIGURE 1.16 Inland waterways freight transport by main type of goods, EU-28, 2016. *Eurostat Statistical Books. (2018).* Energy, transport and environment indicators. *<https://ec. europa.eu/eurostat/web/products-statistical-books/-/KS-DK-18-001>.*

The modal share of inland waterways in freight transport in Europe ranged between 6.2% and 6.9% in 2016. In 2017, inland waterways shipped more than 558 million metric tons of cargo through the 250 inland ports.

A map of the European inland waterway transport network is shown in Fig. 1.17.

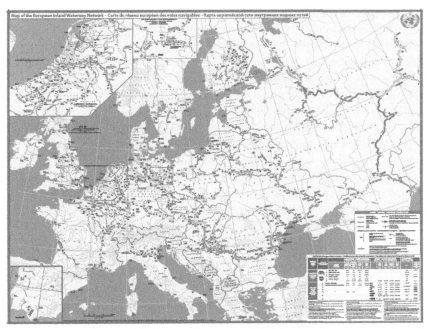

FIGURE 1.17   European inland waterway network. *The United Nations Economic Commission for Europe. (2012).* UNECE—European waterways. *<https://commons.wikimedia.org/wiki/File: UNECE-European-waterways-2012.jpg>.*

1.4.4   Ports in the European Union

Europe's ports are crucial for accommodating goods movement. In 2017, European ports handled 4 billion metric tons of freight, including 74% of extra-EU goods and 37% of the intra-EU freight traffic.

Over 1200 commercial ports operate along the EU's 70,000 km coasts (European Commission, 2019). The TEN-T system comprises 319 seaports that are characterized as essential for the efficient functioning of the internal market and the economy. These ports handle 96% of goods that transit through the EU ports. Of these, 83 are classified as core network ports.

The busiest container ports in Europe for the year 2018 are listed in Table 1.4. The table shows the top 15 container ports based on container throughput expressed in 1000 TEU.

TABLE 1.4 Top 15 container ports in Europe, 2018.

Rank	Rank	Port	2018	Growth
2018	2017		('000 TEU)	2017/2018
1	1	Rotterdam (NL)	14,513	5.7%
2	2	Antwerp (BE)	11,100	6.2%
3	3	Hamburg (DE)	8730	−1.0%
4	4	Bremerhaven (DE)	5467	−1.3%
5	5	Valencia (ES)	5104	5.6%
6	8	Piraeus (EL)	4908	20.9%
7	6	Algeciras (ES)	4772	8.9%
8	7	Felixstowe (United Kingdom)	4161	(2017)
9	10	Barcelona (ES)	3423	15.3%
10	9	Marsaxlokk (MT)	3310	5.1%
11	11	Le Havre (FR)	2884	0.0%
12	12	Genoa (IT)	2609	−0.5%
13	13	Gioia Tauro (IT)	2301	−6.0%
14	14	Southampton (United Kingdom)	1995	(2017)
15	−	Gdansk (PL)	1949	23.3%

Source: Adapted from Top 15 Container Ports in Europe in 2018. <http://www.porteconomics.eu/wp-content/uploads/2019/02/2019-Top15-container-ports-in-Europe-2018.png>.

Of the 20 ports highlighted in Fig. 1.18, 10 are located on the Mediterranean, eight on the North Sea coast, and two on the Atlantic coast.

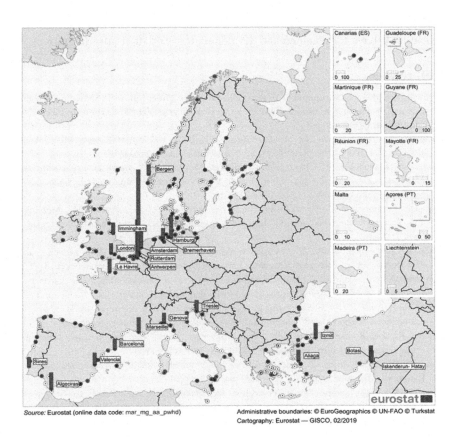

Source: Eurostat (online data code: mar_mg_aa_pwhd)   Administrative boundaries: © EuroGeographics © UN-FAO © Turkstat
Cartography: Eurostat — GISCO, 02/2019

Top 20 ports are named and their handling activity shown as bars.

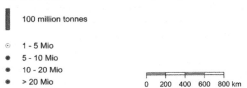

FIGURE 1.18   Top 20 cargo ports and other main cargo ports in 2017. *Eurostat Statistical Books.* Top cargo ports in 2017. *<https://ec.europa.eu/eurostat/web/products-eurostat-news/-/DDN-20190711-1>*.

1.5 Organization of this book

The following two parts of this book analyze the evolution of North American and European trade in these two regions, trade demand characteristics, and the transportation infrastructure, or the supply that serves the demand. The final part of the book provides an analysis of future implications that changes in global trade have for planning and developing transportation infrastructure.

References

Baldwin, R. (2006). *Globalisation: The great unbundling(s)*. Prime Minister's Office Economic Council of Finland. Retrieved from: https://repository.graduateinstitute.ch//record/295612/files/Baldwin_06-09-20.pdf.

Burns, T. S. (2003). *Rome and the Barbarians, 100 B.C.−A.D.400*. Baltimore, MD: Johns Hopkins University Press. Retrieved from: https://muse.jhu.edu/book/3464.

Cámara de Diputados del H. Congreso de la Unión de México. (2015, March 2). *Reglamento de la ley de navegación y comercio marítimos*. Retrieved from: <http://www.diputados.gob.mx/LeyesBiblio/regley/Reg_LNCM_040315.pdf>.

European Commission. (2017). *EU transport in figures Statistical Pocketbook 2017*. Mobility and Transport. Retrieved from: <https://ec.europa.eu/transport/sites/transport/files/pocketbook2017.pdf>.

European Commission. (2018). *EU Transport in figures Statistical Pocketbook 2018*. Mobility and Transport. Retrieved from: https://ec.europa.eu/transport/sites/transport/files/pocketbook2018.pdf.

European Commission. (2019, May 5). *Communication from the Commission to the European Parliament, the Council, the European Economic and Social Committee and the Committee of the Regions 2019 Communication on EU Enlargement Policy*. Retrieved from: <https://ec.europa.eu/neighbourhood-enlargement/sites/near/files/20190529-turkey-report.pdf>.

Findlay, R., & O'Rourke, K. H. (2009). *Power and plenty: Trade, war, and the world economy in the second millennium*. Princeton, NJ: Princeton University Press.

Fogel, R. W. (1964). *Railroads and American economic growth: Essays in econometric history*. Baltimore, MD: John Hopkins University Press.

Furst, T. A. (2012). Safety compass newsletter. *Safe Roads for a Safer Future Investment in Roadway Safety Saves Lives*, 6(3), 1−24. Retrieved from: https://safety.fhwa.dot.gov/newsletter/safetycompass/2012/winter/winter2012.pdf.

Government of Canada. (2019, April 10). *Coasting Trade Act*. Canada. Retrieved from: <https://laws-lois.justice.gc.ca/eng/acts/c-33.3/page-1.html>.

Hummels, D. L. (2007). Transportation costs and international trade in the second era of globalization. *Journal of Economic Perspectives*, 21(3), 131−154. Retrieved from: https://www.aeaweb.org/articles?id = 10.1257/jep.21.3.131.

Jacks, D. S., Meissner, C. M., & Novy, D. (2008). Trade costs, 1870−2000. *American Economic Review*, 98(2), 529−534. Retrieved from: https://pdfs.semanticscholar.org/d607/7c41ea1156332ccf94d5c4875a75f121d8f7.pdf.

Lewandowski, K. (2016). Growth in the size of unit loads and shipping containers from antique to WWI. *Packaging Technology and Science*, 29(8−9), 451−478.

Maddison, A. (2008). The west and the rest in the world economy: 1000−2030. *World Economics*, 9(4), 75−99. Retrieved from: https://www.researchgate.net/publication/237678324_The_West_and_the_Rest_in_the_World_Economy_1000-2030_Maddisonian_and_Malthusian_interpretations.

Marine Insight (2019, February 25). *Top 10 world's largest container ships in 2019.* Retrieved from: <https://www.marineinsight.com/know-more/top-10-worlds-largest-ontainer-ships-in-2019/>.

Mayo, A., & Nohria N. (2005, October 3). The Truck driver who reinvented shipping. *Harvard Business School Working Knowledge.* Retrieved from: <https://hbswk.hbs.edu/item/the-truck-driver-who-reinvented-shipping>.

McNichol, D. (2006). The roads that built America: The incredible story of the US interstate system ((p. 71)) New York: Sterling Publishing, ISBN: 1-4027-3468-9.

Mokyr, J. (1992). *The lever of riches: Technological creativity and economic progress.* Oxford: Oxford University Press.

Ospina-Ortiz, E., Beltekain, D., & Roser, M. (2018). Trade and globalization. *Our World in Data.* Retrieved from: https://ourworldindata.org/trade-and-globalization.

Pettersson J. (2018, October). *Trans-European Road Network, TEN-T (Roads) 2017 performance report. Conference of European Directors of Roads.* Retrieved from: <https://www.cedr.eu/download/Publications/2018/TEN-T-Performance-report-2017.pdf>.

Secretaría de Comunicaciones y Transportes. (2017). *Anuario Estadísitco Sector Comunicaciones y Transportes. 2016.* Retrieved from: <http://www.sct.gob.mx/fileadmin/DireccionesGrales/DGP/estadistica/Anuarios/Anuario_2016.pdf>.

United Nations. (1980, May 24). *United Nations Convention on International Multimodal Transport of Goods; Article 1 definitions.* Retrieved from: <https://www.jus.uio.no/lm/un.multimodal.transport.1980/doc.html#20>.

US Army Corps of Engineers. (n.d.). *Inland waterway navigation; Value to the nation.* Retrieved from: <https://www.mvp.usace.army.mil/Portals/57/docs/Navigation/InlandWaterways-Value.pdf>.

US Department of Transportation, Federal Highway Administration. (2017, April 7). *Ask the Rambler: What is the longest road in the United States?.* Washington, DC. Retrieved from: <https://www.fhwa.dot.gov/infrastructure/longest.cfm>.

Wikipedia the free Encyclopedia. (2019). *Maritime republics.* Retrieved from: <https://en.m.wikipedia.org/wiki/Maritime_republics>.

Wirtz, C. (2018). *Energy, transport and environment indicators.* Statistical Books Eurostat. Retrieved from: https://ec.europa.eu/eurostat/documents/3217494/9433240/KS-DK-18-001-EN-N.pdf/73283db2-a66b-4d34-9818-b61a08883681.

World Trade Organization. (2018). *World Trade Report 2018.* Retrieved from: <https://www.wto.org/english/res_e/publications_e/world_trade_report18_e.pdf>.

Part II

Trade and Transportation in North America

Chapter 2

Trade evolution in North America

2.1 Introduction

North America's trade evolution is directly interrelated with the North American Free Trade Agreement (NAFTA) that officially went into effect on January 1, 1994, creating the largest free market in the world. NAFTA's main goal was to eliminate tariffs in order to stimulate trade among its members (Bondarenko, 2019). Before NAFTA was implemented, Canada and the United States already had an agreement that had been implemented in 1987, the Canada–US Free Trade Agreement (CUSFTA). A few years later, CUSFTA was extended to include Mexico. The CUSFTA included the elimination of tariffs and the reduction of many nontariff barriers, and it was among the first trade agreements to address trade in services. It also included a dispute settlement mechanism for the fair and expeditious resolution of trade disputes (Government of Canada, 2018).

In the early to mid-1980s, after decades of protectionist trade and investment policies, Mexico was facing a severe debt crisis. The government started taking unilateral steps to open and modernize its economy. In 1986 Mexico joined the General Agreement on Tariffs and Trade (GATT), and policy changes enabled the country's economy to become one of the most open economies in the world. Mexico has now 12 free trade agreements (FTAs) involving 46 countries (Mexican Government's Ministry of Economy, 2015; for more information, see Villarreal, 2017).

This chapter presents a brief description of how trade tariff levels were modified over time during the implementation of NAFTA, key milestones of the treaty, and the side agreements on labor and the environment. A summary of NAFTA renegotiations during 2018 and 2019 and the potential implications for transportation are discussed. Statistical information on global and NAFTA trade is presented, with an emphasis on trade flows in the NAFTA bloc. The evolution of China's trade with the world and in particular with the United States is presented as a key component of world trade development. The final section of the chapter presents a description of offshoring and nearshoring and their impacts on NAFTA trade.

International Trade and Transportation Infrastructure Development.
DOI: https://doi.org/10.1016/B978-0-12-815741-1.00002-4

2.2 North America Free Trade Agreement tariffs and timeline

Some of the key NAFTA highlights that have a significant impact on North American trade and transportation practices include:

- *Tariff elimination for qualifying products.* Before NAFTA, tariffs of 30% or higher on export goods to Mexico were common, as were long delays caused by paperwork. Additionally, Mexican tariffs on US-made products were, on average, 250% higher than US duties on Mexican products. NAFTA addressed this imbalance by phasing out tariffs over 15 years. Approximately 50% of the tariffs were abolished immediately when the agreement took effect, and the remaining tariffs were targeted for gradual elimination. Among the areas specifically covered by NAFTA are construction, engineering, accounting, advertising, consulting/management, architecture, health care management, commercial education, and tourism.

  In 1993 the average of US duties for imports from Mexico was 2.07%, while Mexico's average tariffs on all imports from the United States was 10% (Canada's was 0.37%) (Executive United States. President, 1997; Mexican Government's Ministry of Economy, 2015). In agriculture, Mexico's trade-weighted tariff on US products averaged about 11%, and both countries' sanitary and phytosanitary (SPS) rules were impacting trade in 1993 (Villarreal & Fergusson, 2017). By 1996, US and Mexican tariffs were substantially reduced (Fig. 2.1).

- *Elimination of nontariff barriers by 2008.* This included opening the border and interior of Mexico to US truckers and streamlining border processing and licensing requirements. Nontariff barriers were the biggest obstacle to conducting business in Mexico that small exporters faced. Tariff reductions were also made for motor vehicles and auto parts and automobile rules of origin.

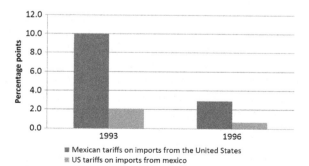

FIGURE 2.1 Average applied tariff levels in Mexico and the United States (1993 and 1996). *Data from Executive Office of the President. (July 1999).* Study on the operation and effects of the North American Free Trade Agreement. *p. 7. <https://digitalcommons.ilr.cornell.edu/cgi/viewcontent.cgi?article = 2939&context = key_workplace>.*

- *Reduced textile and apparel barriers.*
- *More free trade in agriculture.* Mexican import licenses were immediately abolished, with most additional tariffs phased out over a 10-year period.
- *Liberalized regulation of land transportation* (Inc., n.d.). Since the inception of NAFTA, US and Mexican officials have implemented several pilot programs to open the border for cross-border trucking. As of 2019, cross-border operations at the US−Mexico border have not changed much since before NAFTA. Chapter 4, Cross-border transportation infrastructure in North America (transportation supply), presents a description of how truck border crossings operated.

It is important to note the elimination of tariffs on several important commodities that are now the main supply chains in North America. For example, the auto industry partially eliminated tariffs in 1994 and eliminated the remaining tariffs in 2003. Mexican tariffs on US and Canadian corn were eliminated in 2008. In 2017 the renegotiation of the treaty started, and by the end of 2018, those negotiations were concluded (Fig. 2.2). As of May 2019, the new treaty, or US−Mexico−Canada Agreement (USMCA), has yet to be ratified by the three governments (McBrite & Foster, n.d.).

2.3 North America Free Trade Agreement side agreements on labor and the environment

The three NAFTA countries addressed labor and environmental issues in negotiating formal side agreements. On the same date that NAFTA went into effect, two other agreements went into force: the North American Agreement on Labor Cooperation (NAALC) and the North American Agreement on Environmental Cooperation (NAAEC). The creation of the NAAEC led to the creation of the Commission for Environmental Cooperation (CEC) in 1994. To alleviate concerns that NAFTA, the first regional trade agreement between a developing country and two developed countries, would have negative environmental impacts, the commission was mandated to conduct an ongoing ex post environmental assessment (Carpentier, 2006).

In terms of international trade and transportation, the CEC commissioned a study on "Sustainability and Freight Transportation in North America" (Texas Transportation Institute, Texas A&M University System, 2010) that served as the Foundation Paper section of a larger report by the CEC under Article 13, "Towards Sustainable Freight Transportation in North America" (Communications Department of the CES Secretariat, 2011). The objective of the Foundation Paper was to provide basic facts and figures on the freight transportation system in North America, as they relate to greenhouse gas (GHG) emissions, along with an overview of the related issues that exist or are expected to arise. In 2011 the CEC Secretariat published "Destination

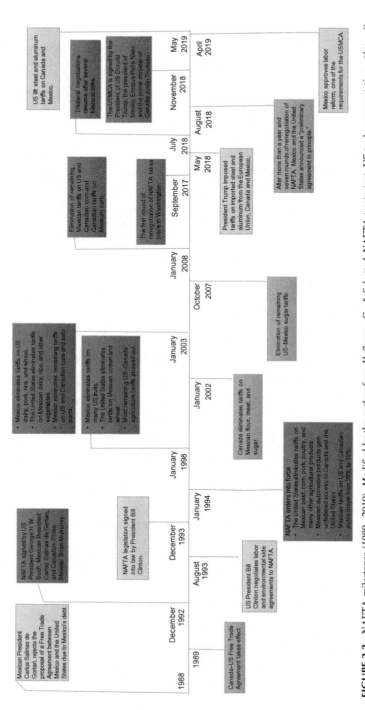

FIGURE 2.2 NAFTA milestones (1989—2019). *Modified by the author from Hufbauer, C., & Schott, J. NAFTA treaty text, US trade representative. <https://fas.org/sgp/crs/row/R42965.pdf>.*

Sustainability: Reducing Greenhouse Gas Emissions from Freight Transportation in North America," which calls for urgent cross-border cooperation to improve the environmental performance of the North American freight system. The report argues that cross-border cooperation measures are necessary not only to enhance environmental sustainability and reduce GHG emissions but also to keep North America competitive with other trade blocs. The report makes six principal recommendations along the following themes:

- Coordination and Networking
- Carbon Pricing and System Efficiency Strategies
- Investments to Improve the Efficiency of the Freight Transportation System and Promote Advanced Technologies
- Supply-chain Management
- Training Eco-drivers
- Gathering and Sharing Data

The labor and environmental side agreements included language to promote cooperation on labor and environmental matters, as well as provisions to address a party's failure to enforce its own labor and environmental laws. The side agreements included dispute settlement processes as a last resort. These processes may impose monetary assessments and sanctions to address a party's failure to enforce its laws (Bolle, 2016; Tiemann, 2004). NAFTA marked the first time that labor and environmental provisions were associated with an FTA. For many, it represented an opportunity for cooperating on environmental and labor matters across borders and for establishing a new type of relationship among NAFTA partners (Gildenhorn & Metzner, 2005).

In addition to the two trilateral NAFTA side agreements, Mexico and the United States entered into a bilateral side agreement related to border environmental cooperation.[1] In this agreement, the two governments committed to cooperate on developing environmental infrastructure projects along the US−Mexico border to address problems regarding the degradation of the environment due to increased economic activity. The agreement established two organizations to work on these issues: the Border Environment Cooperation Commission (BECC), located in Juárez, Mexico, and the North American Development Bank (NADBank), located in San Antonio, Texas. The sister organizations work closely together and with other partners at the federal, state, and local levels in the United States and Mexico to develop, certify, and facilitate financing for water and wastewater treatment, municipal solid waste disposal, and related projects on both sides of the US−Mexico border region (Villarreal & Fergusson, 2017). In 2017 these

---

1. The Agreement Between the Government of the United States of America and the Government of the United Mexican States Concerning the Establishment of a Border Environment Cooperation Commission and a North American Development Bank, November 1993.

two institutions merged into a single institution. The integration preserves the mission, purposes, and functions of both organizations, including their environmental mandate and geographic jurisdiction. NADBank finances environmental infrastructure projects that benefit the residents of the border. Transportation is not an approved sector for NADBank; however, air quality and public transportation are, and most of the air quality projects include paving and roadway improvements to reduce emission.

2.4   North America Free Trade Agreement renegotiation and potential implications for transportation

On October 1, 2018, after 14 months of negotiation, the United States, Canada, and Mexico reached an agreement in principle on a revised NAFTA. The new agreement was renamed the United States—Mexico—Canada Agreement (USMCA).

The final deal has to be ratified by the three countries, but the existing documents indicate that several key industries might change.

2.4.1   Auto industry

Two main changes could impact the North American auto industry. The first one is the provision requiring 75% (up from 62.5% in NAFTA) of the parts going into a vehicle being made in North America to qualify for tariff-free treatment. The intention of this clause is to boost auto production in North America.

The second important change is the requirement for 40%—45% of a vehicle to be made by workers earning at least US$16 an hour. This measure is aimed to discourage auto firms from shifting work to Mexico, where wages are much lower than in the United States or Canada.

2.4.2   Canada's dairy industry

The US will be able to export the equivalent of 3.6% of Canada's dairy market, up from the existing level of about 1%. This measure also scraps a Canadian milk-pricing policy that was negatively impacting US producers in US states like Wisconsin and New York.

2.4.3   Technological companies and online trade

The new USMCA agreement raises duty-free shopping limits to US$100 to enter Mexico and C$150 (US$115) to enter Canada without facing import duties. This is higher than the US$50 previously allowed by Mexico and C$20 permitted by Canada.

This measure will be good for Mexican and Canadian shoppers and for shipping companies and e-commerce firms. It is expected that delivery time will be reduced by having fewer customs inspections.

2.4.4   Steel and aluminum tariffs

In June 2018 the Trump administration imposed a 25% tariff on steel and 10% duties on aluminum imports from key allies in Europe, as well as from Canada and Mexico. On May 17, 2019, the Trump Administration lifted the steel and aluminum tariffs on Canada and Mexico. This change clears a key hurdle for ratification of Trump's replacement for NAFTA with the new USMCA after officials from Canada and Mexico had been adamant that they would not ratify the new agreement until the metal tariffs were removed.

2.5   Global and North America Free Trade Agreement trade

2.5.1   Global trade

The three most important trade blocs worldwide are Asia, the European Union, and the North American counties under NAFTA. The world's merchandise trade reached close to US$36 trillion in 2017, growing at an annual average of 6.6% in the 1993–2017 period. China's trade grew at a higher rate than any other trade bloc, with a 13.5% annual average, while the European Union's trade grew at an annual average rate of 5.9%, followed closely by NAFTA at 5.8% in the same period.

In 2017 the 28 members of the European Union traded one-third (US$11,782 billion) of total world merchandise trade, while NAFTA accounted for 15.8% (US$5661 billion), and China traded 11.5% (US$4105 billion) in the same period (World Trade Organization, International Trade and Market Access Online, 2018) (Fig. 2.3).

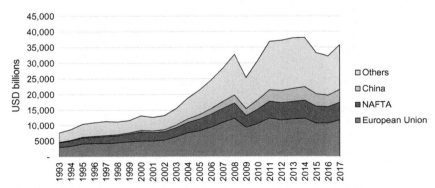

FIGURE 2.3   Global total merchandise trade. *Developed by the author with data from World Trade Organization.* Global total merchandise trade. *<http://stat.wto.org/StatisticalProgram/ WSDBViewData.aspx?Language = E>.*

The European Union is the largest trading bloc with US$11,782 billion in total merchandise trade in 2017 and relatively balanced trade (imports and exports). The second largest trade bloc is North America (United States, Canada, and Mexico) with US$5660 billion in merchandise trade, with the United States contributing to 70% of the total trade of the block. The North American merchandise trade has a negative trade balance, with the United States as the largest contributor to this deficit. China's total merchandise trade was US$4078 billion in 2017, with a positive trade balance. The two accompanying figures (Figs. 2.4 and 2.5) depict merchandise trade by major economy.

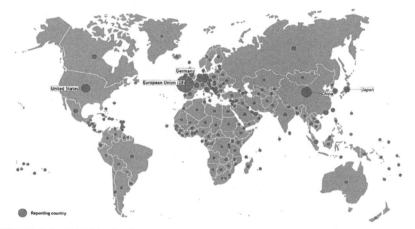

FIGURE 2.4 2017 Merchandise export trade. *World Trade Organization.* International Trade and Market Access Online. *<https://www.wto.org/english/res_e/statis_e/statis_bis_e.htm?>*.

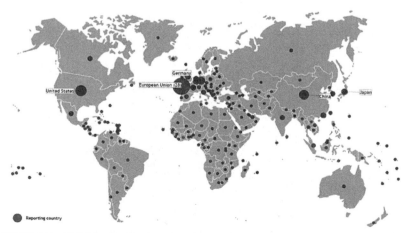

FIGURE 2.5 2017 Merchandise import trade. *World Trade Organization.* International Trade and Market Access Online. *<https://www.wto.org/english/res_e/statis_e/statis_bis_e.htm?>*.

The amount of trade in the EU could be attributed to its large manufacturing production and economic development, as well as its efficient transportation system with efficient waterways, ports, roadways, and rail lines. The United States and China are major players in international trade with strong economies. On the other hand, the southern hemisphere does not have a significant trade bloc.

2.5.2   Trade in the North America Free Trade Agreement Bloc

Total trade of the three NAFTA partners grew 4 times in the 24-year period between 1993 and 2017, from US$293 to US$1190 billion (Fig. 2.6).

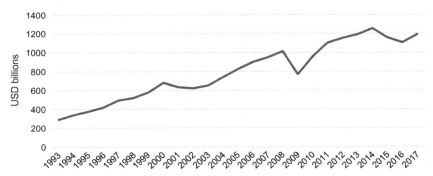

FIGURE 2.6   Intra-NAFTA trade. *Developed by the author with data from United States Census Bureau.* US International Data. *<https://www.census.gov/foreign-trade/data/index. html>.*

Since 1993, US−Mexico trade grew faster than US−Canada trade or trade with other non-NAFTA countries (United States Census Bureau, n.d.). In 2016 after the European Union, Canada was the leading market for US exports, followed by Mexico. Canada and Mexico accounted for 34% of total US exports in 2016. Canada and Mexico ranked third and fourth for US imports, respectively, after China and the EU together. Canada and Mexico accounted for 26% of total US imports (World Trade Organization, International Trade and Market Access Online, 2019) (Fig. 2.7).

The trade between Canada and Mexico is relatively low, compared with their trade with the United States. In 2017 total Canada−Mexico trade was US$26.83 billion with 70% being Mexican exports to Canada. The largest importer and exporter of the three North American countries is the United States with US$477 billion exports and US$624 billion in imports (Fig. 2.7) (Simoes, 2017).

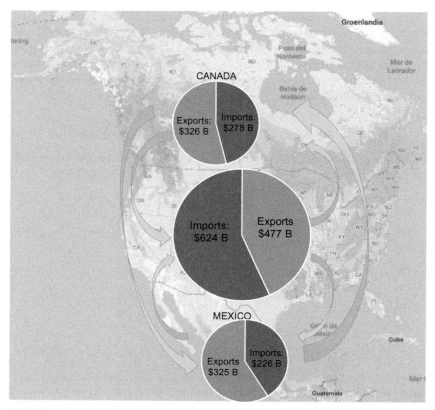

FIGURE 2.7 Trade among North American partners (2017). *Developed by the author with information from the Observatory of Economic Complexity.* Trade among North American partners. *<https://atlas.media.mit.edu/en/resources/data/>*.

North American industries are extremely interrelated. An example is the auto industry, which is the top commodity group in trade among the three countries. Top US imports from Mexico include 9.7% of cars, 7.5% vehicle parts and accessories, and 7.5% trucks and vans. The largest US export commodity category to Mexico is also auto industry related, with 7% vehicle parts and 2.2% accessories and motor vehicle piston engines. US imports from Canada are also concentrated in the same industries with cars representing 14%, and US exports with 18.3% of the total in vehicle parts and accessories, cars, trucks and vans, and motor vehicle piston engines (Simoes, 2017).

As previously mentioned, the United States and Canada already had a trade agreement before NAFTA went into effect. Therefore most of the trade-related effects of NAFTA may be attributed to changes in trade with Mexico. It is important to note that other factors, such as economic growth patterns, also have an impact on trade flows.

Canada and Mexico are highly dependent on US trade, with close to two-thirds of its merchandise trade with the United States. On the other hand, only 30% of US trade is with its two NAFTA partners (Fig. 2.8) (Pérez Ludeña, 2019).

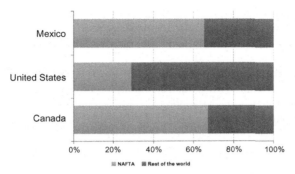

FIGURE 2.8 Canada, United States, and Mexico: intraregional imports and exports as a percentage of 2018 totals. *Data from Pérez, M. (2019).* Vínculos Productivos en América del Norte (LC/MEX/TS.2019/5). *Comisión Económica para América Latina y el Caribe (CEPAL). p. 12.*

2.6   China's trade evolution

2.6.1   China's trade with the world

In June 1971 US President Richard Nixon officially ended the US trade embargo with China, eliminating the legal barriers that had negatively impacted the economic interaction between the two nations since 1950. Between 1971 and 1980, barriers to the flow of goods were lifted, leading to a new trade relationship between the United States and China that allowed China to enter the world economy (Council on Foreign Relations, 2019).

The US–China Relations Act of 2000 provided great benefits to the US–China relationship since it established the following: "To authorize extension of nondiscriminatory treatment (normal trade relations treatment) to the People's Republic of China, and to establish a framework for relations between the United States and the People's Republic of China" (Government Publishing Office of the U.S., 2000). This Act prepared the way for China to join the World Trade Organization (WTO) in 2001.

Deng Xiaoping led China through extensive market-economy reforms by implementing a new brand of thinking that combined socialist ideology with free enterprise, or "socialism with Chinese characteristics." Deng opened China to foreign investment and the global market, policies that led China to become one of the fastest-growing economies in the world (Dernberger, 1993).

One of the key reforms was the adoption of the Industrial Responsibility System in the 1980s that promoted the development of state-owned enterprise by allowing individuals or groups to manage the enterprise by contract.

Private businesses were allowed to operate for the first time since the Communist takeover, and they gradually began to make up an increasing percentage of industrial output (Evans, 1995). One of the key strategies that allowed China to become a trade power was the creation of Special Economic Zones (SEZs) in the 1980s. The SEZs attracted foreign capital by exempting them from taxes and regulations, and they were expanded to cover the entire Chinese coast, drastically increasing foreign direct investment (Bransetter & Lardy, 2008).

China's world trade grew more than 20 times in the 1993−2017 period. The compound annual growth rate of China's total trade in the 1993−2001 period, before China joined the WTO, was 15%. In the same 8-year period from 2002 to 2009, the average annual growth rate of China's trade with the world was 23%. In 1993 China had a trade deficit of US$12 billion, and in 2017, China's trade with the world had a surplus of US$421 billion (Fig. 2.9).

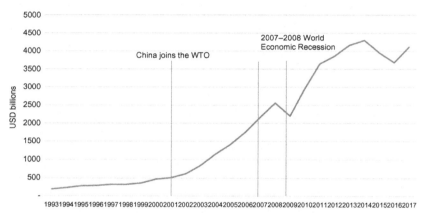

FIGURE 2.9 China total trade. *Developed by the author with data from The Observatory of Economic Complexity.* China Total Trade. *<https://atlas.media.mit.edu/en/profile/country/chn/>*.

2.6.2 US−China trade

US−China trade is the largest bilateral trade in the world, with a historical peak in 2018 of US$660 billion. Trade balance was positive for the United States until 1985, and since then the deficit has grown to a maximum of US$419 billion in 2018 or 64% (United States Census Bureau). Since President Trump took office, the United States has been negotiating with China with the aim of reducing the trade deficit, imposing tariffs on China's imports to the United States (Fig. 2.10).

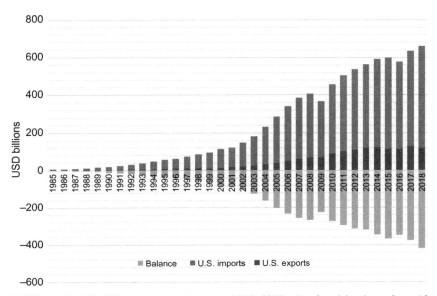

FIGURE 2.10 US–China imports and exports (1985–2018). *Developed by the author with information from the United States Census Bureau. https://www.census.gov/foreign-trade/balance/c0004.html.*

2.6.2.1 Key US–China trade commodities: China's exports

US–China trade has evolved in terms of the commodity mix. An analysis of the 1995–2005 and 2005–15 periods shows that the top commodities have changed drastically, particularly for China's exports to the United States (Table 2.1 and Fig. 2.11). For example, "Textiles," an important export to the United States in 1995, by 2005 and 2015, was not part of the top key commodities. "General industrial machinery and equipment, and parts" did not figure in the top 10 export commodities in 1995, and by 2015 it was ranked as the seventh export commodity with a total value of US$16.3 billion. This represents a growth of 184%. Similarly, "Road vehicles" was not part of the top 10 exports in 1995 or in 2005, and by 2015 it was the eighth largest export with a value of US$14.7 billion, with a growth of 549% in the 2005–15 period (Simones, 2017).

In the 3 years of analysis, only five of China's export commodity groups have maintained constant growth: "Power generating machinery and equipment," "Telecommunications, sound recording and reproducing equipment," "Electric machinery, apparatus and appliances, and parts," "Articles of apparel and clothing accessories," and "Footwear."

One group of China's export commodity groups grew at a much slower pace than the total trade. For example, the "Textile yarn, fabrics, made-up

TABLE 2.1 Top China's exports to the United States (US$ billions).

Commodity group (SITC code)	1995	2005	2015
Power generating machinery and equipment	2.70	38.82	54.58
Telecommunications, sound recording, and reproducing equipment	3.97	31.26	48.54
Electric machinery, apparatus and appliances, and parts	3.23	18.07	38.43
Articles of apparel and clothing accessories	5.55	18.91	35.84
Furniture and parts thereof	0.89	13.79	19.33
Manufactures of metals	1.22	9.94	18.11
General industrial machinery and equipment, and parts	–	5.77	16.39
Road vehicles	–	–	14.80
Footwear	5.42	11.85	13.98
Textile yarn, fabrics, made-up articles, and related products	1.10	5.48	–
Travel goods, handbags, and similar containers	1.54	–	–
Others	17.85	78.22	138.69
Total	43.48	232.11	398.69

articles and related products" commodity category was in the top 10 exports in 1995, and by 2015 it was not relevant, compared to other commodities. Similarly, the "Luggage industry" was in seventh place among China's exports and by 2015 is not in the top commodities traded. "Footwear" showed the lowest growth, mainly because this industry is moving to other countries, for example, Vietnam, India, Indonesia, Malaysia, and other countries that are still located in the Asian continent (Fig. 2.12).

2.6.2.2 Key US−China trade commodities: China's imports

China's imports from the United States have increased at a slower pace than exports. Some commodity groups that, in 1995 or 2005, were not relevant to the binational trade recently increased substantially. For example, "Power generating machinery and equipment" and "Road vehicles" together have a value of US$17.7 billion. The key product within the "Other transport

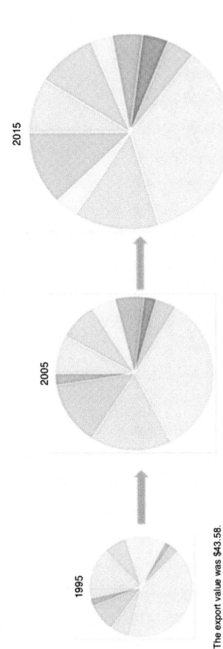

1995

The export value was $43.58.

2005

The export value was $23.28.

2015

The export value was $399B.

* Articles of apparel and clothing accessories
* Footwear
* General Industrial machinery and equipment, and parts
* Others
* Road vehicles
* Textile yarn, fabrics, made-up articles, and related products

* Electric machinery, apparatus and appliances, and parts
* Furniture and parts thereof
* Manufactures of metals
* Power generating machinery and equipment
* Telecommunications, sound recording and reproducing equipment
* Travel goods, handbags, and similar containers

FIGURE 2.11 Top China's exports to the United States by Commodity Group (1995, 2005, and 2015). *Developed by the author with information from the World Trade Organization. (2018). World Trade Statistical Review. <https://www.wto.org/english/res_e/statis_e/wts2018_e/wts2018_e.pdf>.*

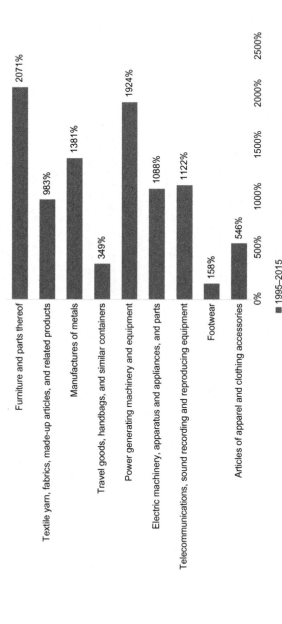

FIGURE 2.12 China's exports to the US growth rates (1995–2015). *Developed by the author with information from the Observatory of Economic Complexity.* China's exports to the U.S. growth rates (1995–2015). *<htps://atlas.media.mit.edu/en/profile/country/chn/>.*

equipment" classification is "aeronautics." "Oil seeds and oleaginous fruit" is an important commodity group of US exports to China, with soybean oil the largest product with a record figure of US$12.7 billion in 2015, when in 1995 it was worth only US$48 million (Table 2.2).

TABLE 2.2 Top China's imports from the United States (US$ billions).

Commodity group (SITC code)	1995	2005	2015
Electric machinery, apparatus and appliances, and parts	0.60	6.28	18.98
Other transport equipment	0.78	3.17	17.74
Oil seeds and oleaginous fruit	0.48	2.85	12.71
Road vehicles	0.23	0.75	13.14
Professional, scientific, controlling instruments, apparatus	0.57	2.46	8.23
General industrial machinery and equipment, and parts thereof	0.86	2.51	5.77
Artificial resins and plastic materials, and cellulose esters, etc.	0.64	2.25	5.52
Machinery specialized for particular industries	1.05	1.45	5.78
Power generating machinery and equipment	0.43	1.51	4.48
Textile fibers (not wool tops) and their wastes (not in yarn)	1.03	1.56	4.65
Metalliferous ores and metal scrap	0.28	2.16	4.38
Organic chemicals	0.38	1.99	3.26
Office machines and automatic data processing equipment	0.54	1.95	1.15
Fertilizers, manufactured	1.17	0.39	0.06
Telecommunications, sound recording and reproducing equipment	0.90	0.84	0.70
Maize, unmilled	0.71	0.003	0.12
Wheat and meslin, unmilled	0.64	0.09	0.20
Others	6.14	16.53	57.61
Total	16.62	46.79	156.75

Between 1995 and 2015, four commodity groups had negative growth rates:

- Fertilizers
- Maize
- Wheat and meslin
- Telecommunications, sound recording and reproducing equipment

On the other hand, three commodities had high growth:

- Electric machinery
- Road vehicles
- Oil seeds

Particularly the oil seeds group, which includes soybean oil, had a tremendous growth in the last 20 years (Fig. 2.13).

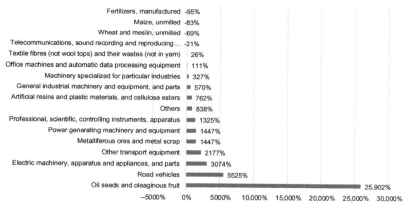

FIGURE 2.13 China's imports from the US Growth Rates (1995–2015). *Developed by the author with information from the Observatory of Economic Complexity.*

US−China trade is handled mostly by ports on the US West Coast, except for oil seeds and grains that are handled by ports in the Gulf of Mexico. Container movement in the West Coast Ports follow similar growth rates as in US−China trade. From 1995 through 2018, loaded container movement in the port of Los Angeles grew 3.26 times. Container trade imbalance has also grown substantially. In 1995 the proportion of US import containers was 60%, and in 2018 it grew to 72%. The largest loaded container trade imbalance at the Port of Los Angeles was in 2004, when it reached 78% (Fig. 2.14).

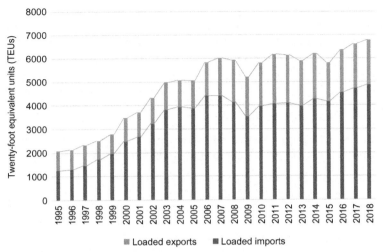

FIGURE 2.14 Port of Los Angeles Container Trade (1995−2018). *Developed by the author with information from the World Trade Organization.* World Trade Statistical Review 2018. <*https://www.wto.org/english/res_e/statis_e/wts2018_e/wts2018_e.pdf*>.

2.7   Impacts of offshoring and nearshoring in North American Free Trade Agreement trade

Offshoring can be defined as the moving of various company operations to another country for reasons such as lower labor costs or more favorable economic conditions in that other country (Webb, 2019). Several decades ago, companies started to transfer operations from North America to Asia, particularly China, because it offered several advantages:

- There was a plentiful supply of workers in China with a steady stream of rural−urban migrants in search of work.
- High unemployment rates drove wages down.
- China developed special economic zones that offered incentives such as reduced tax rates to set up manufacturing operations.

The trend started to revert as wages in China increased to the point that they were no longer enough of an advantage to balance other disadvantages, such as higher logistics costs due to the distance from the North American markets. A company transferring to countries closer to the market is said to be *nearshoring*, which is the transfer of business processes to companies in a nearby country, where producer and consumer expect to benefit from one or more of the following dimensions of proximity: geographic, temporal (time zone), cultural, linguistic, economic, political, or historical linkages (Dictionary of International Trade, 2019). The benefits of nearshoring include:

- *Close geographical proximity*. Nearshoring allows companies to bypass language barriers and cultural learning curves and to reduce travel expenses.

- *Cutting expenses and guaranteeing better controls.* This leads to higher-quality products and also offers access to more skilled workers and lower labor costs, which improves both quality control and customer service.
- *The option for in-person meetings.* The locations of both the original company and the nearshoring location allow this option.
- *Drastic reductions in the costs and times of transport.* Today, this is highly valued, since various e-commerce platforms work with deliveries of 1 or 2 days after the purchase.

Some manufacturing operations have moved back to Mexico, which offers several benefits for US companies (IVEMSA, 2018a):

- It is relatively easy and less expensive to visit your facility in Mexico.
- Communication is simpler to manage because there will be at most 3 hours' difference between US offices and Mexican facilities. (In many cases, they can be kept in the same time zone or in just one zone ahead/behind.)
- Transportation and shipping are quicker, so your products reach your customers faster.

Mexico in particular has some unique solutions that make it an attractive choice for US and other foreign manufacturers:

- The IMMEX/maquiladora program offers tax benefits (deferred import duties on raw goods and materials) to foreign manufacturers.
- The shelter option allows companies to operate in Mexico with reduced legal risk and liability.
- Mexico's free trade agreements, Reciprocal Investment Promotion and Protection Agreements, and other trade agreements with dozens of countries make it a gateway to worldwide markets. Many European and Asian manufacturers have established facilities in Mexico to access North and South American markets.

Many factors have contributed to Canada's emerging as a key nearshore player for US companies. Canada offers political stability and similarities to US laws, making it a low-risk, high-benefit option. Moreover, cost savings, cultural similarities, geographic closeness, and time zone likeness are four fundamental reasons why Canada continues to be a great outsourcing destination for America (IVEMSA, 2018b).

- *Cost savings.* The US dollar has averaged a price 25% higher than the Canadian dollar for five consecutive years, and with a country-wide commitment to making the US dollar even stronger, return on investment is maximized when setting up shop in Canada.
- *Geographic closeness.* Occasional travel is necessary at times for training, audits, and site visits. With Canada and the United States sharing a border and most major Canadian cities being located within 100 miles of the border, travel to Canada is less demanding than flying overseas and may even be quicker than traveling within America.

The NAFTA renegotiation provides more incentives for US companies to operate in Canada and Mexico free of tariffs. The new USMC agreement has updated the 24-year-old terms to include a heavy focus on the automotive industry, agriculture, the digital economy, and labor unions.

References

Bolle, J. M. (February 22, 2016). Overview of labor enforcement issues in Free Trade Agreements. *Congressional Research Service*. https://doi.org/RS22823. Retrieved from <https://fas.org/sgp/crs/misc/RS22823.pdf>.

Bondarenko, P. (2019). *North American Free Trade Agreement; Canada-United States-Mexico (1992)*. *Encyclopedia Britannica*. Retrieved from <https://www.britannica.com/event/North-American-Free-Trade-Agreement>.

Bransetter, L., & Lardy, N. (2008). China's embrace of globalization. In L. Brandt, & T. Rawski (Eds.), *China's great transformation*. Cambridge: Cambridge University Press.

Carpentier, C. L. (December 1, 2006). *IngentaConnect NAFTA commission for environmental cooperation: Ongoing assessment*. Impact Assessment and Project Appraisal.

Communications Department of the CES Secretariat. (2011). Destination sustainability: Reducing greenhouse gas emissions from freight transportation in North America. *Commission for Environmental Cooperation*. ISBN: 978-2-923358-91-8 <http://www3.cec.org/islandora/en/item/4237-destination-sustainability-reducing-greenhouse-gas-emissions-from-freight-en.pdf>.

Council on Foreign Relations. (2019). *U.S. relations with China 1949−2019*. E.U. Retrieved from <https://www.cfr.org/timeline/us-relations-china>.

Dernberger, R. (1993). The drive of the economic modernization and growth: Performance and trends. In M. Y.-M. Kau, & S. H. Marsh (Eds.), *China in the Era of Deng Xiaoping* (pp. 155−224). New York: Library of Congress Catalog-in-Publication Data. Retrieved from <https://books.google.com.mx/books?id = mDS0GW7FH_0C&pg = PA179&redir_esc = y#v = onepage&q&f = false>.

Dictionary of International Trade. (2019). *Nearshoring*. Global Negotiator International Contracts & Documents ready to use. <https://www.globalnegotiator.com/international-trade/dictionary/nearshoring/>.

Evans, R. (1995). *Deng Xiaoping and the making of modern China*. UK: Penguin Books, ISBN: 0-14-013945-1.

Executive United States. President. (1997). *Study on the operation and effects of the North American Free Trade Agreement*. Haus Trust Digital Library. Retrieved from <https://catalog.hathitrust.org/Record/003199072>.

Gildenhorn, J., & Metzner, D. (2005). NAFTA at 10: Progress, potential, and precedents. *Woodrow Wilson International Center for Scholars* (1), 20−30. Retrieved from <https://www.wilsoncenter.org/sites/default/files/NAFTA_long_rev1.pdf>.

Government of Canada. (October 1, 2018). *Canada-U.S. Free Trade Agreement*. Canada. Retrieved from <http://www.international.gc.ca/trade-commerce/trade-agreements-accords-commerciaux/agr-acc/united_states-etats_unis/fta-ale/background-contexte.aspx?lang = eng>.

Government Publishing Office of the U.S. (2000). *One hundred sixth congress of the United States of America. HR 4444*. Authenticated U.S. Government Information. Retrieved from <https://www.govinfo.gov/content/pkg/BILLS-106hr4444enr/pdf/BILLS-106hr4444enr.pdf>.

Inc. (n.d.). *North American Free Trade Agreement (NAFTA)*. Inc. Retrieved from <https://www.inc.com/encyclopedia/north-american-free-trade-agreement-nafta.html>.

IVEMSA. (2018a). *Why nearshoring in Mexico is a key strategy for US manufacturers.* Retrieved from <https://www.ivemsa.com/nearshoring-in-mexico-key-strategy/>.

IVEMSA. (2018b). *Why Canada is a great nearshore outsourcing destination for America.* Retrieved from <https://www.flgfrontline.com/why-canada-is-a-great-nearshore-outsourcing-destination-for-america/>.

McBrite, J. & Foster, D. (n.d.). *NAFTA milestones.* Council on Foreign Relations. Retrieved from <https://www.cfr.org/content/publications/NAFTA-BGR-Timeline-1300x920.jpg>.

Mexican Government's Ministry of Economy. (May 10, 2015). *International trade/countries with treaties and agreements signed with Mexico.* Gob.mx. Retrieved from <http://www.gob.mx/se/acciones-y-programas/comercio-exterior-paises-con-tratados-y-acuerdos-firmados-con-mexico>.

Pérez Ludeña, M. (May 2019). *Vínculos Productivos en América del Norte* (p. 12) Comisión Económica para América Latina y el Caribe (CEPAL). Retrieved from <https://www.cepal.org/es/publicaciones/44609-vinculos-productivos-america-norte>.

Simoes, A. (2017). *What does the United States import from Mexico?* E.U.: The Observatory of Economic Complexity. Retrieved from <https://atlas.media.mit.edu/en/visualize/tree_map/sitc/import/usa/mex/show/2017/>.

Simones, A. (2017). *Products that China exports to the United States (1995, 2005, 2015).* E.U.: The Observatory of Economic Complexity. Retrieved from <https://atlas.media.mit.edu/en/visualize/tree_map/sitc/export/chn/usa/show/1995/>, <https://atlas.media.mit.edu/en/visualize/tree_map/sitc/export/chn/usa/show/2005/>, <https://atlas.media.mit.edu/en/visualize/tree_map/sitc/export/chn/usa/show/2015/>.

Tiemann, M. (March 23, 2004). NAFTA: Related environmental issues and initiatives. *CRS Report for Congress Research Service.* Report 97-291. Retrieved from <https://digital.library.unt.edu/ark:/67531/metacrs6073/m1/1/high_res_d/97-291enr_2004Mar23.pdf>.

United States Census Bureau. (n.d.). *USA trade online.* US: Department of Commerce. Retrieved from <https://usatrade.census.gov/index.php?do = login>.

United States Census Bureau. https://www.census.gov/foreign-trade/balance/c0004.html.

Villarreal, A. (April 25, 2017). Mexico's Free Trade Agreements. *Congressional Research Service.* https://doi.org/R40784. Retrieved from <https://fas.org/sgp/crs/row/R40784.pdf>.

Villarreal, A., & Fergusson, I. (2017). The North American Free Trade Agreement (NAFTA). *Congressional Research Service*, 5−6. https://doi.org/R42965. Retrieved from <https://fas.org/sgp/crs/row/R42965.pdf>.

Webb, J. (2019). *What is offshoring? What is outsourcing? Are they different?* Forbes. Retrieved from <https://www.forbes.com/sites/jwebb/2017/07/28/what-is-offshoring-what-is-outsourcing-are-they-different/#6ceb6c9d2a2e>.

World Trade Organization, International Trade and Market Access Online. (2018). *Time series data base.* Retrieved from <http://stat.wto.org/StatisticalProgram/WSDBViewData.aspx?Language = E>.

World Trade Organization, International Trade and Market Access Online. (2019). *International trade and market access data.* Retrieved from <https://www.wto.org/english/res_e/statis_e/statis_bis_e.htm?solution = WTO&path = /Dashboards/MAPS&file = Map.wcdf&bookmark State = %7b%22impl%22:%22client%22,%22params%22:%7b%22langParam%22:%22en%22%7d%7d>.

Texas Transportation Institute, Texas A&M University System. (March 2010). *Sustainability and freight transportation in North America.* Retrieved from <http://www3.cec.org/islandora/en/item/4094-sustainability-and-freight-transportation-in-north-america>.

Chapter 3

US−Canada and US−Mexico trade demand

3.1 Introduction

Freight transportation demand is given by the consumption or production of goods, and at the international trade level, consumption in one country is understood to attract products from another country that produces those commodities or goods. As discussed in the previous chapters, the economies of Canada, the United States, and Mexico are strongly interlinked, leading to the development of integrated value chains in certain industries. The transportation system in North America, serving the three countries, is also integrated. This chapter presents trade trends information, by mode, between the United States and Mexico and between the United States and Canada. As mentioned in the previous chapter, Canada−Mexico trade is relatively low. The key commodities that are traded among the NAFTA countries are presented, by transportation mode, to identify the most important supply chains that are handled in the subcontinent. The states of origin in the United States and destination provinces in Canada or states in Mexico for those key commodities are presented by land transportation mode.

The total commodity trade between the United States and its two NAFTA partners reached $1229 billion in 2018, a 42% growth in the last 12 years (2006−18). (Note: All dollar amounts in this chapter are US dollars.) The trade balance has remained constant in this period at approximately 55% US imports from Canada and Mexico (Fig. 3.1) (United States Department of Transportation, n.d.).

The following sections describe the details between US−Canada and US−Mexico merchandise trade in the last 12 years.

3.2 US−Canada trade

US trade merchandise with Canada more than doubled in the first decade of FTA/NAFTA (1989−99) from $166.7 to $365.3 billion. US exports to

International Trade and Transportation Infrastructure Development.
DOI: https://doi.org/10.1016/B978-0-12-815741-1.00003-6

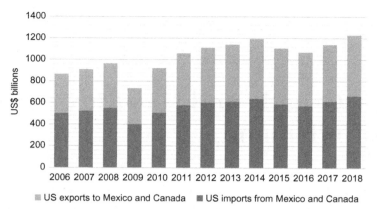

FIGURE 3.1 US merchandise trade with Mexico and Canada (2006−18). *United States Department of Transportation Bureau of Transportation Statistics.* TransBorder Freight Data. *<https://www.bts.gov/transborder>.*

Canada increased from $100.4 billion in 1993 to $312.1 billion in 2014 and then decreased to $298.72 billion in 2018. US imports from Canada increased from $111.2 billion in 1993 to $346.06 billion in 2014 and then decreased to $318.48 billion in 2018.

After a downturn of the economy during the 2001 recession, total US trade with Canada reached a new high of $596.47 billion in 2008, only to fall again due to the financial crisis of 2009, when it fell to $429.6 billion.

The United States has run a trade deficit with Canada since the FTA/NAFTA era, increasing from $9.1 billion in 1989 to $74.64 billion in 2008, before falling back during the 2009 recession. In 2018 the US trade deficit with Canada decreased further to $19.76 billion. While the trade deficit with Canada has been attributed to the FTA/NAFTA, increases have been uneven and may also be attributed to other economic factors, such as changes in energy prices (Trade statistics in this paragraph are derived from data: U.S. International Trade Commission's Interactive Tariff and Trade Data Web, 2019; Villarreal & Fergusson, 2017) (Fig. 3.2).

The three main modes of trade transportation between the United States and Canada are truck, rail, and vessel. The modal split has remained relatively constant in the last 12 years, with trucking handling three-quarters of the merchandise trade, rail 20% and vessel 5% (Fig. 3.3) (United States Department of Transportation, n.d.). Other modes include air, pipeline, mail, and other. In 2018 modes that include "Pipeline, mail, and other" handled 23% of the total US−Canada trade, pipeline being the largest with 11% of the total. Crude oil is the main product traded by pipeline between Canada and the United States.

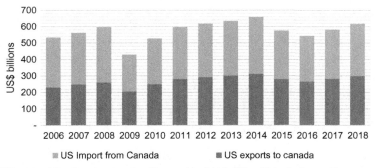

FIGURE 3.2 US—Canada merchandise trade (2006—18). *United States Department of Transportation Bureau of Transportation Statistics.* TransBorder Freight Data. *<https://www.bts. gov/transborder>.*

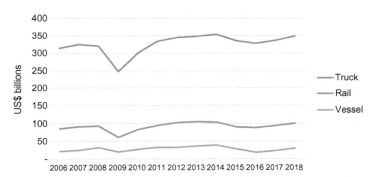

FIGURE 3.3 US—Canada merchandise trade by transportation mode (2006—18). *United States Department of Transportation Bureau of Transportation Statistics.* TransBorder Freight Data. *<https://www.bts.gov/transborder>.*

The main US—Canada trade commodity group is "Vehicles other than railways,"[1] with a 21% capture in 2018. The second largest commodity group is "Computer and related machinery" products, with a 12% of the total truck, rail, and vessel trade by value. A total of 22 commodities make up 80% of the total trade between the United States and Canada by the three transportation modes (Fig. 3.4).

---

1. Note: The commodity flow analysis in these sections comes from the U.S. Department of Transportation, Bureau of Transportation Statistics North American TransBorder Freight Data (https://www.bts.gov/transborder). The commodity classification system used for US—Canada and US—Mexico commodity trade by transportation mode is the Harmonized Tariff Schedule (HTS). Data are available at the two-digit HTS level, and more information is on the HTS at the International Trade Commission (http://www.usitc.gov/).

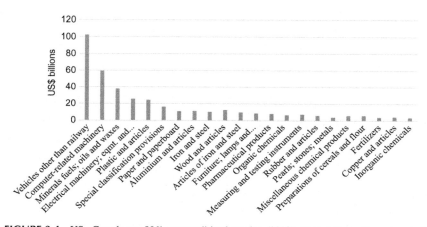

FIGURE 3.4   US–Canada top 80% commodities by value (2018). *United States Department of Transportation Bureau of Transportation Statistics.* TransBorder Freight Data. *<https://www.bts. gov/transborder>*.

Not all traded commodities show a constant growth over time. For example, "Preparations of cereals and flour" imported from Canada to the United States grew 204% in the 2006–18 period, reaching US$3.56 billion, while "Fertilizers" had a very uneven behavior. It reached a peak in 2011 and then fell to US$2.4 billion; that represents a 42% growth in the 2006–18 period. On the other hand, "Iron and steel" imported from Canada to the United States declined during the 2009 crisis, to grow slightly in the last few years (Fig. 3.5).

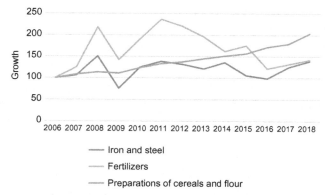

FIGURE 3.5   US imports from Canada: commodity trade variations (2006–18). *United States Department of Transportation Bureau of Transportation Statistics.* TransBorder Freight Data. *<https://www.bts.gov/transborder>*.

Some US exports to Canada experienced very high growth. For example, "Aircraft, spacecraft and parts" had a constant growth since 2006, reaching US$2.8 billion in 2018, or 318%, in the period. "Mineral fuels; oils and waxes" reached a peak in 2014, decreased in 2016, and rebounded again in 2018. US exports of "Iron and steel" to Canada decreased 10% in the 2006−18 period, and the declining trend seems to be continuing (Fig. 3.6).

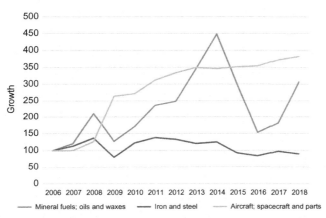

FIGURE 3.6 US exports to Canada: commodity trade variations (2006−18). *United States Department of Transportation Bureau of Transportation Statistics.* TransBorder Freight Data. *<https://www.bts.gov/transborder>.*

3.2.1   US−Canada trade by truck

Truck trade between the United States and Canada follows a similar pattern as the total trade by mode, with "Vehicles other than railways" and "Computer and related machinery" products making up three-quarters of the total trade by value by this mode of transport (Fig. 3.7).

Origin−destination (OD) patterns for the top four commodities exported from the United States to Canada are described in the following sections.

3.2.1.1   US−Canada trade by truck: vehicle other than railway by truck

Sixty percent of the total vehicle exports from the United States to Canada by truck are concentrated in seven states and have destinations in three provinces. The largest flow is between Michigan and Ontario. This US state and Canadian province have the largest concentration of auto industry establishments in the two countries. Indiana, Ohio, and Kentucky are also vehicle exporters to Canada. Indiana is home to several auto plants, like Nissan, Volkswagen, and General Motors. Kentucky has Toyota, Ford, and General Motors plants (Table 3.1).

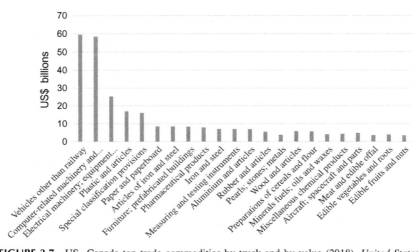

FIGURE 3.7 US–Canada top trade commodities by truck and by value (2018). *United States Department of Transportation Bureau of Transportation Statistics. TransBorder Freight Data.* *<https://www.bts.gov/transborder>*.

TABLE 3.1 US exports to Canada by truck: vehicle other than railway origin–destination matrix (US$ billion).

State of origin/destination province	Ontario	Manitoba	Quebec
Michigan	8.219	0.029	0.035
Indiana	3.508	0.180	0.125
Ohio	3.140	0.054	0.138
Kentucky	1.161	0.022	0.114
Illinois	1.004	0.152	0.009
Texas	0.681	0.061	0.096
Oregon	0.463	0.055	0.191

Source: Developed by the author with data from United States Department of Transportation Bureau of Transportation Statistics: TransBorder Freight Data. https://www.bts.gov/transborder.

Vehicle other than railway imported to the US by truck from Canada originate mainly in Ontario with destinations in Michigan. As mentioned earlier, this state and province are home to a large automotive industry. Other states that attract vehicles are California, Ohio, and Texas (Table 3.2).

TABLE 3.2 US imports from Canada by truck: vehicle other than railway origin–destination matrix (US$ billion).

Province of origin/state of destination	Ontario	Quebec	Manitoba
Michigan	15.58	0.18	0.01
California	2.12	0.17	0.08
Ohio	0.95	0.11	0.01
Texas	0.40	0.48	0.08

Source: Developed by the author with data from United States Department of Transportation Bureau of Transportation Statistics: TransBorder Freight Data. https://www.bts.gov/transborder.

3.2.1.2   US–Canada trade by truck: computer-related machinery and parts

Seven US states originate 80% of the total US exports to Canada of computer-related machinery, which includes all electronic equipment. This commodity group includes parts related to the auto industry; therefore the trade patterns are similar to those in the vehicles trade. California is the port of entry for many electronic products coming from Asia to the ports of Los Angeles and Long Beach, as well as being a large electronic components producer. Texas is the port of entry for many electronic products coming from Mexico, as well as California. These products are assembled in Mexico under the Pitex or maquila program (Table 3.3).[2]

Canadian exports to the United States of computer-related machinery by truck originate in Ontario, Quebec, and Alberta. The highest volume by value is between Ontario and Michigan, followed by Ontario to Texas (Table 3.4).[3]

---

2. The Mexican Maquila (Maquiladora) Program, now IMMEX Program, is an instrument that allows the temporary importation of goods that are used in an industrial process or service to produce, transform, or repair foreign goods imported temporarily for subsequent export or provision of export services, without covering the payment of a general import tax, value-added tax, and, where appropriate, countervailing duties. Secretaría de Economía, http://www.2006-2012. economia.gob.mx/industry/foreign-trade-instruments/immex.

3. It is important to note that the statistical information does not always represent the true origin or destination of the commodities. The information is collected by customs agencies based on the trade manifest, and sometimes the declared origin or destination state province is the one where the merchandise leaves the country and enters the other. Michigan, Texas, and California show large volumes of exports as these states have important land border crossings.

TABLE 3.3 US exports to Canada by truck: computer-related machinery and parts origin–destination matrix (US$ billion).

State of origin/destination province	Ontario	Manitoba	British Columbia
Ohio	3.919	0.137	0.059
Illinois	1.508	0.670	0.475
Michigan	2.646	0.073	0.031
California	1.855	0.023	0.466
Texas	1.332	0.179	0.132
North Carolina	1.203	0.167	0.091
Tennessee	1.233	0.146	0.131

Source: Developed by the author with data from United States Department of Transportation Bureau of Transportation Statistics: TransBorder Freight Data. https://www.bts.gov/transborder.

TABLE 3.4 US imports from Canada by truck: computer-related machinery and parts origin–destination matrix (US$ billion).

Province of origin/state of destination	Ontario	Quebec	Alberta
Michigan	3.767	0.094	0.005
Texas	0.761	0.207	0.700
Ohio	1.098	0.192	0.023
New York	0.474	0.533	0.006
Illinois	0.557	0.106	0.059
Indiana	0.552	0.048	0.011
Alabama	0.147	0.408	0.003
Pennsylvania	0.363	0.125	0.053
Missouri	0.498	0.036	0.003
Kentucky	0.275	0.267	0.004
California	0.294	0.108	0.048
Georgia	0.270	0.183	0.015
Connecticut	0.065	0.426	0.002

Source: Developed by the author with data from United States Department of Transportation Bureau of Transportation Statistics: TransBorder Freight Data. https://www.bts.gov/transborder.

TABLE 3.5 US exports to Canada by truck: electrical machinery; equipment and parts origin–destination matrix (US$ billion).

State of origin/destination province	Ontario	Quebec	British Columbia
California	2.371	0.051	0.414
Texas	2.353	0.034	0.105
Illinois	0.946	0.015	0.042
Michigan	1.097	0.009	0.006
Pennsylvania	0.911	0.095	0.019
Ohio	0.964	0.012	0.020
Tennessee	0.823	0.011	0.014
Vermont	0.002	0.802	0.001

Source: Developed by the author with data from United States Department of Transportation Bureau of Transportation Statistics: TransBorder Freight Data. https://www.bts.gov/transborder.

3.2.1.3   US–Canada trade by truck: electrical machinery; equipment and parts

The third largest US export to Canada by truck is "Electrical machinery; Equipment and parts," with eight US states representing 58% of the total exports of this commodity. This shows that the production of this commodity is spread out throughout the country. California and Texas have the highest values for the same reasons as described in the previous paragraph (Table 3.5).

"Electrical machinery; Equipment and parts" imports from Canada to the United States by truck come mainly from three provinces: Ontario, Quebec, and British Columbia (like US exports). The states of destination have a different mix than US exports, with important flows from Ontario to New York (Table 3.6).

3.2.1.4   US–Canada trade by truck: plastics and articles

The fourth largest US export to Canada by truck is "Plastics and articles," with 11 states participating in 58% of the total exports of this commodity. As with the "Electrical machinery," the production is spread out throughout the country. The Ohio–Ontario trade is the highest by value (Table 3.3). Ohio is home to nearly 10% of all North American Tier-1 automotive suppliers, manufacturing parts for motor vehicles with easy access to both northern and southern automotive facilities. Pennsylvania and New Jersey have a large plastics industry. Pennsylvania is home to plastics manufacturers and establishments engaged in plastics processing, ranked 7th in plastics industry employment in the United States, and New Jersey is the 16th (Table 3.7) (Plastics Industry Association, 2019; Porter, 2018).

TABLE 3.6 US imports from Canada by truck: electrical machinery; equipment and parts origin–destination matrix (US$ billion).

Province of origin/state of destination	Ontario	Quebec	British Columbia
New York	0.276	0.446	0.016
Michigan	0.643	0.017	0.004
Texas	0.243	0.050	0.034
Vermont	0.006	0.344	0.000
Illinois	0.253	0.060	0.013
Georgia	0.260	0.034	0.005
California	0.203	0.040	0.033
Ohio	0.200	0.014	0.007
Indiana	0.138	0.015	0.007
Pennsylvania	0.094	0.029	0.005

Source: Developed by the author with data from United States Department of Transportation Bureau of Transportation Statistics: TransBorder Freight Data. https://www.bts.gov/transborder.

TABLE 3.7 US exports to Canada by truck: plastics and articles origin–destination matrix (US$ billion).

State of origin/destination province	Ontario	British Columbia	Quebec
Ohio	0.890	0.026	0.007
Texas	0.526	0.058	0.017
Pennsylvania	0.484	0.017	0.089
New Jersey	0.443	0.014	0.109
Illinois	0.504	0.021	0.016
Michigan	0.538	0.007	0.003
Indiana	0.484	0.012	0.002
Wisconsin	0.361	0.014	0.005
New York	0.262	0.008	0.088
Georgia	0.223	0.016	0.020
Kentucky	0.257	0.008	0.010

Source: Developed by the author with data from United States Department of Transportation Bureau of Transportation Statistics: TransBorder Freight Data. https://www.bts.gov/transborder.

US imports from Canada of "Plastics and articles" by truck originate in Ontario, Quebec, and British Columbia, and 11 US states participate, with 60% of the total trade of this commodity by value. Imports by truck follow the same OD patterns as exports, with Ontario-to-Ohio showing the highest volume, followed by Ontario to Illinois (Table 3.8).

TABLE 3.8 US imports from Canada by truck: plastics and articles origin−destination matrix (US$ billion).

Province of origin/state of destination	Ontario	Quebec	British Columbia
Ohio	0.393	0.116	0.009
Pennsylvania	0.271	0.226	0.004
Illinois	0.333	0.125	0.006
Texas	0.215	0.105	0.011
New York	0.293	0.144	0.004
California	0.184	0.094	0.070
Michigan	0.340	0.060	0.001
Wisconsin	0.191	0.091	0.004
Indiana	0.214	0.079	0.002
New Jersey	0.164	0.082	0.004
Georgia	0.142	0.089	0.003
Massachusetts	0.132	0.096	0.001
Tennessee	0.145	0.084	0.001

Source: Developed by the author with data from United States Department of Transportation Bureau of Transportation Statistics: TransBorder Freight Data. https://www.bts.gov/transborder.

3.2.2 US−Canada trade by rail

Trade by rail between Canada and the United States is concentrated in fewer commodities, led by "Vehicles other than railway" with 42% of the total trade by rail, followed by "Mineral fuels, oils and waxes" with 10%. Nine commodity groups make 80% of the total trade, by rail, by value (Fig. 3.8).

3.2.2.1 US−Canada trade by rail: vehicle other than railway by truck

Sixty-five percent of the total vehicle exports from the United States to Canada by rail are concentrated in five states and have destination at two provinces. As with trucking, the largest flow is between Michigan and

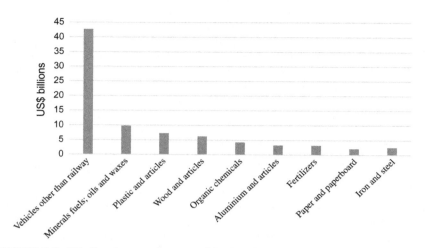

FIGURE 3.8 US—Canada top trade commodities by rail and by value (2018). *United States Department of Transportation Bureau of Transportation Statistics.* TransBorder Freight Data. *<https://www.bts.gov/transborder>.*

Ontario, followed by origins in Kentucky, Indiana, Tennessee, and Missouri. Kentucky and Indiana have several auto assembly plants as noted earlier with regard to truck flows. Tennessee is an important player in the auto industry, with three major auto manufacturing plants (Nissan, Toyota, and Volkswagen) and nearly 1000 auto suppliers (Grigsby, 2018). Missouri has been among the top 10 states for automotive vehicle production with Ford and GM plants (Parson, 2018) (Table 3.9).

TABLE 3.9 US exports to Canada by rail: vehicle other than railway origin—destination matrix (US$ billion).

State of origin/destination province	Ontario	Alberta
Michigan	3.960	0.00002
Kentucky	2.053	0.0059
Indiana	1.712	0.0594
Tennessee	1.637	0.0013
Missouri	1.597	0.0051

Source: Developed by the author with data from United States Department of Transportation Bureau of Transportation Statistics: TransBorder Freight Data. https://www.bts.gov/transborder.

US imports from Canada of "Vehicles other than railway" by rail account for 99% of the total flow by rail, and they have an origin in Ontario, with destinations in the states of California and Michigan. The 2018 value of this trade was US$25.72 billion.

3.2.2.2   U.S–Canada trade by rail: mineral fuels; oils and waxes

Sixty-two percent of the total "Mineral fuels; Oils and waxes" exports from the United States to Canada by rail are concentrated in six states and have destinations in three provinces. The largest flow is between Texas and Ontario. Texas has a large oil industry producing refined products (Table 3.10).

TABLE 3.10 US exports to Canada by rail: mineral fuels; oils and waxes origin–destination matrix (US$ billion).

State of origin/destination province	Ontario	Alberta	Manitoba
Texas	0.149	0.102	0.020
Ohio	0.135	0.031	0.000
Pennsylvania	0.086	0.066	0.001
Illinois	0.057	0.041	0.002
North Dakota	0.0005	0.089	0.016
Louisiana	0.030	0.017	0.008

Source: Developed by the author with data from United States Department of Transportation Bureau of Transportation Statistics: TransBorder Freight Data. https://www.bts.gov/transborder.

US imports from Canada by rail of "Mineral fuels; Oils and waxes" come from Alberta to Louisiana, Texas, Delaware, and Washington. Alberta is a major oil producer, and these US states have refinery capacity (Table 3.11).

TABLE 3.11 US imports from Canada by rail: mineral fuels; oils and waxes origin–destination matrix (US$ billion).

State/province	Alberta	Ontario
Louisiana	1.653	0.086
Texas	0.803	0.047
Delaware	0.882	0.002
Washington	0.754	0.023
Oklahoma	0.577	0.001
Alabama	0.334	0.007

Source: Developed by the author with data from United States Department of Transportation Bureau of Transportation Statistics: TransBorder Freight Data. https://www.bts.gov/transborder.

3.2.3 US−Canada trade by vessel

US−Canada trade by vessel is concentrated in one commodity group, "Mineral fuels; Oils and waxes." This trade accounts for 81% of the total maritime trade between the United States and Canada.

3.3 US−Mexico trade

The United States is by far Mexico's leading partner in merchandise trade. US exports to Mexico rose rapidly since NAFTA, increasing from $41.6 billion in 1993 to $265.01 billion in 2018, an increase of 484%. US imports from Mexico increased from $39.9 billion in 1993 to $346.53 billion in 2018, an increase of 687%. The US trade balance with Mexico went from a surplus of $1.7 billion in 1993 to a deficit of $81.52 billion in 2018 (Fig. 3.9) (United States Department of Transportation, n.d.).

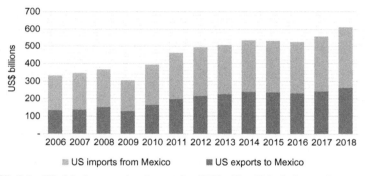

FIGURE 3.9 US−Mexico merchandise trade (2006−18). *United States Department of Transportation Bureau of Transportation Statistics.* TransBorder Freight Data. *<https://www.bts. gov/transborder>.*

Trade by mode between the United States and Mexico is dominated by truck, with an average of 72% participation in the last 12 years, with rail and vessel at 14% each. The vessel participation proportion is higher in the US−Mexico trade than between United States and Canada because most of the petroleum and petroleum products traded between Mexico and the United States are transported by vessel, compared to pipeline in the US−Canada trade. A large proportion of Mexican oil is refined or sold to the United States, and gasoline and other refined products are imported to Mexico from the United States (Fig. 3.10).

Other modes of US−Mexico trade include air, pipeline, mail, and other. In 2018 these modes handled 7% of the total US−Mexico trade. Comparing these modes at the US−Mexico and the US−Canada trade, the main difference is that US−Canada handed 11% of trade by value by pipeline, and Mexico only 1% (Fig. 3.11).

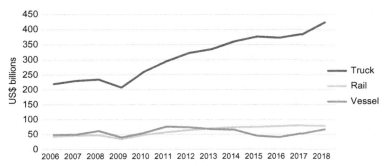

FIGURE 3.10 US—Mexico merchandise trade by transportation mode (2006—18). *United States Department of Transportation Bureau of Transportation Statistics.* TransBorder Freight Data. *<https://www.bts.gov/transborder>*.

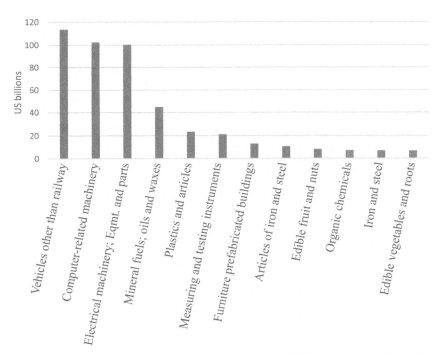

FIGURE 3.11 US—Mexico top 80% commodities by value (2018). *Developed by the author with data from United States Department of Transportation Bureau of Transportation Statistics.* TransBorder Freight Data. *<https://www.bts.gov/transborder>*.

The three main US—Mexico trade commodity groups are "Vehicles other than railway," "Computer and related machinery," and "Electrical machinery, equipment and parts" with 20%, 18%, and 18%, respectively, of the total trade by truck, rail, and vessel between the United States and Mexico by value. Twelve commodities make up 80% of the total trade between the United States and Mexico by the three transportation modes (Fig. 3.12).

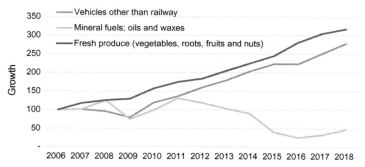

FIGURE 3.12   US imports from Mexico: commodity trade variations (2006–18). *United States Department of Transportation Bureau of Transportation Statistics.* TransBorder Freight Data. *<https://www.bts.gov/transborder>*.

Two US imports from Mexico have had a considerable increase since 2006: "Vehicles other than railway" and "Fresh produce (vegetables, roots, fruits and nuts)." These two commodity groups increased three times since 2006. On the other hand, "Mineral fuels; Oils and waxes" trade declined 50% since 2006 (Fig. 3.13).

"Mineral fuels; Oils and waxes," exported from the United States into Mexico grew six timed since 2006, reaching US$29 billion in 2018. Cereal exports to Mexico doubled in value, while "Organic chemicals" showed a slight but constant increase in the 2006–18 period (Fig. 3.13).

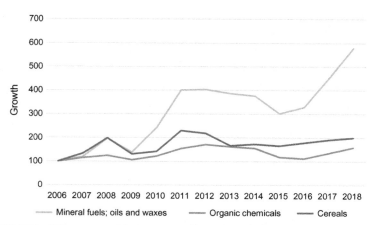

FIGURE 3.13   US exports to Mexico: commodity trade variations (2006–18). *United States Department of Transportation Bureau of Transportation Statistics.* TransBorder Freight Data. *<https://www.bts.gov/transborder>*.

3.3.1   US—Mexico trade by truck

Truck trade by commodity between Mexico and the United States have the same three top commodities as the total trade; however, the difference is that "Electrical machinery" is the top commodity with 23% of the total trade by truck, followed by "Computer and related machinery" (22%) and "Vehicles other than railway" (14%). Eleven commodities make 80% of the total trade between the United States and Mexico by truck (Fig. 3.14).

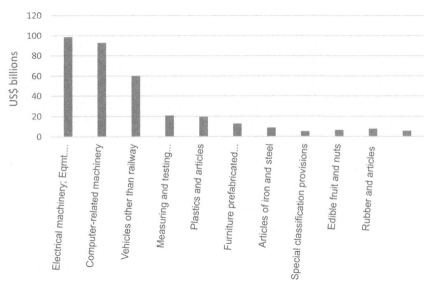

FIGURE 3.14   US—Mexico top trade commodities by truck and by value (2018). *United States Department of Transportation Bureau of Transportation Statistics.* TransBorder Freight Data. *<https://www.bts.gov/transborder>.*

3.3.1.1   US exports to Mexico by truck: electrical machinery; equipment and parts

The largest flows of "Electrical machinery; Equipment and parts" from the United States into Mexico by truck is between Texas and the Mexican border states of Chihuahua and Tamaulipas and between California and Baja California. Ciudad Juarez in Chihuahua and Tijuana in Baja California are two border cities in Mexico with large concentrations of maquiladora plants. Truck flows between the United States and Mexico at these two border cities carry mainly "Electrical machinery; Equipment and parts." The flow between

Texas and Tamaulipas is partially to maquila plants along the border in Tamaulipas, but mainly through the Laredo, Texas/Nuevo Laredo, Tamaulipas, which is the largest port of entry in North America and a gateway for products flowing south to Central Mexico (Table 3.12).

TABLE 3.12 US exports to Mexico by truck: electrical machinery, equipment and parts origin−destination matrix (US$ billion).

State of origin in the United States/ destination state in Mexico	Chihuahua	Tamaulipas	Baja California	Nuevo Leon	Estado de Mexico
Texas	6.6584	5.2689	0.0664	0.7714	1.0196
California	1.7419	0.0087	3.3154	0.1803	0.6751
Arizona	0.0128	0.0004	0.0395	0.0243	0.0432
Illinois	0.0544	0.0379	0.3427	0.1566	0.2967
Michigan	0.1998	0.0731	0.0069	0.2104	0.0268
Massachusetts	0.0185	0.0959	0.8688	0.0208	0.0386
Wisconsin	0.1373	0.0007	0.0097	0.3693	0.0714
Pennsylvania	0.0914	0.0018	0.0227	0.1360	0.0237
Georgia	0.0246	0.0298	0.0946	0.2852	0.0335

Source: Developed by the author with data from United States Department of Transportation Bureau of Transportation Statistics: TransBorder Freight Data. https://www.bts.gov/transborder.

3.3.1.2   US exports to Mexico by truck: computer-related machinery and parts

"Computer-related machinery and parts" exports by truck from the United States into Mexico are concentrated in flows from Texas to Chihuahua. As previously mentioned, this takes place mainly at the El Paso, Texas−Ciudad Juarez, Chihuahua passage. Other flows occur at California−Baja California and Texas−State of Mexico, which is home to a large high-tech manufacturing cluster (Table 3.13).

TABLE 3.13 US exports to Mexico by truck: computer-related machinery and parts origin–destination matrix (US$ billion).

State of origin in the United States/ destination state in Mexico	Chihuahua	Nuevo Leon	Estado de Mexico	Baja California	Distrito Federal
Texas	14.17874	0.65047	1.38619	0.02027	1.07267
California	0.18571	0.09444	0.22644	2.19108	0.27037
Michigan	0.13534	0.25377	0.07346	0.00674	0.05567
Illinois	0.02793	0.34190	0.11826	0.06677	0.04970
New York	0.00552	0.75987	0.03781	0.00560	0.07687
Ohio	0.01637	0.12425	0.20452	0.00660	0.04732
Tennessee	0.11719	0.06464	0.02617	0.31242	0.25274
New Mexico	0.68945	0.00092	0.01217	0.00003	0.00116
Indiana	0.00438	0.30076	0.05102	0.02085	0.03378

Source: Developed by the author with data from United States Department of Transportation Bureau of Transportation Statistics: TransBorder Freight Data. https://www.bts.gov/transborder.

3.3.1.3   US exports to Mexico by truck: vehicles other than railway

"Vehicles other than railway" exports by truck from the United States into Mexico originate in automotive industry states in the United States like Michigan, Indiana, Illinois, among others. The states of Texas and California have automobile production. However, as previously mentioned, the information is collected in a way that the state of origin in the United States might not represent the true origin but rather the state where the commodity is exported into Mexico. States in Mexico that receive "Vehicles other than railway" are Baja California, Nuevo Leon, Estado de Mexico, Guanajuato, Coahuila, and Distrito Federal (now Mexico City). All these Mexican states have large population centers or auto assembly plants, where vehicles are received and are prepared to go to final market (Table 3.14).

TABLE 3.14 US exports to Mexico by truck: vehicles other than railway origin–destination matrix (US$ billion).

State of origin in the United States/destination state in Mexico	Baja California	Nuevo Leon	Estado de Mexico	Guanajuato	Coahuila	Distrito Federal
Texas	0.0165	0.2036	0.8940	0.6500	0.5764	0.6798
California	1.8587	0.0323	0.0448	0.0019	0.0022	0.0073
Michigan	0.0109	0.1540	0.0702	0.1924	0.2361	0.0584
Indiana	0.0862	0.1810	0.0796	0.0323	0.1238	0.0027
Ohio	0.0561	0.1245	0.0438	0.0792	0.0882	0.0222
Illinois	0.0079	0.1169	0.0241	0.0600	0.0390	0.0776
South Carolina	0.0255	0.0360	0.0015	0.0671	0.0001	0.0007
Kentucky	0.0198	0.1132	0.0101	0.0468	0.0132	0.0149
Tennessee	0.0087	0.0691	0.0250	0.0123	0.0121	0.1038
North Carolina	0.0115	0.1186	0.0128	0.0689	0.0111	0.0412
Wisconsin	0.0079	0.0683	0.0101	0.0291	0.0817	0.0021
Pennsylvania	0.0096	0.1276	0.0248	0.0157	0.0248	0.0003
Minnesota	0.0046	0.2089	0.0020	0.0001	0.0077	0.0002

Source: Developed by the author with data from United States Department of Transportation Bureau of Transportation Statistics; TransBorder Freight Data. https://www.bts.gov/transborder.

3.3.2 US–Mexico trade by rail

"Vehicles other than railway" is the main commodity that is handled by rail between Mexico and the United States, with 52% of the total trade by value (Fig. 3.15).

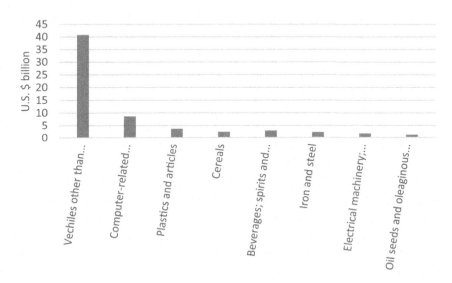

FIGURE 3.15 US–Mexico top trade commodities by rail and by value (2018). *United States Department of Transportation Bureau of Transportation Statistics.* TransBorder Freight Data. *<https://www.bts.gov/transborder>.*

3.3.2.1 US exports to Mexico by rail: vehicles other than railway

"Vehicles other than railway" exports from the United States to Mexico originate in the United States auto industry–related states, including Michigan, Illinois, Indiana, and Ohio. The largest volume by value is between Michigan and Mexico City (Distrito Federal), one of the largest metropolitan areas in the world with an increasing automobile fleet. Michigan-to-Guanajuato has an important volume. Guanajuato is home to multiple auto plants, including General Motors, Honda, Mazda, Toyota, and Hino Motors (Table 3.15).

TABLE 3.15 US exports to Mexico by rail: vehicles other than railway origin—destination matrix (US$ billion).

State of origin in the United States/destination state in Mexico	Distrito Federal	Guanajuato	Estado de Mexico	Jalisco
Michigan	0.55363	0.40381	0.02724	0.00143
Texas	0.07877	0.02807	0.43896	0.00344
Illinois	0.08724	0.23907	0.01169	NDA
Indiana	0.03088	0.00736	0.00207	0.16069
Ohio	0.01628	0.03491	0.00277	0.09996
Georgia	0.01779	0.00018	–	0.00002
Kentucky	0.22691	0.00225	–	0.00042
Tennessee	0.06696	0.00261	0.00287	

Source: Developed by the author with data from United States Department of Transportation Bureau of Transportation Statistics: TransBorder Freight Data. https://www.bts.gov/transborder.

3.3.2.2   US exports to Mexico by rail: computer-related machinery and parts

The largest flow of "Computer-related machinery and parts" between the United States and Mexico is from Texas to the State of Mexico (Estado de Mexico). The State of Mexico surrounds Mexico City and has a large population as well as a large industrial and manufacturing cluster (Table 3.16).

3.3.2.3   US exports to Mexico by rail: plastics and articles

"Plastics and articles" trade from the United States into Mexico by rail comes from Texas, Louisiana, Michigan, Illinois, Pennsylvania, and New Jersey. All these states have plastic production industries. The automobile industry is a large consumer of plastics for parts. The Mexican states that receive this commodity by rail include states with large population centers and the automobile industry (Table 3.17).

Mexico is the second largest market for US grain. The main states of origin for cereal are Illinois, Nebraska, Kansas, Iowa, and Missouri. In 2018 Mexico was the top US export destination for corn, wheat, and rice by volume (United States Department of Agriculture, Foreign Agricultural Service, 2019) (Table 3.18).

TABLE 3.16 US exports to Mexico by rail: computer-related machinery and parts origin–destination matrix (US$ billion).

State of origin in the United States/ destination state in Mexico	Estado de Mexico	Guanajuato	Distrito Federal	Coahuila	San Luis Potosi
Texas	1.4820252	0.1321014	0.1249202	0.0015575	0.1273576
Indiana	0.0001758	0.0058981	0.0379153	–	–
Michigan	0.0164016	0.0651795	0.0035138	0.0389296	0.0167296
Illinois	0.0342590	0.0761399	–	0.1106759	0.0376667
Wisconsin	–	0.0012467	0.0001730	0.0499788	0.0000002
Arizona	0.0000003	–	0.0389841	–	–
Ohio	0.0007435	0.0096175	0.0072970	–	0.0018149
Tennessee	0.0101289	0.0022479	–	–	–
Alabama	–	0.0146211	–	–	–
Kentucky	–	0.0005019	0.0045278	0.0000258	0.0001582

Source: Developed by the author with data from United States Department of Transportation Bureau of Transportation Statistics: TransBorder Freight Data. https://www.bts.gov/transborder.

TABLE 3.17 US exports to Mexico by rail: plastics and articles origin–destination matrix (US$ billion).

State of origin in the United States/destination state in Mexico	Estado de Mexico	Nuevo Leon	Guanajuato	Distrito Federal
Texas	0.5938	0.2217	0.0717	0.0970
Louisiana	0.0959	0.0384	0.0774	0.0178
Michigan	0.1465	0.0195	0.0106	0.0425
Illinois	0.0574	0.0483	0.0107	0.0002
Pennsylvania	0.0412	0.0239	0.0092	0.0022
New Jersey	0.0398	0.0235	0.0295	0.0003

Source: Developed by the author with data from United States Department of Transportation Bureau of Transportation Statistics: TransBorder Freight Data. https://www.bts.gov/transborder.

TABLE 3.18 US exports to Mexico by rail: cereal origin–destination matrix (US$ billion).

State of origin in the United States/ destination state in Mexico	Aguascalientes	Jalisco	Estado de Mexico
Illinois	0.23	0.12	0.02
Nebraska	0.03	0.19	0.05
Kansas	0.26	0.04	0.03
Iowa	0.25	0.09	0.01
Missouri	0.16	0.03	0.05

Source: Developed by the author with data from United States Department of Transportation Bureau of Transportation Statistics: TransBorder Freight Data. https://www.bts.gov/transborder.

3.3.3 US–Mexico trade by vessel

Compared to US–Canada trade by vessel, US–Mexico trade handled commodities other than "Mineral fuels; oils and waxes." Even though this is the top commodity group, "Vehicles other than railways" is the second largest commodity group (Fig. 3.16). Mexico is a large manufacturer of finished vehicles that are handled by rail and vessel to the United States.

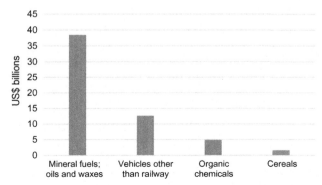

FIGURE 3.16 US–Mexico Top Trade commodities by vessel and by value (2018). *United States Department of Transportation Bureau of Transportation Statistics.* TransBorder Freight Data. *<https://www.bts.gov/transborder>*.

3.3.4   US imports by truck and rail

The Bureau of Transportation Statistics, TransBorder Freight Data does not provide information on the state of origin in Mexico for US imports. However, the available information provides a good picture of the key commodities' states of entry in the United States, and it includes commodity weight and value. As weight is important for transportation, the information was analyzed by weight for truck and rail.

One of the largest US imports from Mexico by truck is fresh produce (including commodities in the "Edible vegetables, roots, fruit and preparations" category), and the main states of destination are Texas, California, and Arizona. Arizona imports large amounts of tomatoes and other vegetables from the state of Sinaloa on the Mexican west coast. Another key commodity is finished vehicles that are assembled in central Mexico in the states of Guanajuato, State of Mexico, Coahuila and Nuevo Leon. Other commodities are shown in Table 3.19.

Two commodities concentrate a large portion of US imports from Mexico by rail: "Vehicles other than railway" and "Beverages; Spirits and vinegar." This second group is mainly beer that is produced at various locations near the US–Mexico border and is sent to the United States by rail. Most likely the US importer of these two commodities is registered in Michigan and Illinois; therefore the statistical data show these states as destinations. However, as previously mentioned, the true destination is spread throughout the United States (Table 3.20).

3.4   Key North American Free Trade Agreement supply chains

With the elimination of many tariffs and no-tariff barriers, North American industries became more integrated. Supply chains are now interlinked across

TABLE 3.19 Main US imports from Mexico by truck (thousand metric tons).

Commodities	Texas	California	Arizona	Michigan	Illinois	Georgia	Ohio	Kentucky	Pennsylvania
Vehicles other than railway	2212.61	973.35	19.71	1167.39	130.35	73.42	213.63	187.32	149.67
Edible vegetables, roots, fruit, and preparations	3717.55	2929.32	2588.99	345.85	152.51	51.22	25.01	16.76	38.14
Salt; sulfur; plaster and cement	3423.68	193.14	36.31	596.68	21.38	6.73	20.02	204.07	0.73
Computer-related machinery and parts	1116.72	227.34	103.54	440.13	136.24	132.83	247.47	149.43	61.18
Electrical machinery; equipment and parts	1019.36	397.01	205.05	212.21	154.46	183.90	81.41	43.23	119.15
Beverages; spirits and vinegar	738.86	170.85	52.16	0.07	481.27	399.43	0.002	48.50	0.02
Articles of iron and steel	747.64	112.97	24.92	49.72	48.66	28.40	30.42	35.64	23.53
Furniture; prefabricated buildings	358.85	204.71	13.92	278.53	33.90	84.75	35.71	49.26	12.99
Plastics	332.98	236.25	24.29	32.56	38.91	13.05	44.52	25.74	95.44
Ceramic products	781.58	100.84	8.13	2.82	18.46	37.66	22.63	0.03	24.61
Glass	370.05	111.42	6.13	11.90	6.16	7.79	45.11	9.60	19.80
Iron and steel	557.70	127.69	14.68	4.55	11.58	3.38	18.77	1.33	7.66
Stone; plaster; cement and asbestos	363.91	147.49	35.82	2.39	5.65	69.06	1.34	0.63	91.02

Source: Developed by the author with data from United States Department of Transportation Bureau of Transportation Statistics: TransBorder Freight Data. https://www.bts.gov/transborder.

TABLE 3.20 US imports from Mexico by rail (thousand metric tons).

Commodities	Michigan	Illinois	Texas	California	Arizona
Vehicles other than railway	3689.650	31.808	179.208	263.503	0.002
Beverages; spirits and vinegar	–	3299.948	0.008	4.473	–
Iron and steel	1.552	12.768	696.987	18.865	11.659
Salt; sulfur; plaster and cement	9.970	5.762	457.886	160.392	17.816
Inorganic chemicals	–	34.998	93.896	11.390	307.547
Computer-related machinery and parts	190.270	53.466	13.140	53.978	0.019

Source: Developed by the author with data from United States Department of Transportation Bureau of Transportation Statistics: TransBorder Freight Data. https://www.bts.gov/transborder.

the NAFTA countries, leading to massive trade growth in some commodity groups, as just shown. The transportation system in North America is well developed, particularly the highway and rail networks, to provide an efficient means to handle trade. Industries in North America take advantage of its transportation systems and production sites to identify the best source locations and to reduce production costs. A large share of NAFTA trade consists of intermediate products that are shipped from one country to another at different stages of production, which involves having a product shipped back and forth across the same borders multiple times.

Auto parts or computer components that are used in the production of final goods are intermediate parts that are traded in the NAFTA region, and a great deal of the trade takes place within firms. The automobile industry is a good example of this type of trade, which lowers the cost of cars to the consumer and makes firms more globally competitive, accounting for 60% of majority-owned affiliate trade.

The following sections present three case studies on key NAFTA supply chains.

3.4.1 Auto industry

In 2017 approximately 17.5 million cars and trucks were produced throughout North America. An example of a simplified North American auto production supply chain is shown in (Fig. 3.17). The vehicle engine is manufactured in Mexico and shipped by truck all the way to Canada, where

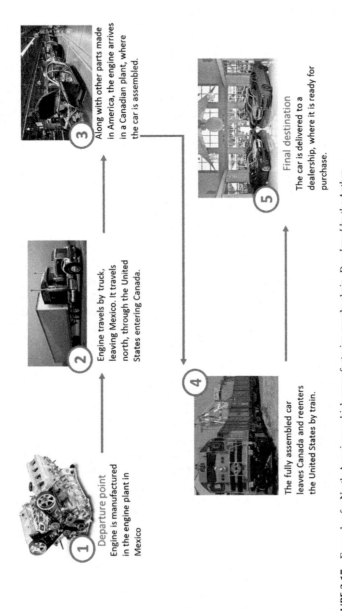

Departure point
Engine is manufactured in the engine plant in Mexico

2 Engine travels by truck, leaving Mexico. It travels north, through the United States entering Canada.

3 Along with other parts made in America, the engine arrives in a Canadian plant, where the car is assembled.

4 The fully assembled car leaves Canada and reenters the United States by train.

5 **Final destination**
The car is delivered to a dealership, where it is ready for purchase.

FIGURE 3.17 Example of a North American vehicle manufacturing supply chain. *Developed by the Author.*

the car is assembled with other parts from the United States and Canada. The finished vehicle is shipped by rail to a distribution center in the United States and from there to the dealership via truck car carrier.

NAFTA total cars production grew 39% between 1990 and 2017. Mexico experienced the largest growth rate in that period with a 164% increase (International Organization of Motor Vehicle Manufacturers, n.d.). US light vehicle production grew only 1.3% between 2015 and 2016, while Canada's production grew 5.2%, and Mexico's 2.5%. Since 2008, Mexican light vehicle production was higher than Canada's (Fig. 3.18) (Center for Automotive Research, 2017).

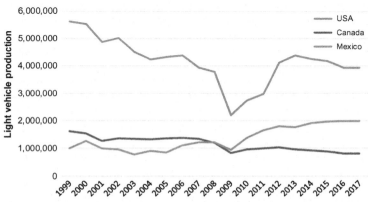

FIGURE 3.18   Light vehicle production in the NAFTA region (1999–2017). *Developed by author based on: International Organization of Motor Vehicle Manufacturers. (2018). Production Statistics. <http://www.oica.net/2018-production-statistics/>.*

Car manufacturing in the United States is concentrated in 13 of the 48 contiguous states (listed in order by number of plants):

1. Michigan
2. Ohio
3. Alabama
4. Illinois
5. Kentucky
6. Tennessee
7. Indiana
8. Mississippi
9. Missouri
10. South Carolina
11. Texas
12. Georgia
13. Kansas

The concentration in Michigan and adjacent states, including the province of Ontario in Canada, reflects the industry's historic base. Newer plants have located in the US Southern states, which are mostly foreign owned. These new locations were picked due to lower labor costs, nonunionized labor, state government incentives, and proximity to Mexico. Good rail and highway connectivity is an important decision factor in locating auto manufacturing plants, which depend on efficient supply chains.

Similarly, Mexico's auto plants are located in the northern and central parts of the country. The northern plants located in Nuevo Leon, Coahuila, Chihuahua, Sonora, and Baja California prefer this location due to its proximity to the US auto part supplier and finished vehicle markets. Most recently, Asian manufacturers have established new plants in central Mexico to take advantage of the large supply of skilled workforce, as well as access to Mexico's largest domestic consumer market, which is concentrated in the golden triangle formed by Mexico City, Guadalajara, and Monterrey (Pavlakovich-Kochi, 2017a).

The US Big Three auto manufacturers (General Motors, Chrysler, and Ford Motor Company) are still the largest producers of finished vehicles in North America. In 2015 they operated 43 plants, of which 27 car and truck assembly plants are located in the United States, 11 in Mexico, and 5 in Canada. The number of Asian and European plants in North America has been growing. In 2015 29 plants were in operation (18 in the United States and 11 in Mexico, including plants for Honda, Nissan, Toyota, Hyundai-Kia, Mercedes-Benz, and Volkswagen/Audi) (Pavlakovich-Kochi, 2017a) (Fig. 3.19).

Mexico's auto industry has grown significantly since the inception of NAFTA. As of 2015, 10 of the largest light and heavy vehicle manufacturers have operations in Mexico: General Motors, Ford, FCA, Volkswagen, Nissan, Honda, BMW, Toyota, Volvo Trucks, and Mercedes-Benz Trucks. In the 2016−18 period, other brands started operations in Mexico, including Audi, BMW, Mercedes-Benz, Infiniti, and Kia Motors. Heavy vehicle manufacturers with operations in Mexico include Daimler, Kenworth, Hino, Isuzu, Mercedes-Benz, Volvo, and Man, among others. Fig. 3.20 presents the location of these auto manufacturers (Pro Mexico, Ministry of Economy, 2016).

A large number of auto parts suppliers are headquartered in Michigan and Ontario, while one-quarter of them are in car assembly plants in other parts of the United States: Ohio, Illinois, Kentucky, Indiana, Tennessee, Georgia, South Carolina, and Texas.

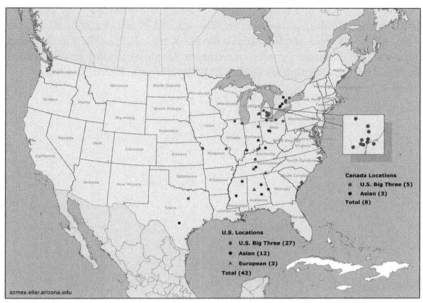

FIGURE 3.19   North American car manufacturing plants, United States and Canada (2015). *Economic and Business Research Center, Eller College of Management, The University of Arizona: Arizona, Mexico, and North America "Auto-Alley", by Vera Pavlakovich-Kochi, PhD https://www.azeconomy.org/2017/03/border-economy/arizona-mexico-and-north-americas-auto-alley/.*

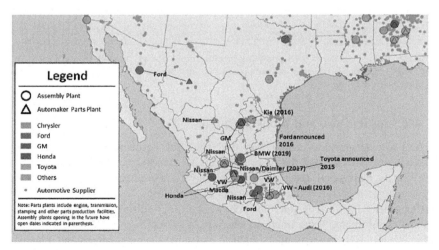

FIGURE 3.20   Mexican Automakers Assembly Plans and Automakers-owned Plants as of June 2016. *The Growing Role of Mexico in the North American Automotive Industry. Trends, Drivers and Forecasts. Center for Automotive Research for Automotive Communities Partnership. July 2016.*

A few suppliers in California and Arizona are associated with assembly plants in Baja California and Sonora. The state of Nuevo Leon is also home to one of the 100 top suppliers (Pavlakovich-Kochi, 2015). The top auto part suppliers have multiple facilities throughout North America and are located near the manufacturing plants (Fig. 3.21) (Pavlakovich-Kochi, 2017b).

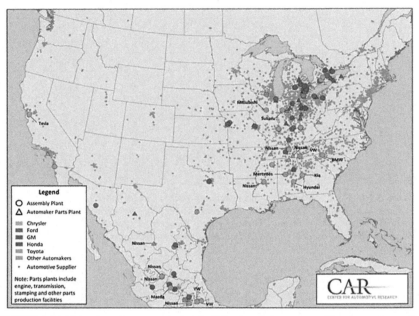

FIGURE 3.21   Location of parts-producing facilities in relation to assembly plants. *Center for Automotive Research*. Location of parts-producing facilities in relation to assembly plants. *<https://www.cargroup.org/>*.

3.4.2   Agriculture and foods products

NAFTA's agricultural treaty has two bilateral agreements: one between Canada and Mexico and the other between Mexico and the United States. As previously mentioned, the United States and Canada already had a free trade agreement; therefore the US—Canada provisions continued to apply (Alexander, 1993). As for the US—Mexico agriculture trade agreement, NAFTA eliminated most nontariff barriers in agricultural trade over a period of 15 years. Sensitive products such as sugar and corn received the longest phase-out periods. Approximately one-half of US—Mexico agricultural trade became duty-free when the agreement went into effect (The Trade Partnership, 2004; Villarreal & Fergusson, 2017).

Agricultural product trade in North America is very important because it provides a local source of food demand throughout the year. NAFTA agricultural trade provides the best possible prices by moving products from where they are grown and produced to where they are consumed. The supply chain is efficient, bringing equilibrium to supply and demand in the region. Fresh produce and fruits grown in Mexico during the winter are shipped north to satisfy the demand, while grain from Canada and the United States is shipped to Mexico to satisfy grain requirements, mainly corn.

The agricultural supply chain is complicated as it involves the participation of multiple stakeholders throughout the process from "dirt to dinner." The multiple phases and stakeholders in the agricultural supply chain include farms, crops, transportation, water usage, labor, and processing. Unlike manufactured products, agricultural products are not often grown in the same locations as they are consumed.

Fig. 3.22 presents a typical North American food supply chain. A typical NAFTA chain is exemplified by a typical American breakfast with bacon that probably starts its life as a piglet in Manitoba, Canada; is then trucked to southern Minnesota where it is fed corn from Iowa and where it is processed into bacon; and is finally sent to a US grocery store or back to Canada. Feeder pigs are primarily born in Canada (most often in Manitoba) and then shipped to the United States when they are about 40 pounds (Stitzer, 2018).

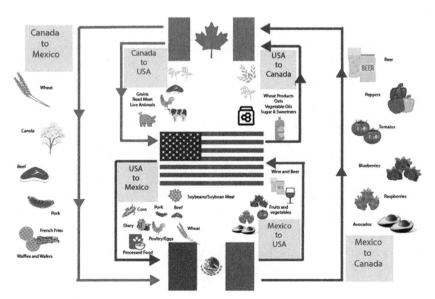

FIGURE 3.22 Agriculture industry NAFTA supply chain example (Stitzer, 2018). *Stitzer, L. M. What is NAFTA?* <*https://www.dirt-to-dinner.com/what-is-nafta/*>.

In 2017 Canada and Mexico were the number one and number three top destinations of US agricultural exports, respectively. The United States exported to Canada US$25.4 billion of agricultural products and imported US$25.1 billion, a relatively balanced trade. US–Canada total agricultural trade grew 4.5 times between 1992 and 2017, from US$11.6 to US$52 billion (United States Census Bureau, n.d.).

Key agricultural US exports to Canada include fruits and vegetables, and Canadian exports to the United States include flour, fish, and meat (Figs. 3.23 and 3.24).

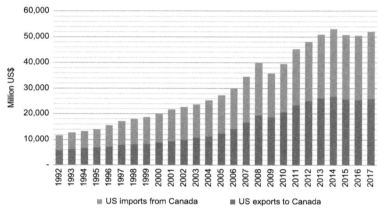

FIGURE 3.23   US–Canada agricultural trade (1992–2017). *United States Department of Transportation Bureau of Transportation Statistics.* TransBorder Freight Data. *<https://www.bts. gov/transborder>.*

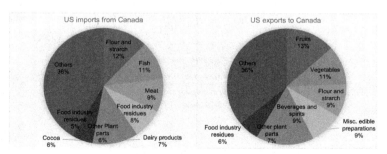

FIGURE 3.24   US–Canada agricultural trade products (2017). *Developed by the author with data from United States Department of Transportation Bureau of Transportation Statistics.* TransBorder Freight Data. *<https://www.bts.gov/transborder>.*

The United States exported to Mexico US$17.7 billion of agricultural products and imported US$24.78 billion, giving Mexico a trade surplus of more than US$7 billion. US—Mexico total agricultural trade grew 7 times from US$6.4 to US$45 billion between 1992 and 2017 (Fig. 3.25) (United States Census Bureau, n.d.).

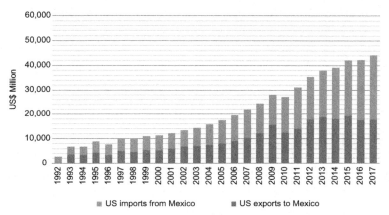

■ US imports from Mexico   ■ US exports to Mexico

FIGURE 3.25 US—Mexico agricultural trade (1992—2017). *United States Department of Transportation Bureau of Transportation Statistics.* TransBorder Freight Data. *<https://www.bts. gov/transborder>.*

With the implementation of NAFTA, US—Mexico agricultural product trade with the United States grew much faster than US—Canada trade. A U.S. Department of Agriculture (USDA) report mentioned:

> *Mexico does not produce enough grains and oilseeds to meet internal demand, so the country's food and livestock producers import sizable volumes of these commodities to make value-added products, primarily for the domestic market. In turn, U.S. fruit and vegetable imports from Mexico are closely tied to Mexico's expertise in producing a wide range of produce, along with its favorable climate and a growing season that largely complements the U.S. growing season (United States Census Bureau, n.d.).*

Key agricultural US exports to Mexico include cereals and meat. Cereals are mainly corn and wheat, which is handled by rail though the North American railroad system. Mexico exports fruits and vegetables to the United States, mostly by truck, and beverages and spirits, mainly beer by rail (Fig. 3.26).

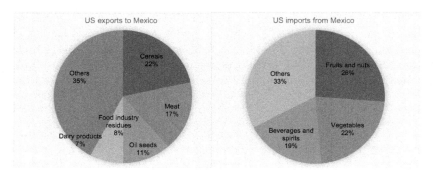

FIGURE 3.26 US—Mexico agricultural trade products (2017). *United States Department of Transportation Bureau of Transportation Statistics.* TransBorder Freight Data. *<https://www.bts. gov/transborder>.*

US corn exports to Mexico expanded at a compound annual rate of 19.7% between 1993 and 2017, a growth of 7477%. Wheat expanded at a compound annual rate of 8.03% in the same period with a total growth of 538 from 1993 to 2017 (United States Census Bureau, n.d.).

3.4.3   Energy

The energy industry is the second major U.S. sector that relies on NAFTA intermediate imports. The United States is a major importer of crude oil from Canada, and to a lesser extent Mexico. In 16 states—including Illinois, Texas, Minnesota, Oklahoma, Washington, Montana, and Colorado—crude oil is the largest intermediate good import from North America. Pipelines carry oil from Alberta, Canada into the northern and western United States where it is refined and sent into markets throughout the west .Canada is one of the world's largest crude oil producers and it exported an average of more 3.7 million barrels per day (bbls/d) to the United States, and received 378,000 bbls/d of U.S. crude oil exports in 2018. U.S.-Canada refined product trade was relatively balanced with Canada exporting 582,000 bbls/d to the U.S. and importing 517,000 bbls/d in 2018.

Historically, energy trade between Mexico and the U.S. has been of Mexico's crude oil exports and recently imported back to Mexico as refined products. In 2018, Mexico exprtoed 665,000 bbls/d of crude oil and imported 1.2 million bbls/d of refined products. Mexican petroleum is handled by vessel through the Gulf of Mexico to major refining and chemical manufacturing hubs in Texas, Louisiana and Mississippi (Fig. 3.27) (Parilla, 2017).

In 2016, 81 US refineries imported crude oil from either Canada or Mexico, as US refineries are configured to process heavy crudes from Canada and Mexico. Canada is the US number one source for imported crude oil; imports of

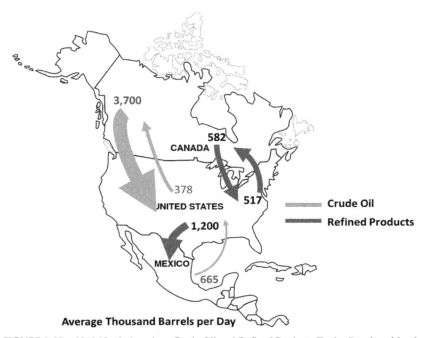

Average Thousand Barrels per Day

FIGURE 3.27 2018 North American Crude Oil and Refined Products Trade. *Developed by the author with information from the U.S. Energy Information Administration: https://www.eia.gov/ todayinenergy/detail.php?id = 39172, Natural Resources Canada, Crude oil facts, https://www. nrcan.gc.ca/science-data/data-analysis/energy-data-analysis/energy-facts/crude-oil-facts/20064#L7, U.S. Energy Information Administration, Country Analysis Executive Summary: Canada, October 7, 2019, https://www.eia.gov/international/content/analysis/countries_long/Canada/canada_CAXS.pdf.*

Canadian crude increased 61% between 2000 and 2016. US refineries that import Mexican crude also supply refined products to the domestic market, as well as exports back to Mexico (American Petroleum Institute, 2017).

In 2013, Mexico made a Constitutional Reform opening the country to private investment in the oil and gas sector. To meet current demand for refined products, Mexico imports a large portion of refined products from refineries on the U.S. Gulf Coast and arrive by ship. However, for the last few years, some of these products are imported by rail. Kansas City Southern de Mexico in coordination with Kansas City Southern railroad are handling refined products from Texas to Central Mexico. The total number of manifest train service has been increasing on a month to month basis and it is expected to continue growing 15 percent per year for the next 5 years. The service includes origins in Corpus Christi and Beaumont, Texas, serving Monterey (Salinas Victoria Terminal), the Port of Altamira in the Gulf of Mexico, San Luis Potosi, San Jose Iturbide, and Querétaro (Fig. 3.28).

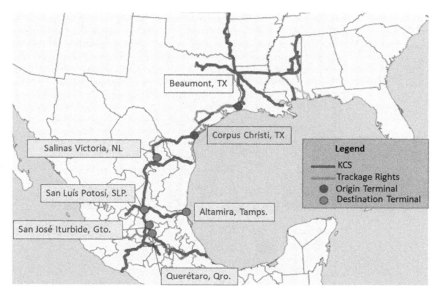

FIGURE 3.28   KCS-Served Fluid Terminals. Developed by the Author with information from Kansas City Southern, Investor Relations General Book, Last Updated April 17, 2019. https://investors.kcsouthern.com/ ~ /media/Files/K/KC-Southern-IR-V2/documents/ir-general-book-170419.pdf. Map *source: https://es.wikipedia.org/wiki/Archivo:Kansas_City_Southern_Railway_system_map.svg.*

References

Alexander, D. (1993). The North American Free Trade Agreement: An overview. *Berkeley Journal of International Law*, *11*(1), 12. Retrieved from <https://scholarship.law.berkeley.edu/cgi/viewcontent.cgi?article = 1124&context = bjil>.

American Petroleum Institute. (2017). *Energy benefits of NAFTA*. API. Retrieved from <https://www.api.org/ ~ /media/files/policy/trade/energy-benefits-of-nafta.pdf>.

Center for Automotive Research. (January 2017). *NAFTA briefing: Trade benefits to the automotive industry and potential consequences of withdrawal from the agreement*. CAR. Retrieved from <https://www.cargroup.org/wp-content/uploads/2017/01/nafta_briefing_january_2017_public_version-final.pdf>.

Grigsby, K. (2018). *Tennessee's huge auto industry: 7 things you may not know*. Nashville, TN: Tennessean. Retrieved from <https://www.tennessean.com/story/money/cars/2018/03/27/tennessee-auto-industry-smyrna-nissan-gm-spring-hill-vw-chattanooga/447779002/>.

International Organization of Motor Vehicle Manufacturers. (n.d.). *2016 Production Statistics*. OIACA. Retrieved from <http://www.oica.net/category/production-statistics/2016-statistics/>.

Parilla, J. (2017). *How US states rely on the NAFTA supply chain*. Brookings, OR. Retrieved from <https://www.brookings.edu/blog/the-avenue/2017/03/30/how-u-s-states-rely-on-the-nafta-supply-chain/>.

Parson, L. M. (2018). *Established auto industry*. Missouri Department of Economic Development. Retrieved from <https://ded.mo.gov/auto/why-missouri/established-auto-industry>.

Pavlakovich-Kochi, V. (2015). *Auto News Data Center*. The University of Arizona. Retrieved from <https://www.azeconomy.org/2017/03/border-economy/arizona-mexico-and-north-americas-auto-alley/>.

Pavlakovich-Kochi, V. (March 31, 2017a). *Arizona, Mexico and North America's "Auto Alley."* The University of Arizona. Retrieved from <https://www.azeconomy.org/2017/03/border-economy/arizona-mexico-and-north-americas-auto-alley/>.

Pavlakovich-Kochi, V. (March 31, 2017b). *Arizona, Mexico and North America's "Auto Alley."* Arizona's Economic and Business Research Center. Retrieved from <https://www.azeconomy.org/2017/03/border-economy/arizona-mexico-and-north-americas-auto-alley/>.

Plastics Industry Association. (2019). *Facts & figures of New Jersey*. E.U. Retrieved from <https://www.plasticsindustry.org/factsheet/new-jersey>.

Porter, E. M. (2018). *Ohio*. Boston: Clustering mapping. Retrieved from <http://clustermapping.us/region/state/ohio>.

Pro Mexico, Ministry of Economy. (2016). *The Mexican automotive industry: Current situation, challenges and opportunities*. Retrieved from <https://www.promexico.mx/documentos/biblioteca/the-mexican-automotive-industry.pdf>.

Stitzer, L.M. (February 22, 2018). *What is NAFTA? Dirt to dinner; food matters*. Retrieved from <https://www.dirt-to-dinner.com/what-is-nafta/>.

The Trade Partnership. (February 2004). *NAFTA: A decade of growth* (p. 35) Washington, DC: Business Roundtable. Retrieved from <http://tradepartnership.com/wp-content/uploads/2014/06/NAFTA_Decade_of_Growth.pdf>.

United States Census Bureau. (n.d.). *USA trade online*. U.S. Department of Commerce. Retrieved from <https://usatrade.census.gov/index.php?do = login>.

United States Department of Agriculture, Foreign Agricultural Service. (2019). *Mexico: Grain and feed annual*. Retrieved from <https://www.fas.usda.gov/data/mexico-grain-and-feed-annual-3>.

United States Department of Transportation. (n.d.). *TransBorder Freight Data*. Bureau of Transportation Statistics. Retrieved from <https://www.bts.gov/transborder>.

U.S. International Trade Commission's Interactive Tariff and Trade Data Web. (2019). Retrieved from <http://dataweb.usitc.gov>.

Villarreal, A., & Fergusson, I. (2017). The North American Free Trade Agreement (NAFTA). *Congressional Research Service*. https://doi.org/R42965. Retrieved from <https://fas.org/sgp/crs/row/R42965.pdf>.

Chapter 4

Cross-border transportation infrastructure in North America (transportation supply)

4.1 Introduction

Freight transportation infrastructure is an important element in handling international trade across international borders. In this context, *infrastructure* includes not only the physical facilities at the land border crossings, roadways, and rail lines approaching the border that support freight transportation but also the processes that are involved in the exchange of goods between the countries in North America.

As mentioned in previous chapters, most of the trade among Canada, Mexico, and the United States is handled by land modes of transport, primarily truck and rail. This chapter presents a description of the transportation infrastructure that serves trade between the United States and Mexico and between the United States and Canada. The first part of this chapter describes the highway infrastructure characteristics in each country, including main corridors that handle freight and funding mechanisms for these assets. A description of the rail network in North America is also included, covering characteristics and markets served by each of the main railroads in the region.

The second part of this chapter describes the critical nodes of the international trade networks in North America, which are land ports of entry (POEs) or border crossings. The physical characteristics of the POEs at the US−Canada and US−Mexico crossings are presented, followed by a description of the highway and rail border crossing processes. The description includes the physical movement of goods, as well as the information exchange processes, and the technology that has been implemented to facilitate trade. An assessment of the stakeholders' role in border crossing process and its implications for trade movement is discussed. The current US−Mexico cross-border truck rules and implications are also analyzed, identifying potential improvements.

International Trade and Transportation Infrastructure Development.
DOI: https://doi.org/10.1016/B978-0-12-815741-1.00004-8

4.2   Roadway system in Canada

Canada's National Highway System (CNHS) is an evolution of the Trans-Canada Highway (TCH) concept originally launched in 1949. In 2016, the CNHS comprised 38,049 km (23,642 miles) of highways, of which 95% is owned and operated by provincial and territorial governments. The remaining 5% is comprised of roads under federal control, which are those through national parks and the Alaska Highway, with 3%, and the other 2% are roads under municipal control.

The CNHS is divided into three categories:

1. *Core Route*. Key interprovincial and international corridor routes that include links to intermodal facilities and important international border crossings.
2. *Feeder Routes*. Links to the core routes from population and economic centers.
3. *Northern and Remote Routes*. Key linkages to core and feeder routes that provide the primary means of access to northern and remote areas, economic activities, and resources (Council of Ministers Responsible for Transportation and Highway Safety, 2016).

Fig. 4.1 presents a map depicting the Canadian National Highway System.

In 2007, the Government of Canada released the National Policy Framework for Strategic Gateways and Trade Corridors. This policy is aimed to improve the capacity and efficiency of Canada's transportation system to support international trade. The Government of Canada identified the link between the efficient movement of trade and increased competitiveness of the economy.

The Strategic Gateways and Trade Corridors Framework includes a government-wide approach to develop and optimize Canada's transportation system, emphasizing its geographic advantages. The Framework includes long-term planning and public–private collaboration and applies an integrated approach to evaluating and implementing transportation infrastructure, as well as policy and operational measures.

Canada's gateways are divided into three regions. Each region has its unique characteristics; therefore specific strategies have been developed for each region. It is important to note that these three gateways are complementary to one another. The three regional strategies are discussed in the following sections.

4.2.1   Canadian Asia–Pacific gateway and corridor strategy

The objective of this particular strategy is to strengthen Canada's competitive position by establishing the best transportation network between Asia

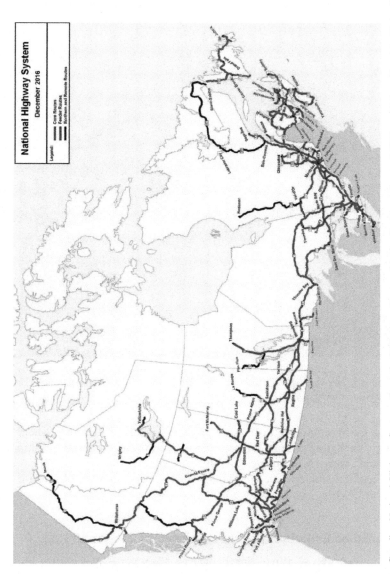

FIGURE 4.1 Canadian National Highway System. *Council of Ministers Responsible for Transportation and Highway Safety. Canada's National Highway System—annual report 2016.* *<https://comt.ca/english/nhs-report-2015.pdf>*.

and North America. This gateway links the ports of Vancouver and Prince Rupert in the Pacific Coast with Canada's inland supply chain and the rest of North America (Fig. 4.2).

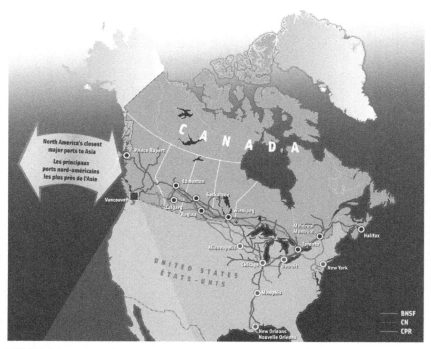

FIGURE 4.2 Asia−Pacific gateway and corridor. *Association Professionnelle des Gérants et Courtiers en Immuebles de Genève.* Canada's Asia−Pacific gateway and corridor initiative. *<http://www.apgci.gc.ca/apgc.html>*.

Multiple transportation infrastructure projects have been identified under this strategy, including actions from the federal government in partnership with all four western Canadian provinces (Alberta, British Columbia, Manitoba, and Saskatchewan), as well as other public and private sector partners.

4.2.2 Canadian Ontario−Quebec Continental Gateway strategy

This gateway provides a critical link between all key gateway facilities and the Canada−US border crossings. The Ontario−Quebec Continental Gateway strategy is directed toward developing a sustainable, secure, and efficient multimodal transportation system that supports business opportunities (Fig. 4.3).

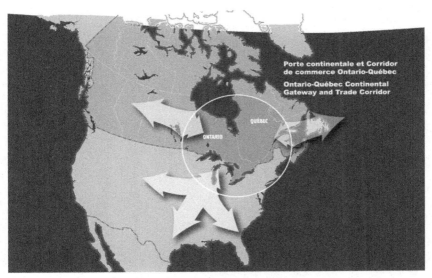

FIGURE 4.3 Ontario–Quebec Continental Gateway. *Environmental Assessment, official Blog of the Concordia University Master of Environment Students.* The Canadian Environmental Assessment Fallacy. *<https://mastereia.wordpress.com/2012/04/11/the-canadian-environmental-assessment-fallacy/>.*

4.2.3 Canada's Atlantic gateway and trade corridor strategy

This corridor connects North America to markets in Europe, the Caribbean, Latin America, and Asia via the Suez Canal through its deepwater ports. The strategy of this multimodal corridor was developed in partnership between government entities and private sector stakeholders, including the Canadian Federal Government and the provincial governments of Nova Scotia, New Brunswick, Prince Edward Island, Newfoundland, and Labrador (Government of Canada, 2017a) (Fig. 4.4).

4.2.4 Canada's highway funding

Transport Canada is the agency responsible for transportation policies and programs in Canada, promoting safe, secure, efficient, and environmentally responsible transportation (Government of Canada, 2018a). According to Transport Canada, Highways in Canada, including the TCH and the CNHS, fall within provincial/territorial jurisdiction; therefore responsibility for the planning, design, construction, operation, maintenance, and financing of highways lies with each province or territory (Government of Canada, 2010a).

The Canadian federal government has a long history of providing assistance for highway construction in Canada. Federal taxes, including the excise tax on gasoline and diesel fuel, go into the general coffers and help sustain a

FIGURE 4.4 Atlantic gateway and trade corridor. *Atlantic Gateway and Trade Corridor Strategy. Connecting Canada with the World.* <*http://www.halifaxgateway.com/site-ghp2/media/HalifaxGateway/AGW1.pdf*>.

number of federal programs. Federally funded infrastructure programs that assist in funding highways and roads are primarily structured through bilateral cost-sharing agreements with specific provinces and territories. The majority of these infrastructure funds are administered by Infrastructure Canada (Padova, 2006).

Under Infrastructure Canada, a C$8.8 billion fund was established under the 2007 Building Canada plan. The fund makes investments in public infrastructure owned by provincial, territorial, and municipal governments and, in certain cases, private sector and nonprofit organizations. Funding is allocated to each province and territory based on population (Government of Canada, 2010b).

At the provincial level, fuel taxes and other road-related fees such as motor vehicle licensing and registry fees, as well as fines, contribute to covering a large portion of highway-related construction and maintenance costs.

Canada has not made significant use of tolls or congestion charges and other road pricing mechanisms. However, some provinces are considering introducing these types of mechanisms to complement shrinking gas tax revenues to fund transportation infrastructure projects.

In 2017, the government of Canada proposed to invest C$10.1 billion over the next decade in trade and transportation projects. This investment will help build stronger and more efficient transportation corridors to international markets and help Canadian businesses compete, grow, and create more jobs.

Transport Canada is leading the overall investment in trade and transportation infrastructure under the Trade and Transportation Corridors Initiative (TTCI). This initiative will prioritize investments to address congestion and bottlenecks along vital corridors and around transportation hubs and ports providing access to world markets (Government of Canada, 2018b).

The main goals of the TTCI are:

- *Supporting trade corridors.* Invest C$2 billion over 11 years for the National Trade Corridors Fund, which is a merit-based program to make Canada's trade corridors more efficient and reliable. This program will reduce bottlenecks, address capacity issues, make the transportation system more resilient to the effects of climate change, and make sure it is able to support new technologies and innovation.
- *Transportation innovation.* Stay on top of changing trends by updating regulations, certifications, and standards. The TTCI is planning to invest C$50 million to develop regulations for the safe use of connected and automated vehicles and unmanned air vehicles, to establish pilot projects, and to establish standards and certifications for the safe use of these new technologies.
- *Data exchanges on transportation information.* Invest C$50 million to create a new Canadian Centre on Transportation Data. This center will gather the information needed to make targeted investments in trade corridors, which will support growth and the creation of good, well-paying jobs (Government of Canada, 2019).

4.3   Roadway system in the United States

4.3.1   National Highway System in the United States

The National Highway System (NHS) consists of roadways important to the nation's economy, defense, and mobility. It was developed by the Department of Transportation (DOT) in cooperation with the states, local officials, and metropolitan planning organizations (MPOs). The NHS includes the following roadway subsystems:

- *Interstate.* The Eisenhower Interstate System of highways, which retains its separate identity within the NHS.
- *Other principal arterials.* Highways in rural and urban areas providing access between an arterial and a major port, airport, public transportation facility, or other intermodal transportation facility.
- *Strategic Highway Network (STRAHNET).* A network of highways that are important to the United States' strategic defense policy and that provide access, continuity, and emergency capabilities for defense purposes.
- *Major strategic highway network connectors.* Highways providing access between major military installations and highways, part of the Strategic Highway Network.
- *Intermodal connectors.* Highways that provide access between major intermodal facilities and the other four subsystems making up the NHS (U.S. Department of Transportation, Federal Highway Administration, 2017).

It is important to note that a specific highway route may be on more than one subsystem. Fig. 4.5 presents the 2015 United States NHS.

4.3.2   The United States National Highway Freight Network

The Fixing America's Surface Transportation (FAST) Act is a funding and authorization bill to govern US federal surface transportation spending that became law in December 2015. The FAST Act directed the FHWA to establish a National Highway Freight Network (NHFN) to strategically direct federal resources and policies toward the improved performance of highway portions of the US freight transportation system.

The freight network of the United States includes 985,000 miles (1.58 million kilometers) of federal-aid highways and other modes of transport that link ports, airports, cities, manufacturing centers, farms, mines, and other economic activity sites. The Interstate System carries one-half of truck travel and three-fourths of travel by freight-hauling trucks serving places at least 50 miles apart (U.S. Department of Transportation, Federal Highway Administration, 2017a).

The NHFN includes the following roadway subsystems:

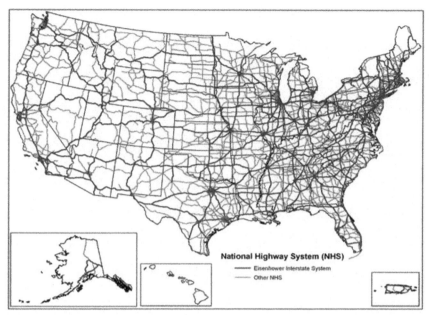

FIGURE 4.5 United States National Highway System. *Wikipedia.* The Free Encyclopedia: National Highway System (United States). *<https://en.wikipedia.org/wiki/National_Highway_ System_(United_States)>.*

- *Primary Highway Freight System (PHFS).* A network of highways identified as the most critical highway portions of the US freight transportation
  system. The network consist of 41,518 miles (66,429 km), including
  37,436 miles (59,898 km) of Interstate and 4082 miles (6531 km) of non-
  Interstate roads.
- *Other Interstate portions not on the PHFS.* Highways consisting of the
  remaining portion of Interstate roads not included in the PHFS. These
  routes provide important continuity and access to freight transportation
  facilities. These portions amount to an estimated 9511 miles (15,303 km)
  of Interstate, nationwide, and will fluctuate with additions and deletions
  to the Interstate Highway System.
- *Critical Rural Freight Corridors (CRFCs).* Public roads not in an urbanized area that provide access and connection to the PHFS and to the
  Interstate with other important ports, public transportation facilities, or
  other intermodal freight facilities.
- *Critical Urban Freight Corridors (CUFCs).* Public roads in urbanized
  areas that provide access and connection to the PHFS and to the
  Interstate with other ports, public transportation facilities, or other inter-
  modal transportation facilities (U.S. Department of Transportation,
  Federal Highway Administration, 2017b) (Fig. 4.6).

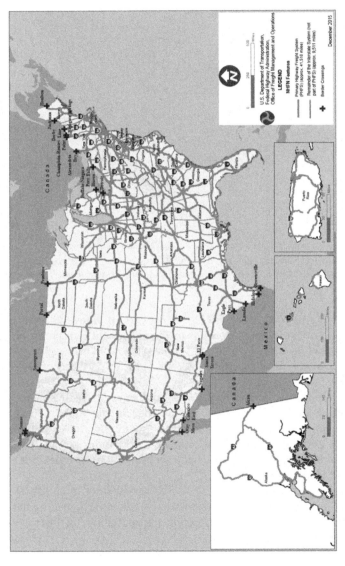

FIGURE 4.6 National Highway Freight Network. *U.S. Department of Transportation.* Federal Highway Administration. *<https://ops.fhwa.dot.gov/freight/ infrastructure/nfn/maps/nhfn_map.htm>.*

4.3.3 Highway funding in the United States

The United States federal government provides some form of highway funding to the states through the Federal-Aid Highway Program (FAHP). Funds are apportioned to the states by formula, and the implementation is the responsibility of the state departments of transportation (state DOTs). The federal government provides 80%, and the states need to match that amount with 20% for non-Interstate System road projects. The federal government provides 90% for Interstate System projects. Federal funds can be spent only on designated federal-aid highways.

The FAHP is an "umbrella" program that contains various separate highway programs administered by the FHWA. In order to have access to these programs, each state is required to have a State Transportation Improvement Plan (STIP). In the STIP, state DOTs determine funding priorities. Metropolitan planning organizations (MPOs), which are federally mandated and federally funded transportation policy-making organizations that are made up of representatives from local government and governmental transportation authorities, also have an important role in project decision-making in urban areas. However, federal funding flows through state DOTs and then to MPOs.

The Highway Trust Fund (HTF) is a transportation fund that receives money from a federal fuel tax of 18.4 cents per gallon of gasoline and 24.4 cents per gallon of diesel fuel and related excise taxes. It is important to note that the tax amount is fixed, not a percentage of the fuel price. The HTF currently has two accounts: the Highway Account, which funds road construction and other surface transportation projects, and a smaller Mass Transit Account, which supports mass transit. Separate from the HTF, there is the Leaking Underground Storage Tank Trust Fund, which receives an additional 0.1 cent per gallon of gasoline and diesel, making the total amount of tax collected 18.5 cents per gallon on gasoline and 24.5 cents per gallon on diesel fuel.

The FAHP is different from other federal programs because it does not rely on appropriated budget authority. The FHWA is funded through the HTF and may obligate (promise to pay) funds for projects funded with contract authority prior to an appropriation. Once funds have been obligated, the federal government has a legal commitment to provide the funds. Because highway projects usually span more than several years, this approach shields highway construction projects from annual appropriations decisions.

The HTF rates on motor fuels have not changed since 1993 and thus have failed to keep pace with price increases for gasoline and diesel fuel. Revenue from the federal excise tax on gasoline and on diesel fuel accounts for 86% of the total. Other smaller amounts come from sales taxes on tractors and heavy trucks, an excise tax on tires for heavy vehicles, and an annual use tax on those vehicles. In addition to dedicated tax revenue, the trust fund receives a small amount of interest on trust fund reserves (Tax Policy Center, 2018) (Fig. 4.7).

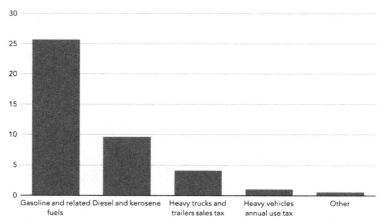

FIGURE 4.7 Highway Trust Fund Revenue by Source (2017) (billions of dollars). *Tax Policy Center Urban Institute & Brookings Institution.* Key elements of the U.S. tax system. <*https://www.taxpolicycenter.org/briefing-book/what-highway-trust-fund-and-how-it-financed*>.

As vehicles become more efficient in terms of fuel consumption due to more hybrid or electric vehicles on the road, fuel tax revenues have been going down, while travel-miles have remained constant or are increasing. This situation has created a gap between the cost of surface transportation spending and revenues from the HTF. The US Congress has filled these gaps with transfers mainly from the Treasury's general fund (Tax Policy Center, 2018). The projected gap between dedicated surface transportation revenues and spending from fiscal year 2021 to fiscal 2026 will average $20.1 billion annually (Congressional Budget Office, 2016).

Various alternative approaches to solve the highway funding gap are being analyzed. These alternatives include indexing the motor fuel tax rates to the price of fuel or to inflation or charging drivers for the distance they travel. This distance-based-user-charges alternative is favored by economists; however, its implementation procedures need to be defined and agreed on by all stakeholders.

Tolling highways is another user fee alternative for highway operation and funding. Most of the state DOTs public—private partnership efforts are being devoted to the development of toll roads. The FHWA has a tolling program under the FAST Act that is managed under the Center for Innovative Finance Support (Build America Transportation Investment Center, n.d.).

One of the first toll roads in the United States was the Carlisle-to-Irwin segment of the Pennsylvania Turnpike that opened in 1940. A financial success prompted other states to use the same financing method. Each state established a toll authority to issue bonds, and revenues from the bonds provided up-front funds to pay for construction. Toll revenue was used by the toll authority to repay bondholders with interest, for finance administration, and for the maintenance and operation of the highway. Multiple states developed tolled turnpikes in roadways that had been designated as part of the Interstate System. By law, these turnpikes were built without any federal-aid highway funds or other federal tax dollars. As of 2015, there were 3296 miles (5303 km) of toll roads in the Interstate System, and 2260 miles (3636 km) of toll roads in the non-Interstate network (U.S. Department of Transportation, Federal Highway Administration, 2016, 2017c).

4.4   Roadway system in Mexico

The Mexican National Highway Network (NHN) had 393,473 km (244,492 miles) in 2016. Thirteen percent of the NHN is the main Federal Network, 24% are feeder roads, 45% are rural highways, and 18% minor asphalt roads. The NHN can also be classified based on the surface as shown in (Fig. 4.8) (Secretaría de Comunicaciones y Transportes, 2017). Close to 80% of the total NHN length is either paved or has an asphalt surface. There is still one-fifth of the network with unpaved roadways.

Fig. 4.9 presents the Mexican NHN.

4.4.1   Highway classification in Mexico for freight movement

In Mexico, the federal government, through the Ministry of Communications and Transport (Secretaría de Comunicaciones y Transportes [SCT]), establishes truck size and weight regulations for operation on the federal highway system.

Not all commercial vehicles can operate throughout the roadway network. Official Regulation NOM-012-SCT-2-2017, published in the *Diario Oficial* (*Federal Gazette*) on June 7, 2017, and developed by the SCT, establishes the following highway classifications: ET, A, B, C, and D.

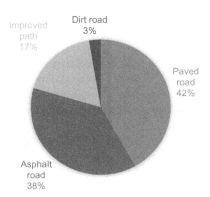

FIGURE 4.8 Mexican Highway Network by Surface. *Developed by the author with information from the Secretaría de Comunicaciones y Transportes.* Anuario Estadístico 2016 (Statistical Yearbook 2016). *<http://www.sct.gob.mx/fileadmin/DireccionesGrales/DGP/estadistica/Anuarios/Anuario_2016.pdf>.*

FIGURE 4.9 Mexican National Highway Network. *Instituto Nacional de Geografía y Estadística–INEGI.* Principales carreteras en México (Mexican National Highway Network). *<https://www.inegi.org.mx/>*.

- *Highway Type ET–Eje de Transporte.* "Transportation axis" highways are the highest category of roadways in Mexico. ET highways are those with geometric and structural characteristics that can accommodate the operation of vehicles with the maximum dimensions, capacity, and weight. Additionally, the SCT authorizes other general interest vehicles to operate on ET highways. ET highways can be designated ET2 (two lanes) or ET4 (four lanes).
- *Highway Type A.* Type A highways allow for the operation of all vehicles authorized with the maximum dimensions, capacity, and weight, except those that by their dimensions and weight are only allowed on ET highways. Type A highways can be designated as A2 (two lanes) or A4 (four lanes).
- *Highway Type B.* Type B highways have lower design standards than Type A highways, but they are included in the primary network, which, due to their geometric and structural characteristics, serve interstate transportation. Type B highways can be designated as B2 (two lanes) or B4 (four lanes).
- *Highway Type C.* Type C highways form the secondary roadway network. Due to their design characteristics, they serve medium trip lengths within states, establishing connections and links with the primary network.

- *Highway Type D.* Type D highways form the feeder network and serve traffic within municipalities. They serve relatively short trip lengths, establishing connections with the secondary network (Type C highways).

Long combination vehicles (LCVs), or double trailer trucks, are commonly used in Mexico. LCVs with a tractor with three axles, a two-axle semitrailer, and a four-axle trailer (T3-S2-R4) are allowed to travel only on ET and A roads and have a maximum gross vehicular weight of 75.5 metric tons (166,449 pounds) and a total length of 31 meters (101.7 feet). Fig. 4.10 presents a typical T3-S2-R4 configuration operating in Mexico.

FIGURE 4.10   T3-S2-R4 truck configuration operating in Mexico.

4.4.2   Highway corridors in Mexico

The SCT identified 15 roadway corridors that provide north−south and east−west connectivity. Some of these corridors are already developed, and others are under development, improving roadway conditions. These corridors connect to all state capitals, the main metropolitan concentrations, the medium cities, the relevant maritime ports, and the accesses to international border crossings with the United States in the north and with Belize and Guatemala in the south of the country (Secretaría de Comunicaciones y Transportes, 2017).

Fig. 4.11 presents the main highway corridors in Mexico.

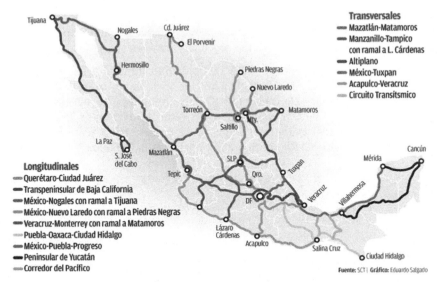

Transversales
- Mazatlán-Matamoros
- Manzanillo-Tampico
  con ramal a L. Cárdenas
- Altiplano
- México-Tuxpan
- Acapulco-Veracruz
- Circuito Transítsmico

Longitudinales
- Querétaro-Ciudad Juárez
- Transpeninsular de Baja California
- México-Nogales con ramal a Tijuana
- México-Nuevo Laredo con ramal a Piedras Negras
- Veracruz-Monterrey con ramal a Matamoros
- Puebla-Oaxaca-Ciudad Hidalgo
- México-Puebla-Progreso
- Peninsular de Yucatán
- Corredor del Pacífico

Fuente: SCT | Gráfico: Eduardo Salgado

FIGURE 4.11 Main highway corridors in Mexico. *Secretaría de Comunicaciones y Transportes.* Anuario Estadístico del Sector Comunicaciones y Transportes 2016 *(Statistical Yearbook of the Communications and Transportation Sector 2016).* <http://cicm.org.mx/wp-content/files_mf/presentaci%C3%B3nherramientasprogramafni201926.01.19.pdf>.

4.4.3 Highway funding in Mexico

The Mexican highway network is built mostly by the federal government with revenues from the annual federal budget. The federal government can also give grants or concessions for building and operating roads to individuals, states, or municipalities.

Since the year 2000, Mexican roadway expansion has been funded mainly by private sector investments through various types of public—private partnerships (3P). Part of the tolled network is managed by an agency called Federal Roads and Bridges and Related Services (CAPUFE), which in 2014 handled approximately 40% of the total tolled network in the country.

The Mexican private toll road program was one of the first in the world, and it faced some design issues that led to the government bailout of some of the concessions. However, in the 1989—94 period, the toll roadway network almost doubled to 9900 km (6153 miles) with 53 concessions and an investment of $13 billion.

In the original toll road program, the Mexican federal government partially guaranteed the cost of construction and traffic growth projections. The concessions were awarded to the bidder with the shortest concession period that resulted in high toll levels. This made tolls difficult to pay by most users, and traffic volumes were extremely lower than original estimates. The government bailed out 23 of the concessions and assumed the bank liabilities and temporary ownership. The federal government created a trust fund that manages the debt of the rescued toll roads (World Bank & Public—Private Infrastructure Advisory Facility, 2003).

In 2016, the main corridor network included 9818 km (6100 miles) of toll roads and 40,681 km (25,278 miles) of nontoll roads. The toll roads constitute 19.44% of the main corridor highway network, while the nontoll highways represent 80.56%.

4.5 Summary: North American highway systems

The highway network in Canada, the United States, and Mexico has relatively good geographical coverage in all three countries and provides an efficient system for handling freight and international trade. Several differences in the way the three countries operate and fund the highway network could impact overall system performance. In Canada, the vast majority of the system is owned and operated by provincial and territorial governments, while in the United States, the states perform planning and construction with federal funding that goes to each state on a formula basis. In Mexico, the federal government has the leading role in the planning, construction, and operation of highways.

For funding, Mexico has relied on a concession system for construction and operation of the highway system. In the United States funding comes mainly from the Highway Trust Fund; however, this funding mechanism needs to be revised to continue as a feasible long-term alternative funding source. Canada's federal government assists funding highways and roads through bilateral cost-sharing agreements with specific provinces and territories, administered by Infrastructure Canada.

The three North American countries have programs to address the movement of freight and trade in the highway system. Canada's Strategic Gateways and Trade Corridors program was specifically developed to improve the capacity and efficiency of Canada's transportation system to support international trade. In the United States, the National Highway Freight Network is being developed to strategically direct federal resources and policies toward the improved performance of highway portions of the US freight transportation system. Mexico has defined 15 strategic corridors that link the Pacific Ocean and Gulf of Mexico coasts, as well as the southern and northern borders.

Truck configurations and maximum weights vary across the three North American countries. In Mexico, the double trailer is a common sight on main roadways. In Canada, LCVs usually operate on a special permit basis, and Canadian provinces have the authority to regulate truck size and weight, so the limits under which commercial vehicles operate vary significantly among provinces. Canadian long-combination vehicles are not directly comparable with US or Mexican vehicles due to differences in regulatory regimes and the operating environment. In the United States, the most common long-haul truck configuration is the 53-foot tractor-trailer.

4.6 Railroads in North America

The rail system in North America connects nearly all major cities and maritime ports in Canada, the United States, and Mexico. The system has the same standard gauge (1435 mm, or 4 ft $8^1/_2$ in) and, because the freight system is not electrified as in Europe, all freight rail companies use diesel locomotives and railcars that are interchangeable and can therefore serve the manufacturing and distribution industries throughout North America.

Compared to the highway systems in all three North American countries, which are built mainly by the federal or state governments, the railroad system is owned and operated mainly by private sector companies, except for Mexico where the government has granted a 50-year concession for the right to operate and maintain specific rail lines.

4.6.1 Railroad classification

The Surface Transportation Board (STB) of the United States classifies railroad companies based on annual operating revenues. Class I railroads are those with an annual revenue higher than \$447,621,226. Other railroads include Class II with an annual operating revenue of less than \$447,621,226 and more than \$35,809,698 and Class III railroads with annual operating revenues of less than \$35,809,698.

The Association of American Railroads (AAR) has similar classifications; however, these classifications include the track length under each railroad operation. The AAR classifications are as follows:

- *Class I railroad.* The AAR matches the STB's classification threshold for Class I railroads.
- *Regional railroad.* Regional railroads are line-haul railroads below the Class I revenue threshold that operate at least 350 miles of road and earn at least \$20 million in revenue or that earn revenue between \$40 million and the Class I revenue threshold regardless of mileage.
- *Local railroad.* Local railroads include freight railroads that are not Class I or regional. The local railroad category can be further subdivided into local line-haul carriers and switching and terminal carriers. This latter category is composed of railroads that primarily provide switching and/or terminal services for other railroads (U.S. Surface Transportation Board, n.d.).

There are seven Class I railroads in the United States and Canada:

1. Union Pacific
2. Burlington Northern and Santa Fe (BNSF)
3. CSX
4. Norfolk Southern
5. Canadian National
6. Canadian Pacific
7. Kansas City Southern

Ferromex is the largest railroad in Mexico but does not own track in the United States; therefore, it is not classified as a Class I Railroad. The AAR classifies Ferromex as a Class I Special Member (non-US) for interchange purposes.

- *Union Pacific Railroad (UP).* UP operates 32,000 miles of track west of Chicago and New Orleans. It became the largest railroad in North America in terms of track miles after a 1996 merger with Southern Pacific. UP serves the Pacific Coast ports handling rail intermodal containers to these important gateways. UP also hauls coals from the Powder River Basin and grain from the US Midwest for domestic consumption, as well as exports through the US–Mexico border or exports by barge or ocean ports.
- *Burlington Northern Santa Fe (BNSF).* BNSF's 32,000 miles of track serve the western two-thirds of the United States. The current structure is the result of the 1995 merger of Burlington Northern and the Atchison, Topeka and Santa Fe railroads. BNSF serves the US Midwest and Western States, as well as three Canadian Provinces: Manitoba, Saskatchewan, British Columbia. One of BNSF's main markets is grain. It serves over 1500 grain elevators in the US Midwest. Grain is hauled west to the Pacific Northwest for exports or south to ports in Texas and the Gulf of Mexico or for export to Mexico through land border crossings.
- *CSX Transportation (CSX).* CSX operates a 21,000-mile network in 23 states, the District of Columbia east of the Mississippi, as well as the Canadian provinces of Ontario and Quebec. CSX connects to over 230 short line and regional railroads and more than 70 ocean, river, and lake ports.
- *Norfolk Southern (NS).* NS operates more than 20,000 miles of track, serving every major port on the US East Coast between New York City and Jacksonville, Florida. Coal is the main market for NS, and it also has the largest rail intermodal network in eastern North America, handling auto parts and finished vehicles.
- *Canadian National (CN).* CN is Canada's largest railway in terms of revenue and track length. Its transcontinental track spans from Nova Scotia in the Atlantic Ocean to British Columbia on the Pacific Ocean. In the United States, CN purchased the Illinois Central railroad in 1998, as well a number of smaller railroads. CN also has trackage rights along the Mississippi River valley from the Great Lakes to the Gulf of Mexico.
- *Canadian Pacific (CP).* Canadian Pacific operates parallel to CN's transcontinental corridor with over 15,000 miles of track in six Canadian Provinces and 13 states in the United States. CP connects ports on the Pacific and Atlantic Coasts with major North American distribution centers and every Class I railroad. In 2009, CP acquired the Dakota, Minnesota and Eastern Railroad (DME/ICE) and the Iowa, Chicago and Eastern Railroad (IC&E). The combined DME/ICE system serves North and South Dakota, Minnesota, Wisconsin, Nebraska, and Iowa. It also has connection to Kansas City, Missouri, and Chicago, Illinois.

- *Kansas City Southern (KCS)*. KCS includes three railroads: Kansas City Southern Railway Company (KCSR), Kansas City Southern de México (KCSM), and Panama Canal Railway Company (PCRC). It is the smallest of the US and Canadian Class I railroads with approximately 6000 miles of track in the United States and Mexico. KCS purchased Transportación Ferroviaria Mexicana, its Mexican partner in the original concession in 1998. The so-called Nafta railroad serves the United States and Mexico markets with a north–south route. Mexican operations are an important component of KCS revenues.
- *Ferromex (FXE)*. Ferromex is the largest railroad in Mexico with 7500 miles of track serving Mexico's Pacific Northwest, Central Mexico, and the Gulf of Mexico. Ferromex connects to five border crossings with the United States in California, Arizona, and Texas, handling grain, auto parts, and finished vehicles and mining products. UP has a 26% ownership in Ferromex.

Fig. 4.12 presents the eight major railroads in North America.

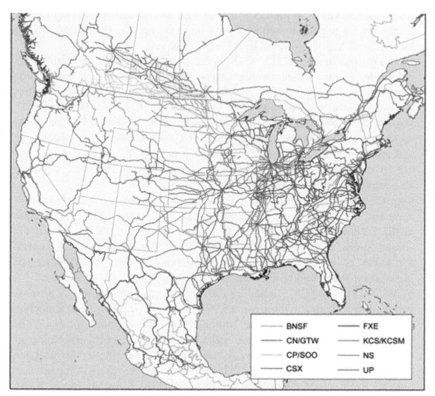

FIGURE 4.12 Class I railroads in North America. *Wikipedia.* The free encyclopedia: Class I railroads of North America. *<https://en.wikipedia.org/wiki/File:Class1rr.png>*.

4.7 Land border crossings

Cross-border transportation is important for regional and national economics. Border crossing infrastructure allows the movement of people and goods that impact not only the local economies at the actual border region but whole nations that share land borders. At the local level, the movement of travelers generates economic development, providing goods and services for day-to-day activities. The movement of freight also generates transportation, logistics, and trade-related jobs in the region close to the border. At the national level, good and efficient trade movement through land ports of entry improves the countries' competitiveness, attracting local and foreign investments in those industries producing goods that are traded through land ports of entry.

The border crossing facility includes specialized infrastructure with personnel and equipment, and each crossing has specific procedures to control the flow of pedestrians, privately owned vehicle (POV) or passenger vehicle crossings, truck or commercial vehicle (CV) crossings, and rail crossings. Border crossing facilities are important as they house multiple agencies from two countries that are responsible for enforcing federal laws related to immigration and the commercial movement of goods, plants, and animals at the border.

This section provides a description of the land border crossing environment at the US—Canada and US—Mexico land ports of entry. The description includes the location of each border crossing, border crossing processes, and stakeholders participating in each process and their roles. Security policies and programs impact the border crossing process; therefore, a description of several programs that have been implemented at the North American land border crossings is included, as well as an analysis of their impact in cross-border trade.

4.7.1 US—Canada border crossings infrastructure

The total US—Canada border has 8891 km (5525 miles), of which 2475 km (1538 miles) constitute Canada's border with Alaska. So 6416 km (3987 miles) of border, exclusive of the Alaska border, include seven Canadian provinces (British Columbia, Alberta, Saskatchewan, Manitoba, Ontario, Quebec, and New Brunswick), and 12 US states (Washington, Idaho, Montana, North Dakota, Minnesota, Michigan, Ohio, Pennsylvania, New York, Vermont, New Hampshire, and Maine).

There are more than 100 land border crossings between Canada and the United States. However, 28 main crossings handle most of the commercial and privately owned vehicles. Of those 28 crossings, 22 handle commercial vehicles. Table 4.1 shows the major US—Canada international border crossings, identifying the type of service provided (Canada DUI Entry Law, n.d.).

The map in Fig. 4.13 shows the locations of the major US—Canada trucking land border crossings.

TABLE 4.1 Major US—Canada border crossings.

No.	Canadian state	US state	Name	US City/Canadian City	POV	CV
1	British Columbia	Washington	Boundary Bay	Point Roberts/Delta	✓	
2			Douglas (Peace Arch)	Blaine/Surrey	✓	✓
3			Pacific Highway	Blaine/Surrey	✓	✓
4			Huntingdon	Sumas/Huntingdon	✓	✓
5			Osoyoos-Oroville	Oroville/Osoyoos	✓	✓
6	Alberta	Montana	Coutts	Sweetgrass/Coutts	✓	✓
7	Saskatchewan	North Dakota	North Portal	Portal/North Portal	✓	✓
8	Manitoba		Emerson	Pembina/Emerson	✓	✓
9	Ontario	Minnesota	Fort Frances Bridge	International Falls/Fort Frances	✓	✓
10		Michigan	Sault Ste. Marie International Bridge	Sault Ste. Marie/Sault Ste. Marie	✓	✓
11			Blue Water Bridge	Port Huron/Sarnia	✓	✓
12			Detroit—Windsor Tunnel	Detroit/Windsor	✓	✓
13			Ambassador Bridge	Detroit/Windsor	✓	✓
14		New York	Peace Bridge	Buffalo/Fort Erie	✓	✓
15			Whirlpool Bridge	Buffalo/Niagara Falls	✓	
16			Rainbow Bridge	Niagara Falls/Niagara Falls	✓	
17			Lewiston-Queenston Bridge	Lewinton/Queenston	✓	✓
18			Thousand Island Bridge	Alexandria Bay/Lansdowne	✓	✓
19			Cornwall/International Bridge	Massena, Rooseveltown/Cornwall	✓	✓
20			Prescott-Ogdensburg	Ogdensburg/Prescott	✓	✓
21	Quebec		St-Bernard-de-Lacolle	Champlain/Lacolle	✓	✓

#	State/Province	Station	Port		
22	Vermont	Highgate Springs	Highgate Springs/St. Armand	✓	✓
23		Rock Island	Derby Line/Stanstead	✓	✓
24		Stanhope-Norton	Norton/Stanhope	✓	✓
25	Maine	Armstrong-Jackman	Jackman/Armstrong	✓	✓
26		Woodstock Road	Houlton/Belleville	✓	✓
27	New Brunswick	St. Stephen/Milltown	Calais/St. Stephen	✓	
28		St. Stephen/Ferry Point	Calais/St. Stephen	✓	

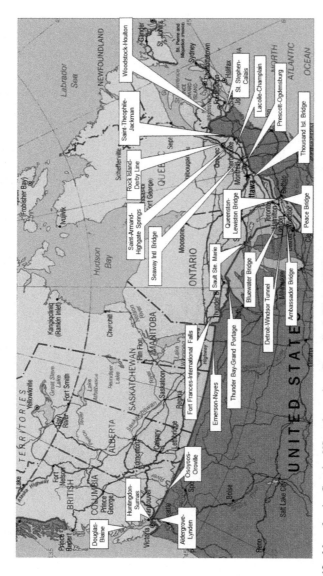

FIGURE 4.13 Map of major Canada—US truck crossings (Donnelly & Gliebe, 2002). *Developed by the author with information from Transport Canada, map from On the World Map. http://ontheworldmap.com/canada/canada-road-map.jpg.*

The flow of commercial vehicles from Canada into the United States has been increasing at a very low rate since the 2009 recession. In 2017, 5.77 million trucks crossed the US−Canada border into the United States. The volume reached a peak in 2004 with 6.84 million crossings (Fig. 4.14).

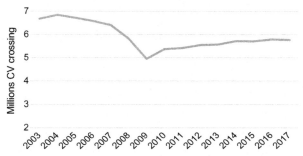

FIGURE 4.14 Canada to the US CV crossings (2003−17). *Developed by the author with information from the U.S. Department of Transportation.* Bureau of Transportation Statistics. *<https://explore.dot.gov/t/BTS/views/BTSBorderCrossingAnnualData/BorderCrossingTableDashboard?:embed = y&:showShareOptions = true&:display_count = no&:showVizHome = no>.*

In 2017, 26.4 million passenger vehicles crossed from Canada into the United States. The POV volume has declined considerably from 32.9 million vehicles in 2013 (Fig. 4.15).

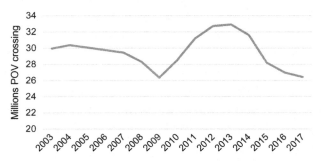

FIGURE 4.15 Canada to the US POV crossings (2003−17). *Developed by the author with information from the U.S. Department of Transportation.* Bureau of Transportation Statistics. *<https://explore.dot.gov/t/BTS/views/BTSBorderCrossingAnnualData/BorderCrossingTableDashboard?:embed = y&:showShareOptions = true&:display_count = no&:showVizHome = no>.*

4.7.2 US−Canada rail crossings

There are 10 major rail crossings at the US−Canada border. The two Canadian Class I railroads (Canadian National and Canadian Pacific) serve all of them, except for the Blaine−Douglas crossing that is served by the BNSF railroad on both sides of the border. Detroit−Windsor, Buffalo/Niagara Falls−Fort Erie and Port Huron−Sarnia are the three crossings with the highest trade volume by value (Table 4.2).

TABLE 4.2 Top 10 highest volume (US$) Northern border rail freight crossings.

No.	US city	US state	Canadian city	Canadian province	Connecting railroads
1	Detroit	Michigan	Windsor	Ontario	CP
2	Port Huron	Michigan	Sarnia	Ontario	CN
3	International Falls	Minnesota	Fort Frances	Ontario	CN
4	Buffalo	New York	Fort Erie–Niagara Falls	Ontario	NS/CP–CN/CP
5	Portal	North Dakota	North Portal	Saskatchewan	CP
6	Blaine	Washington	Douglas	British Columbia	BNSF
7	Pembina	North Dakota	Emerson	Manitoba	CN/CP–BNSF
8	Rouses Point	New York	Lacolle	Quebec	CP/NS/CN
9	Eastport	Idaho	Kingsgate	British Columbia	CP–UP
10	Sweetgrass	Montana	Coutts	Alberta	CP–BNSF

- Buffalo-Niagara Falls, New York—Fort Erie—Niagara Falls, Ontario
- Port Huron, Michigan—Sarnia, Ontario

The locations of the 10 rail international crossings at the Canada—US border are presented in Fig. 4.16.

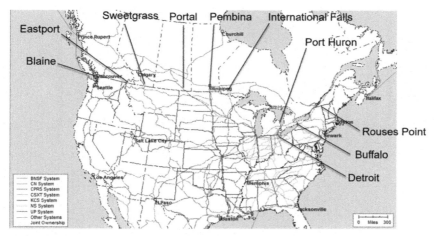

FIGURE 4.16   US—Canada rail border crossings.

4.7.3   US—Mexico border crossings infrastructure

The US—Mexico border has 3142 km (1953 miles) and covers from the Pacific Ocean in Tijuana—San Ysidro to the Gulf of Mexico in Matamoros—Brownsville. The US—Mexico border region has four states in the United States (California, Arizona, Nuevo Mexico, and Texas) and six states in Mexico (Baja California, Sonora, Chihuahua, Coahuila, Nuevo Leon, and Tamaulipas). The Rio Grande covers 64% of the total border between the two countries and the Texas—Mexico border. All crossings spanning the Rio Grande are international bridges, and the majority are tolled.

There are 45 crossings at the US—Mexico border that handle POVs and CVs. Forty-three of them serve POVs, and 25 serve CVs. Two crossings serve only commercial vehicles: the World Trade Bridge in Laredo, Texas—Nuevo Laredo, Tamaulipas and the San Luis II crossing in Arizona—Sonora. Table 4.3 presents the list of the POV and CV crossings at the US—Mexico Border.

The map in Fig. 4.17 presents the location of the US—Mexico land border crossings.

TABLE 4.3 Major US—Mexico privately owned vehicle border.

No	Mexican state	US state	Name	US City/Mexican City	POV	CV
1	Tamaulipas	Texas	Veterans International Bridge	Brownsville/Matamoros	✓	✓
2			Gateway International Bridge	Brownsville/Matamoros	✓	
3			B&M Bridge	Brownsville/Matamoros	✓	
4			Free Trade Bridge	Los Indios/Lucio Blanco	✓	✓
5			Progreso International Bridge	Progreso/Nuevo Progreso	✓	✓
6			Donna International Bridge	Donna/Rio Bravo	✓	
7			Pharr—Reynosa Intl. Bridge on the Rise	Pharr/Reynosa	✓	✓
8			McAllen—Hidalgo—Reynosa Bridge	Hidalgo/Reynosa	✓	
9			Anzalduas International Bridge	Mission/Reynosa	✓	
10			Los Ebanos Ferry	Los Ebanos/Gustavo Díaz Ordaz	✓	
11			Rio Grande City—Camargo Bridge	Rio Grande City/Camargo	✓	✓
12			Roma—Ciudad Miguel Aleman Bridge	Roma/Ciudad Miguel Aleman	✓	✓
13			Lake Falcon Dam Crossing	Falcon Heights/Ciudad Guerrero	✓	
14			Juarez—Lincoln Bridge	Laredo/Nuevo Laredo	✓	
15			Gateway to the Americas Bridge	Laredo/Nuevo Laredo	✓	
16			World Trade Bridge	Laredo/Nuevo Laredo		✓

#	State	Crossing	City pair		
17	Nuevo León	Laredo–Colombia Solidarity Bridge	Laredo/Colombia	✓	✓
18	Coahuila	Camino Real International Bridge	Eagle Pass/Piedras Negras	✓	✓
19		Eagle Pass Bridge I	Eagle Pass/Piedras Negras		✓
20		Del Rio–Ciudad Acuna International Bridge	Del Rio/Ciudad Acuña	✓	✓
21		Lake Amistad Dam Crossing	Del Rio/Ciudad Acuña		✓
22	Chihuahua	Presidio Bridge	Presidio/Ojinaga	✓	✓
23		Fort Hancock–El Porvenir Bridge	Fort Hancock/El Porvenir		✓
24		Tornillo–Guadalupe Bridge	Fabens/Caseta	✓	✓
25		Ysleta–Zaragoza Bridge	El Paso/Ciudad Juarez	✓	✓
26		Bridge of the Americas	El Paso/Ciudad Juarez	✓	✓
27		Good Neighbor Bridge	El Paso/Ciudad Juarez		✓
28		Paso del Norte Bridge	El Paso/Ciudad Juarez		✓
29	Nuevo México	Santa Teresa	Doña Ana/Ciudad Juarez	✓	✓
30		Columbus	Columbus/Puerto Palomas	✓	✓
31		Antelope Wells	Antelope Wells/Berrendo		✓

(Continued)

TABLE 4.3 (Continued)

No	Mexican state	US state	Name	US City/Mexican City	POV	CV
32	Sonora	Arizona	Douglas	Douglas/Agua Prieta	✓	✓
33			Naco	Naco /Naco	✓	✓
34			Nogales Deconcini	Nogales/Nogales	✓	
35			Nogales Mariposa	Nogales/Nogales	✓	✓
36			Sasabe	Sasabe/El Sasabe	✓	✓
37			Lukeville	Lukeville/Sonoyta	✓	✓
38			San Luis II	San Luis/San Luis Rio Colorado		✓
39			San Luis I	San Luis/San Luis Rio Colorado	✓	
40	Baja California	California	Andrade	Andrade/Los Algodones	✓	
41			Calexico East	Calexico/Mexicali	✓	✓
42			Calexico West	Calexico/Mexicali	✓	
43			Tecate	Tecate/Tecate	✓	
44			Otay Mesa	Otay Mesa/Tijuana	✓	✓
45			San Ysidro	San Ysidro/Tijuana	✓	

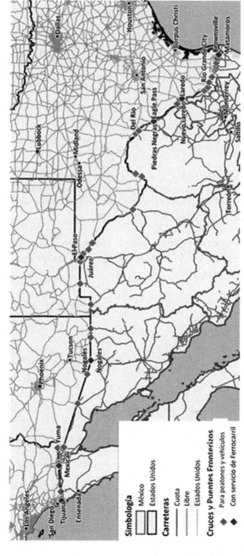

FIGURE 4.17 US—Mexico land border crossing locations. *Secretaría de Relaciones Exteriores: 2016. U.S. Customs and Border Protection (CBP).* <*https:// www.cpb.gov/contact/ports*>.

Truck traffic at the US—Mexico border has been increasing at a relatively steady rate since the end of the 2009 economic crisis. Trucks traveling from Mexico into the United States reached a pick in 2017 of 6 million trucks, up 40% from 4.29 million on 2009 (Fig. 4.18).

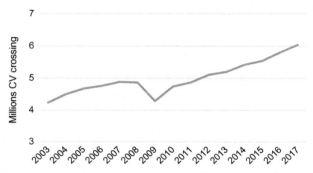

FIGURE 4.18 Mexico to the US CV crossings (2003—17). *Developed by the author with information from the U.S. Department of Transportation.* Bureau of Transportation Statistics. *<https://explore.dot.gov/t/BTS/views/BTSBorderCrossingAnnualData/BorderCrossingTableDashboard?:embed = y&:showShareOptions = true&:display_count = no&:showVizHome = no>.*

Close to 80 million privately owned vehicles crossed from Mexico into the United States in 2017. The volume of POVs crossing the border has decreased from 9.5 million in 2005 (Fig. 4.19).

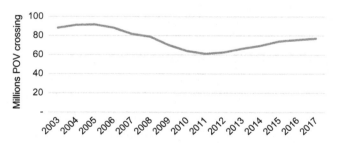

FIGURE 4.19 Mexico to the US POV crossings (2003—17). *Developed by the author with information from the U.S. Department of Transportation. Bureau of Transportation Statistics.* *<https://explore.dot.gov/t/BTS/views/BTSBorderCrossingAnnualData/BorderCrossingTableDashboard?:embed = y&:showShareOptions = true&:display_count = no&:showVizHome = no>.*

4.7.4 US—Mexico rail border crossings

Seven crossings are in operation at the US—Mexico border. In El Paso—Ciudad Juarez, there are two international bridges. Five of the seven crossings are served by Ferromex on the Mexican side of the border, and six of the seven crossings are served by UP on the US side of the border. The San Ysidro—Tijuana border crossing is served by two short lines on both sides of the border. An additional rail border crossing is under reconstruction and is expected to be operational in a few years. This crossing is on Ojinaga, Chihuahua—Presidio Texas and is served by Ferromex (FXE) on the Mexican side of the border and by the Texas Pacifico in the US side of the border (Table 4.4 and Fig. 4.20).

TABLE 4.4 US-Mexico 2018 Operating Rail Crossings.

No.	US city	US state	Mexican city	Mexican state	Connecting railroads
1	Laredo	Texas	Nuevo Laredo	Tamaulipas	KCS/UP—KCSM
2	Eagle Pass	Texas	Piedras Negras	Coahuila	UP/BNSF—FXE
3	El Paso	Texas	Cd. Juarez	Chihuahua	UP—FXE
					BNSF—FXE
4	Nogales	Arizona	Nogales	Sonora	UP—FXE
5	Brownsville	Texas	Matamoros	Tamaulipas	UP—KCSM
6	Calexico	California	Mexicali	Baja California	UP—FXE
7	San Ysidro	California	Tijuana	Baja California	San Diego & Imperial Valley Railroad—Tijuana/Tecate Short Line

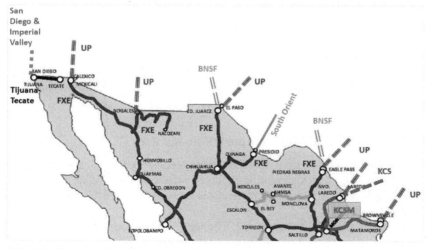

FIGURE 4.20   Map of the US—Mexico rail border crossing locations.

4.8 Stakeholders in the North American border crossing environment

Many private sector and federal, state, and local agencies are involved in the movement of goods and people across land borders in North America. The most relevant stakeholders and their functions are described in the following sections.

4.8.1 Federal customs agencies

North American customs agencies are the main stakeholders at land border crossings. They are in charge of the operation of the facilities and coordinate activities with other federal and local agencies.

4.8.1.1 US Customs and Border Protection

CBP is part of the US Department of Homeland Security (DHS) with a mission to "safeguard America's borders thereby protecting the public from dangerous people and materials while enhancing the Nation's global economic competitiveness by enabling legitimate trade and travel." CBP takes a comprehensive approach to border management and control, combining customs, immigration, border security, and agricultural protection into one coordinated and supportive activity (Department of Homeland Security, 2019).

4.8.1.2 Canadian Border Services Agency

The Canada Border Services Agency (CBSA) is a federal institution that is part of the Public Safety portfolio that ensures Canada's security and prosperity by facilitating and overseeing international travel and trade across Canada's border.

4.8.1.3 Servicio de Administración Tributaria (Aduana de México)

At land border crossings, the Mexican customs agency controls the entry and exit of goods to and from the country and verifies that foreign merchandise entering the country follows legal procedures.

4.8.2 Federal and local transportation agencies

Federal and state/provincial transportation agencies are in charge of planning, developing, and maintaining roadway infrastructure leading to the border crossings. There are a few differences among the three North American countries.

Transport Canada supports the efficient, safe, sustainable, and secure movement of goods and people across the Canada—US border and continues to leverage its investments and expertise in transportation/infrastructure (Government of Canada, 2016).

The US Department of Transportation (USDOT) ensures that the US transportation system meets national needs and interests and improves quality of life. At the border crossings, it oversees all other federal transportation agencies, including the Federal Highway Administration (FHWA) and the Federal Motor Carrier Safety Administration (FMCSA). FMCSA's staff is located at the border performing commercial vehicle safety screening and inspections.

The Mexican Ministry of Communications and Transportation (Secretaría de Comunicacione y Transportes [SCT]) plans the infrastructure required for new border crossing projects and grants concessions for the construction, operation, and maintenance of border crossings through public–private partnerships.

State Departments of Transportation and Provincial Ministries of Transportation are agencies that coordinate with federal transportation planning departments to plan, develop, and maintain roadway infrastructure approaching border crossing facilities.

4.8.3   Border crossing operators

In all three North American countries, some international border crossings are operated by private sector entities, public local agencies, or public––private partnerships. At the Texas–Mexico border, the US side of the international bridges is usually owned by the city, and the operation, which includes toll collection, is done by city employees. On the Mexican side of the border, the international crossings are usually managed and operated by the federal toll operator, Federal Roads and Bridges Agency (Caminos y Puentes Federales de Ingresos y Servicios Conexos [CAPUFE]), a state agency, or a private entity under a build-operate-transfer (BOT) concession from the federal or state governments. In Canada, the operation of bridges and tunnels is administered by diverse agencies. For example, the Federal Bridge Corporation Limited is responsible for operating and managing the Seaway International Bridge in Cornwall, Ontario; the Sault Ste. Marie International Bridge in Sault Ste. Marie, Ontario; and the Thousand Islands International Bridge in the Thousand Islands. The Ambassador Bridge at Detroit–Windsor is privately owned by the Detroit International Bridge Company.

4.8.4   Private sector carriers, customs brokers, and logistics operators

Motor carriers, rail companies, customs brokers, and other logistics companies play an important role in the cross-border movement of goods. Usually these companies have operations at both sides of the border in order to coordinate the movement of goods and the repositioning of transportation equipment.

At the US—Mexico border, the customs brokers play an important role, as they are liable for the correct documentation of goods entering Mexico. Therefore, all shipments have to be processed by a licensed Mexican customs broker. Mexican-domiciled motor carriers are not allowed to travel beyond a 25-mile commercial zone in the United States; therefore a drayage or transfer tractor picks up a load in Mexico and drops it within the commercial zone so that a US-based carrier can take the load to the final destination beyond the commercial zone.

4.8.5 Other organizations

Multiple organizations are involved in the planning, development, and improvement of cross-border transportation. For example, two binational groups have been working together for several decades.

The US—Mexico Joint Working Committee on Border Transportation Planning initiated operations shortly after NAFTA in 1994, with the intention of promoting "effective communication related to transportation planning between US—Mexico Border States" and working to "develop a well-coordinated land transportation planning process along the border" (U.S. Department of Transportation, Federal Highway Administration, 2015).

A similar group at the US—Canada border is the Transportation Border Working Group (TBWG) with a mission to facilitate the safe, secure, efficient, and environmentally responsible movement of people and goods across the Canada—US border. The TBWG brings together multiple transportation and border agencies, as well as other organizations, to coordinate transportation planning, policy implementation, and the deployment of technology to enhance border infrastructure and operations (TBWG, 2005).

Although multiple agencies and private sector companies are operating international border crossings, there is a relatively high degree of collaboration and coordination among stakeholders to ensure efficient border operations. As previously mentioned, customs agencies in each of the three North American countries take control of the flow of people and goods across international border crossings.

4.9 Border crossing processes

The border crossing process for passenger and commercial vehicles at the North American land border is complicated due to the number of stakeholders participating in the process. The commercial vehicle crossing is particularly complicated because it requires the exchange of information among public and private sector stakeholders at the federal and local levels. The process at the US–Mexico border requires additional commercial vehicle inspections at the US–Canada border.

4.9.1 Mexico to the US commercial vehicle crossing process

The typical northbound border crossing process requires a shipper or motor carrier in Mexico to file shipment data with both the Mexican and the US federal agencies through the e-Manifest and have an authorized motor carrier available to move the goods from one country to the other. Once the shipment is at the border with the drayage or transfer tractor and an authorized driver, the process flows through three main potential physical inspection areas (Fig. 4.21):

- Mexican export lot
- US Federal Compound
- US state safety inspection facility

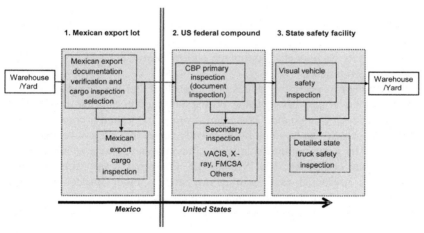

FIGURE 4.21 Flowchart depicting the commercial border crossing process from Mexico to the United States. Villa, J. C. (1966). Status of the US–Mexico commercial border crossing process. *Analysis of Recent Studies and Research.*

4.9.1.1 The Mexican export lot

A drayage driver with the required documentation proceeds into the Mexican Customs (Aduanas) compound. For audit and interdiction purposes, Mexican Customs conducts inspections consisting of a physical review of the cargo of randomly selected outbound freight prior to its export. Shipments that are not selected proceed to the exit gate, cross the border, and continue on to the US port of entry.

Several international crossings along the US−Mexico border are tolled. Tolls are collected in Mexico for northbound traffic and in the United States for southbound traffic. Toll collection is manual (cash) and electronic. All of the crossings along the Texas−Mexico border are bridges that cross the Rio Grande River, and most of them are tolled. Before crossing into the United States, commercial vehicles pay tolls and proceed to the US Federal Compound.

4.9.1.2 The US Federal Compound

At the primary inspection booth, the driver of the truck presents identification and shipment documentation to the processing agent. The US Customs and Border Protection (CBP) inspector at the primary inspection booth uses a computer terminal to cross-check the basic information about the driver, vehicle, and cargo with information sent previously by the carrier via the CBP's Automated Cargo Environment (ACE) electronic manifest (e-Manifest). The CBP inspector then makes a decision to refer the truck, driver, or cargo for a more detailed secondary inspection of any or all of these elements or—alternatively—releases the truck to the exit gate.

Motor carriers electronically submit the e-Manifest, which enables CBP to prescreen the crew, conveyance, equipment, and shipment information before the truck arrives at the border. This allows CBP to focus its efforts and inspections on high-risk commerce and to minimize unnecessary delays for low-risk commerce.

A secondary inspection includes any inspection that the driver, freight, or conveyance undergoes between the primary inspection and the exit gate of the US Federal Compound. Personnel from CBP usually conduct these inspections, which can be done by physically inspecting the conveyance and the cargo or by using nonintrusive inspection equipment (such as X-rays).

Within the compound, FMCSA and US Food and Drug Administration (FDA) have personnel and facilities to perform other inspections when required. A vehicle audit could happen at the Federal Compound or the State Safety Inspection Facility depending on practice.

4.9.1.3 The state vehicle safety inspection facility

In the majority of the land border crossings at the US−Mexico border, the state safety inspection facility is located adjacent to the Federal Compound. State police inspect conveyances to determine whether they are in compliance with US state safety standards and regulations. If their initial visual inspection finds any violation, they direct the truck to proceed to a more detailed inspection at a special facility.

After leaving the state vehicle safety inspection facility, the driver typically drives to the freight forwarder or customs broker yard to drop off the trailer for later pickup by a long-haul tractor bound for the final destination.

4.9.2 US to Mexico commercial vehicle crossing

The Mexico-bound commercial vehicle crossing process has only one inspection station by Mexican Customs. The inspection decision in Mexico is a red light/green light decision in which a loaded commercial vehicle is randomly selected for a secondary inspection if it gets a red light. Empty vehicles cross with no need to stop at the Mexican Customs' booths.

At some land border crossings, US CBP performs random manual inspections on the US side of the border for commercial vehicles crossing into Mexico, aiming to identify illegal shipments of cash and weapons. Land border crossings are not designed for southbound commercial inspection on the US side of the border, and consequently this generates congestion.

4.9.3 Mexico to US privately owned vehicle crossing process

On the Mexican side of the border, passenger vehicles are required to pay tolls at those crossings that have tolls, usually the international bridges. Drivers pay tolls either manually or via electronic collection systems.

Once passenger vehicles pay the toll, they proceed, if necessary, to the US Federal Compound, where POVs go through primary and sometimes secondary inspections. At the primary inspection booths, CBP officers must ask the individuals who want to enter the country to show proper documentation, such as proof of citizenship, and state the purpose of their visit to the United States. If necessary, the vehicle is sent to secondary inspection.

At the primary inspection booth, license plate readers and computers perform queries of the vehicles against law enforcement databases that are continuously updated. A combination of electronic gates, tire shredders, traffic control lights, fixed iron bollards, and pop-up pneumatic bollards ensure physical control of the border crossers and their vehicles.

At the secondary inspection station, a much more thorough investigation of the identity of those wanting to enter the United States, as well as the purpose of their visit, is performed. During this step, individuals may also have to pay duties upon their declared items. Upon completion, access to the United States is either granted or denied.

4.9.4 US to Mexico privately owned vehicle crossing process

Similarly to commercial vehicles, POVs entering Mexico are subject to a random selection process for inspection. When a POV vehicle is selected with a red light, it goes to secondary inspection, where Mexican Customs officers perform a vehicle screening and check for illegal goods being carried into the country.

4.9.5   Canada–US border crossing processes

Compared, to the US–Mexico border crossing process, the US–Canada border crossing process is relatively streamlined. The main difference in the process at both US borders is that commercial vehicles entering the United States from Canada do not have to go through the vehicle safety inspection process, and there is no inspection at the country of origin. POVs and CVs are examined separately. Both can be pulled out for secondary screening. CVs crossing the border have a longer process than POVs as that can involve secondary cargo inspections.

4.10   Trusted traveler and trade programs

CBP, in coordination with authorities in Canada and Mexico, have implemented several programs to expedite clearance at land border crossings. The trusted trader traveler program is aimed at cross-border freight movement, while the trusted traveler program is used for POV users.

4.10.1   FAST program

The Free and Secure Trade (FAST) program offers expedited clearance to carriers that have demonstrated supply chain security and that are enrolled in the Customs–Trade Partnership Against Terrorism (C-TPAT). The FAST program is in operation at most of the major US international land border crossings. The FAST program allows expedited release for US–Canada and US–Mexico partnering importers for qualifying commercial shipments (U.S. Customs and Border Protection, 2019).

CBSA and CBP have the joint FAST program, which enhances border and trade chain security while making cross-border commercial shipments simpler and subject to fewer delays. FAST is a voluntary program that enables the CBSA to work closely with the private sector to enhance border security, combat organized crime and terrorism, and prevent contraband smuggling (Government of Canada, 2017b).

Mexico's version of the C-TPAT is the Authorized Economic Operator (Operador Económico Autorizado [OEA]). OEA-certified carriers and shippers can use special inspection lanes at the Mexican Customs compound called Express lanes, and also the FAST lanes for imports into the United States with fewer inspections and faster clearance at land border crossings (Superintendencia de Administración Tributaria, 2019).

4.10.2   Passenger vehicle border crossing security programs

The Secure Electronic Network for Travelers Rapid Inspection (SENTRI) program is a trusted traveler program for passenger vehicles at the

US—Mexico border, and the NEXUS program is for the US—Canada border. These CBP programs provide expedited travel for preapproved, low-risk travelers through dedicated lanes. Users enrolled in this program receive a NEXUS/SENTRI card that has a radio frequency identification (RFID) transponder. SENTRI users need to register the vehicle at the time of application. When an approved international traveler approaches the border in the SENTRI lane, the system automatically identifies the vehicle and the identity of its occupant(s) by reading the file number on the RFID card. The file number triggers the participant's data to be brought up on the CBP officer's screen at the primary inspection booth. The data are verified by the CBP officer, and the traveler is released or referred for additional inspection (U. S. Customs and Border Protection, 2017).

4.10.3   Unified cargo processing

In 2016, CBP and SAT/Aduanas started working together under a program to have Mexican customs officers working side by side with CBP officers conducting joint cargo inspections at the Mariposa border crossing in Nogales, Arizona—Nogales, Sonora. The pilot program proved to be successful, reducing wait times and creating more efficient inspections, thus lowering the cost of doing business at the US—Mexico border. As of May 2017, the program was implemented at two other border crossing at the US—Mexico border, and the plan is to expand it to so that more locations can benefit from its success

4.10.3.1   US—Mexico cross-border trucking

On top of the additional costs created by the drayage or transfer system caused by the inability of Mexican tractors to cross the border beyond the commercial zone, the inspection process adds another layer of inefficiencies to trucks entering the United States from Mexico. The time required for a shipment to make the complete trip from the yard or the manufacturing plant in Mexico to the exit of the state inspection facility depends on the number of secondary inspections required, as well as the number of inspection booths in service and traffic volume at that specific time of day. There is duplication on the vehicle safety inspection, as US federal and state agencies perform some level of inspection of every truck that crosses from Mexico into the United States.

All shipments into and out of Mexico require a Mexico customs broker, which is a private third-party business, hired to carry out customs-related services such as goods classification, inspection, and counting; acquiring, preparing, and transmitting documents or data; maintaining and reporting records; duty and tax collection and payment; and obtaining drayage services to physically move goods across the border.

The requirement of using a Mexico customs broker by Mexican law makes importing goods by truck into Mexico different from any other North American cross-border truck movements. A Mexican licensed customs broker must submit the customs declaration and must have a power of attorney from the importer. The customs broker is liable for any error concerning the application of the proper customs procedure, the tariff classification of the goods, the correct payment of duties and taxes, and the strict compliance with nontariff barriers.

Truck imports into Mexico not only require the use of a drayage tractor to carry the trailer across the border, but also the Mexico custom broker most likely would be required to classify the shipment and to inspect and count the items in the shipment in order to prepare the required documentation.

The US—Canada truck border crossing process is relatively straightforward compared to the one at the US southern border. No drayage is required for US—Canada shipments as Canadian tractors are allowed beyond the commercial zone in the United States and Canadian and US customs brokers are not required to physically inspect the cargo, as they are not liable for any potential errors on the import/export declaration. The other element that simplifies the crossing for Canadian trucks into the United States is that a truck safety inspection is not required at a separate location with additional waiting time as is done at the US—Mexico border.

US—Mexico cross-border trucking process

NAFTA provisions on cross-border trucking specify that restrictions on the movement of Mexican-domiciled trucks beyond a narrow commercial zone extending 3—20 miles into the United States were to be phased out between 1995 and 2000 (Frittelli, 2014). However, the United States alleged that Mexican commercial drivers and carriers would pose a safety risk to the US public, and the restrictions remained beyond 2000. Mexico contested the decision in 1998, and an international panel ruled in Mexico's favor in 2001. The US Administration vows to comply with the panel decision. However, it includes 22 safety requirements in the Transportation Appropriations Act.

In 2003, several US stakeholders, including unions, nonprofit organizations, and trucking associations, challenged the legality of the moratorium lift, citing environmental reasons, and the Court of Appeals halted the operation of Mexican trucks in the United States The case went to the US Supreme Court, who overturned the Court of Appeals decision, allowing Mexican motor carriers to apply for operating authority. This led to the Bush Administration to start a trial program beginning in September 2007. In 2009, the US Congress defunded the program. Mexico imposed tariffs on certain US goods in response to the program's termination, as permitted by NAFTA. After bilateral negotiations, the

(Continued)

(Continued)

Obama Administration announced a new pilot program to allow long-haul Mexican trucks into the United States in April 2011.

As of 2019, the cross-border trucking operations at the US—Mexico border remain the same as before NAFTA. This is due, for one thing, to the safety requirements imposed on Mexican-domiciled carriers participating in the Pilot Program, which were required to complete a Pre-Authorization Safety Audit (PASA) before being granted operating authority. In addition, they were required to successfully complete a compliance review if they participated in the Pilot Program for 18 months (U.S. Department of Transportation, 2018) (Fig. 4.22).

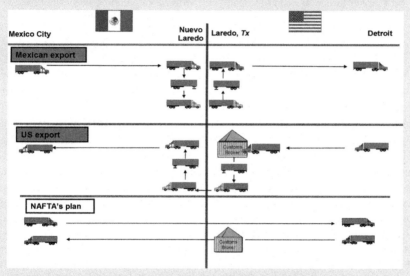

FIGURE 4.22 US—Mexico truck border crossing process: current and NAFTA plan.

The main issue is the commercial cabotage rules. Mexican carriers are allowed to pick up a load in the United States and transport it back to Mexico. Therefore, if the trip from Mexico to the interior of the United States does not have a secure backhaul load, it would make the operation economically inviable.

These circumstances—not allowing Mexican tractors to circulate beyond the commercial zone of the neighboring country—have enabled the use of drayage or transfer trucks to flourish along the border. It is important to clarify that most of the trailers, or "boxes," that are hauled by Mexican tractors are allowed to cross and travel beyond the border commercial zone. The Mexican tractors or power units are the ones that are not allowed to travel internally in the United States.

(Continued)

(Continued)

An export trip from Mexico City to the interior of the United States (e.g., Detroit) requires at least three tractors or power units. The Mexican long-haul carrier picks up the load with the shipper and brings it to the border region (Nuevo Laredo), where the trailer is dropped at a yard. A drayage or transfer tractor picks up that load and crosses with it to the US side of the border (Laredo, Texas) to a yard, where a US carrier picks up the load and takes it to the final destination in the United States.

An import load into Mexico follows a similar process, with an additional process: the Mexican customs broker. Most shipments into Mexico require a customs broker to prepare and file documents with Mexican authorities. The broker receives the shipment on the US side of the border where it inspects it to prepare documents and pay duties if necessary. Once the shipment has the appropriate documentation, the trailer is hauled by a drayage truck to a yard on the Mexican side of the border, where a Mexican long-haul carrier picks up the load and takes it to the final destination in Mexico.

4.11 Border crossing infrastructure development process

4.11.1 US Presidential Permit

Building new border crossings or expanding existing transportation infrastructure at the US−Mexico and US−Canada border is a complex task. The two federal governments have to agree on the actual project and funding for construction, and the operation has to be identified in order for the project to move forward. Once both neighboring governments agree on a specific project, the United States requires a Presidential Permit. The Executive Order 11423 (August 16, 1968, 33 Fed. Reg. 11741) states that "the proper conduct of the foreign relations of the United States requires that executive permission be obtained for the construction and maintenance at the borders of the United States of facilities connecting the United States with a foreign country."

This permission is conveyed through a Presidential Permit, and it is required for the full range of facilities on the border, including land border crossings, bridges, pipelines, tunnels, conveyor belts, and tramways. The US Department of State is the lead agency processing the Presidential Permit applications, and it consults extensively with relevant federal, state, and local agencies, inviting public comment in arriving at the determination whether the proposed project is of national interest.

The permitting, construction, and completion of any project on the US−Canada or US−Mexico border require close coordination and planning with the governments of Canada and Mexico, as well as with sponsors and federal, state, and local authorities in both countries. A summary of the steps of the Presidential Permit application is presented in the following sections.

4.11.2   Step 1: Project categorization

The project is classified according to its complexity and size using three colors:

- *Red.* All new and extensive modifications for existing border crossings
- *Yellow.* Permanent modifications on existing border crossings that affect Mexican operations
- *Green.* Minor changes in the proximity of the border that are not expected to affect Canadian/Mexican operations

4.11.3   Step 2: Application requirements

Applications should include the following:

- *Identifying information.* Information precisely identifying the person or entity that is applying for the permit and that will ultimately be responsible for the crossing. For land border crossings, the General Services Administration (GSA) is generally the permittee.
- *Description of facility.* A detailed description of the proposed facility, including its location, design, the safety standards to be applied, access routes, and details of the proposed construction methods.
- *National interest.* An explanation of how the proposed facility would serve the national interest.
- *Similar facilities.* A list of similar facilities in the area.
- *Traffic information.* If applicable, information about existing and projected levels of international road traffic and a description of the road system that would serve the facility on each side of the border.
- *Construction plan.* A plan for construction of the facility, including an expected schedule for securing other necessary permits and approvals, financing, and construction.
- *Financing.* An explanation of how the applicant will finance the facility, including estimated costs and, if applicable, the proposed toll structure.
- *Approvals from the neighboring country:*
  - *Mexico.* Information showing how the project fits with Mexican development plans and priorities and a description of all steps that the applicant has taken or will take to secure the approval of local, state, and federal officials in Mexico.
  - *Canada.* A description of all steps that have been or will be taken to secure the approval of local, provincial, and federal officials in Canada. Expression of the desire of the Government of Canada that applications for permits to construct cross-border facilities be made at the same time in the two countries.

4.11.4   Step 3: Environmental review

The US lead agency conducts an environmental review process if issuance of a Presidential Permit has the potential to significantly impact the environment. Its Bureau of Oceans and International Environmental and Scientific Affairs (OES) determines whether such a review is necessary and, if so, leads the preparation of an appropriate document.

The US Department of State acts consistently with the National Environmental Policy Act of 1969 (NEPA) in conducting environmental reviews. NEPA calls for agencies to evaluate and disclose the environmental impacts of proposed actions and ensures that environmental factors are included in the decision-making process. NEPA gives agencies a structured, analytical decision-making framework that integrates environmental, social, and economic factors.

4.11.5   Step 4: Agency review and public comment

The applicant is required to provide copies—including all environmental and other documentation—to relevant federal and state agencies for their comment. If during the environmental review DOS finds no significant impact (FONSI), a report is published. Otherwise, additional environmental impact reports are needed before the project is considered further.

4.11.6   Step 5: National interest determination and permit issuance

The US Department of State informs federal agencies of its intention to issue a Presidential Permit. Assuming there are no objections from any of the officials specified in the executive order, the Presidential Permit is issued. In the event of an objection, the Secretary of State will refer the matter directly to the president for a final decision.

4.12   Border crossing infrastructure funding mechanisms

Mexico has developed several funding sources for the construction and operation of border crossing infrastructure. These include public funds as well as public—private partnerships (P3s). Public funding could come from the Mexican Federal Budget that is prepared annually by the Executive Office and approved by the House of Representatives. Construction, expansion, maintenance, and conservation of border crossing projects are classified as capital expenditures under the federal budget.

Mexico has extensive experience in P3s, starting with roadway construction in the 1980s, and this mechanism has proven to be a good alternative for border crossing infrastructure development. Under the P3 mechanism, public sector participants provide access to various financing options, such as national development bank loans by the Mexican Public Works Development Bank (Banco Nacional de Obras y Servicios Públicos [BANOBRAS]). The National Infrastructure Fund (FONADIN) is another funding source for infrastructure development funding within the Mexican federal government. FONADIN provides financial instruments, such as guarantees and subordinate loans, when a private sector partner is involved in the project. The private sector partner brings efficiencies to the project through experience, knowledge, and technology. Border crossing infrastructure projects that include tolled infrastructure have a direct revenue source that could be used to secure loans and other financial instruments. With tolled international crossings, the private sector operator can use the cash flow generated by tolls to recuperate construction cost investments.

In the United States, border crossing infrastructure is funded mainly through two mechanisms. The first is the traditional border crossing funding through federal appropriations. This method includes GSA and CBP working together. GSA is responsible for acquiring the necessary resources and permits needed for construction, while CBP pays for operations of border crossings from its own budget, as well as paying rent to GSA for the maintenance and recapitalization of border crossings (GSA; U.S. General Services Administration, 2018). CBP and GSA produce a five-year plan with a list of projects that are subject to feasibility studies. GSA and the Office of Management Budget review the estimated cost of the project from the feasibility studies, and it is eventually submitted for Congressional approval. Other stakeholders in the process include the USDOT and state departments of transportation, which provides funding and financing for the transportation components of border crossing projects.

CBP does not have the legislative authority to collect tolls for funding border crossing infrastructure; so, in order to have access to an alternative source of funding, CBP and GSA implemented a donation acceptance program that allows these agencies to partner with local governments and private businesses to develop infrastructure through P3s. GSA and CBP can accept proposals of person and real property, as well as services that may include the construction of new improvements, repairs, and alterations (U.S. Customs and Border Protection, 2014). Donation proposals are reviewed under the following three-phase process (U.S. Customs and Border Protection & GSA. U.S. General Services Administration, 2017):

- *Phase I: Proposal evaluation and selection.* A viable donation proposal that has been evaluated and selected for further planning and development by CBP and GSA, as applicable.
- *Phase II: Proposal planning and development.* A fully planned and developed donation proposal that is executable and fulfills CBP's operational needs at an acceptable cost, schedule, and risk.

- *Phase III: Donation acceptance agreement.* A fully executed donation acceptance agreement that formalizes acceptance of the proposed real property, personal property, monetary, or nonpersonal services donation, or any combination of the foregoing, by CBP or GSA, or by both.

Border crossing support infrastructure, including road access networks, vehicle inspection facilities, and right of way for these facilities, is usually funded with state or local sources. States and counties on the US side of the border have access to various credit instruments and may issue bonds with discounted rates and terms. States, counties, cities, and Regional Mobility Authorities (RMAs) can issue bonds guaranteed by toll revenue. At the Texas—Mexico border, most of the international crossings are tolled, and the revenue goes to the city or development agency.

The North American Development Bank (NADB) was created through the Agreement Between the Governments of the United States and Mexico, which went into effect on January 1, 1994, and was amended on August 4, 2004. The NADB was established in San Antonio, Texas, and began operations on November 10, 1994, with the initial capital subscriptions of the US and Mexican governments. The NADB provides direct loans, short-term financing, issuance of municipal bonds, or participation as part of a consortium for projects that are located within 100 km north of the US—Mexico international border and 300 km south of the border (North American Development Bank, 2017). In 2017, the NADB was analyzing the potential of participating in funding a new land border crossing at Otay Mesa in the Tijuana—San Diego region.

References

Build America Transportation Investment Center. (n.d.). *State funding; tolls.* BATIC Institute & AASHTO Center for Excellence. Retrieved from <http://www.financingtransportation.org/funding_financing/funding/state_funding/tolls.aspx>.

Canada DUI Entry Law. (n.d.). *Immigration lawyers: USA—Canada border crossing.* Canada. Retrieved from <http://www.canadaduientrylaw.com/border-crossings.php>.

Congressional Budget Office. (2016, September). *Projections of highway trust fund accounts under CBO's march 2016 baseline.* Retrieved from <https://www.cbo.gov/sites/default/files/51300-2016-03-HighwayTrustFund.pdf>.

Council of Ministers Responsible for transportation and Highway Safety. (2016, September). *Canada's national highway system—Annual report 2015.* Retrieved from <https://comt.ca/english/nhs-report-2015.pdf>.

Department of Homeland Security. (2019). *U.S. customs and border protection.* Retrieved from <https://www.cbp.gov/>.

Donnelly, R., & Gliebe, J. (2002). *Truck freight crossing the Canada—U.S. border.* Parsons Brinckerhoff Quade & Douglas Inc.. Retrieved from <http://ebtc.info/wp-content/uploads/2014/07/final-report.pdf>.

Frittelli, J. (2014). *Status of Mexican trucks in the United States: Frequently asked questions.* Congressional Research Services. Retrieved from <https://fas.org/sgp/crs/misc/R41821.pdf>.

Government of Canada. (2010a, April 1). *Highways, transport Canada*. Canada. Retrieved from <http://www.tc.gc.ca/eng/policy/acg-acgd-menu-highways-2141.htm>.

Government of Canada. (2010b, October 26). *Building Canada fund*. Canada. Retrieved from <http://www.infrastructure.gc.ca/prog/bcf-fcc-eng.html>.

Government of Canada. (2016, November, 4). *Transport Canada; borders*. Canada. Retrieved from <https://www.tc.gc.ca/eng/policy/acg-acgd-menu-borders-2144.htm>.

Government of Canada. (2017a, February 1). *Transport Canada. Gateways and corridors*. Canada. Retrieved from <https://www.tc.gc.ca/eng/policy/anre-menu-3023.htm>.

Government of Canada. (2017b, February 28). *About the free and secure trade program*. Canada. Retrieved from <https://www.cbsa-asfc.gc.ca/prog/fast-expres/about-apropos-eng. html>.

Government of Canada. (2018a, February 15). *About transport Canada*. Canada. Retrieved from <http://www.tc.gc.ca/eng/aboutus-menu.htm>.

Government of Canada. (2018b, September 20). *Trade and transportation infrastructure*. Canada. Retrieved from <http://www.infrastructure.gc.ca/plan/tt-ct-eng.html>.

Government of Canada. (2019, February 1). *Trade and transportation corridors initiative*. Canada. Retrieved from <http://www.tc.gc.ca/eng/trade-transportation-corridors-initiative.html>.

GSA. U.S. General Services Administration. (2018). *Land ports of entry overview*. Official website of the U.S. Government. Retrieved from <https://www.gsa.gov/real-estate/gsa-properties/land-ports-of-entry-overview>.

North American Development Bank. (2017). *Nadbank index*. Retrieved from <http://www.nadbank.org/~nadborg/index.php>.

Padova, A. (2006, February). Federal participation in highway construction and policy in Canada. *Library of Parliament, Economics Division*. Retrieved from <http://www.res.parl. gc.ca/Content/LOP/ResearchPublications/prb0569-e.htm>.

Secretaría de Comunicaciones y Transportes. (2017). *Anuario Estadístico Sector Comunicaciones y Transportes. 2016*. Retrieved from <http://www.sct.gob.mx/fileadmin/ DireccionesGrales/DGP/estadistica/Anuarios/Anuario_2016.pdf>.

Superintendencia de Administración Tributaria. (2019). *Operador Económico Automatizado*. Retrieved from <https://portal.sat.gob.gt/portal/operador-economico-autorizado/>.

Tax Policy Center. (2018). *What is the Highway Trust Fund and how is it financed?* Urban Institute. Retrieved from <http://www.taxpolicycenter.org/briefing-book/what-highway-trust-fund-and-how-it-financed>.

TBWG. (2005). *The Canada-United States, transportation working group*. Retrieved from <http://www.thetbwg.org/index_e.htm>.

U.S. Department of Transportation, Federal Highway Administration. (2015, October, 20). *U. S.–Mexico Joint Working Committee on transportation planning*. Washington, DC. Retrieved from <http://www.borderplanning.fhwa.dot.gov/mexico.asp>.

U.S. Department of Transportation, Federal Highway Administration. (2016, June 27). *Toll facilities in the United States*. Washington, DC. Retrieved from <https://www.fhwa.dot.gov/ policyinformation/tollpage/miletrends.cfm>.

U.S. Department of Transportation, Federal Highway Administration. (2017a, February 1). *Demands on the transportation system*. Washington, DC. Retrieved from <https://ops.fhwa. dot.gov/freight/freight_analysis/freight_story/demands.htm>

U.S. Department of Transportation, Federal Highway Administration. (2017b, February 1). *National Highway Freight Network map*. Washington, DC. Retrieved from <https://ops. fhwa.dot.gov/freight/infrastructure/nfn/maps/nhfn_map.htm>.

U.S. Department of Transportation, Federal Highway Administration. (2017c, August, 09). *Why does the interstate system include toll facilities?* Washington, DC. Retrieved from <https://www.fhwa.dot.gov/infrastructure/tollroad.cfm>.

U.S. Customs and Border Protection. (2014). CBP access newsletter. *Office of Congressional Affairs, 3*(13). Retrieved from <https://www.cbp.gov/sites/default/files/documents/CBP AccessV3.13_101014.pdf>.

U.S. Customs and Border Protection. (2017). *Secure electronic network for travelers rapid inspection.* Official Website of the Department of Homeland Security. Retrieved from <https://www.cbp.gov/travel/trusted-traveler-programs/sentri>.

U.S. Customs and Border Protection. (2019). *FAST: Free and secure trade for commercial vehicles.* Official Website of the Department of Homeland Security. Retrieved from <https://www.cbp.gov/travel/trusted-traveler-programs/fast#>.

U.S. Customs and Border Protection & GSA. U.S. General Services Administration. (2017, August 22). *Section 482 donation acceptance authority proposal evaluation procedures & criteria framework.* Retrieved from <https://www.cbp.gov/sites/default/files/assets/documents/2017Aug/DAP%20Section%20482%20Framework%2020170203.pdf>.

U.S. Department of Transportation. (2018). *U.S.-Mexico cross-border trucking pilot program.* Federal Motor Carrier Safety Administration. Retrieved from <https://www.fmcsa.dot.gov/international-programs/mexico-cross-border-trucking-pilot-program>.

U.S. Department of Transportation, Federal Highway Administration. (2017, June 29). *National Highway System.* Washington, DC. Retrieved from <https://www.fhwa.dot.gov/planning/national_highway_system/>.

U.S. Surface Transportation Board. (n.d.). *Railroad definitions.* Washington, DC: American Short Line and Regional Railroad Association. Retrieved from <https://www.aslrra.org/web/About/Railroad_Definitions/web/About/Short_Line_Definitions.aspx?hkey = f8f1d91d-b99a-4761-8a29-a620f42c16e1>.

World Bank & Public-Private Infrastructure Advisory Facility. (2003). *Private solutions for infrastructure in Mexico: Country framework report for private participation in infrastructure.* Washington, DC. ISBN: 0-8213-5414-0. Retrieved from <http://documents.worldbank.org/curated/en/615701468774861738/pdf/2979600182131541410.pdf>.

Part III

Trade and Transportation in Europe

Chapter 5

Trade and transportation evolution in the European Union

5.1 Description of how the European Union evolved from the original founding members to current status

The European Union (EU) comprises 28 countries, covering a large portion of the European continent as shown in Fig. 5.1. It is an international economic and political organization, founded upon numerous treaties. It has undergone several expansions from the first six Member States of its initial formation.

5.1.1 A brief history of the European Union

The *Treaty on European Union*, known as *Maastricht Treaty*, went into force on November 1, 1993 (European Union, 2019a, 2019b, 2019c). This international agreement established the EU. The first formation of the Union, however, was created after the end of World War II with the aim to end conflicts, strengthen democracy, and restructure the economy of Europe. A timeline of major events leading to the current state of the EU is shown in Fig. 5.2.

The first six European countries that formed an official organization under the *Treaty of Paris* (1951) were Belgium, France, Germany, Italy, Luxembourg and the Netherlands. These countries renounced part of their sovereignty in 1952, founding the *European Coal and Steel Community* (ECSC) and placing their coal and steel production in a common market. The *European Court of Justice* was established under the same Treaty. In 1957 the *European Economic Community* (EEC) (or Common Market) was created by the *Treaty of Rome*, with the aim to bring about economic integration. The *European Atomic Energy Community* (EAEC) was established during the same year by the Euratom Treaty. The *Merger Treaty* of 1965 created the *European Communities* (EC), merging ECSC, EEC and EAEC. The EU expanded with Denmark, Ireland, and the United Kingdom becoming members in 1973; Greece joined in 1981; Portugal and Spain followed in 1986.

International Trade and Transportation Infrastructure Development.
DOI: https://doi.org/10.1016/B978-0-12-815741-1.00005-X
149

FIGURE 5.1   European Union member states by accession date.

The Schengen Agreement was signed in 1985 and came into effect in 1995. The Schengen Area includes 22 of the 28 EU countries (excluding Bulgaria, Croatia, Cyprus, Ireland, Romania and the United Kingdom) and some non-EU nations, the citizens of which are entitled to travel freely among them, operating as a single nation with uniform visa policy for international travel. The *Single European Act* was enacted in 1986 aiming at the establishment of a single European currency and common foreign and domestic policies. In 1994 the *Treaty of Corfu* was signed, with Austria, Sweden and Finland joining the EU in 1995. A *monetary union* came into full force in 2002. The Eurozone is composed of 19 EU Member States (Austria, Belgium, Cyprus, Estonia, Finland, France, Germany, Greece, Ireland, Italy, Latvia, Lithuania, Luxembourg, Malta, the Netherlands, Portugal, Slovakia, Slovenia, and Spain) using the euro currency. In 2003 the *Treaty of Accession* was signed, which went into force in 2004 when the new members joined the EU (Cyprus, Czech Republic, Estonia, Hungary, Latvia, Lithuania, Malta, Poland, Slovakia, and Slovenia). Romania and Bulgaria joined the EU in 2007 and Croatia followed in 2013. In 2007 the Lisbon Treaty, known as the Treaty on the Functioning of the EU (TFEU) was signed.

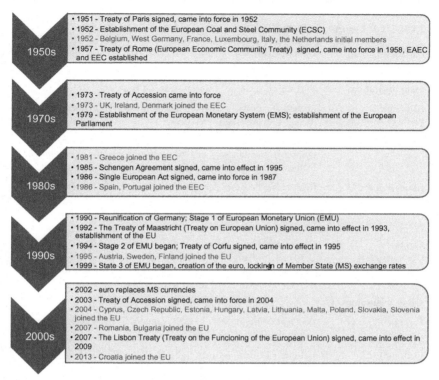

FIGURE 5.2   Timeline of the European Union.

5.1.2   Decision-making at European Union level and the European institutions involved

Actions taken by the EU are founded on treaties, which present the objectives of the EU, set the rules for how the EU institutions operate and how decisions are made. They outline the relationship between the EU and its Member States (European Union, 2017). Not all Member States participate in all EU policy areas, as is the case of the Euro area and the Schengen area previously noted.

While the EU Member States remain sovereign and independent states, they delegate some of their decisions on matters of common interest to the shared institutions they have created (European Union, 2017). According to Article 13 of the Treaty on EU (Official Journal of the European Union, 2016) the institutional framework comprises seven institutions (European Union, 2018) as shown in Table 5.1.

TABLE 5.1 European institutions.

European institution	Description
Main institutions	
European Parliament	Represents the EU's citizens, is directly elected by them and is the EU's lawmaking body
European Council	Defines the EU's overall political direction and priorities, and comprises the heads of state or government of the EU Member States, its President and the European Commission President
Council of the EU (Council)	Represents the executive governments of the EU's Member States, is part of the EU legislature, and, along with the European Parliament, is the main decision-making body of the EU
European Commission	Represents the interests of the EU as a whole and is a politically independent executive body of the EU, proposing legislation, implementing decisions of the European Parliament and the Council of the EU
Other institutions	
European Court of Auditors	Looks after the interests of EU taxpayers, as EU's independent external auditor
Court of Justice of the EU	Interprets EU law, ensures that it is applied in the same way in all EU countries, and settles legal disputes between national governments and EU institutions
European Central Bank	Manages the euro and frames and implements the EU economic and monetary policy

EU, European Union.

Decisions made at the EU level involve the institutions as follows (European Parliament, 2019a, 2019b):

1. Heads of state and government make decisions on general policies in the European Council.
2. The Commission makes proposals for new laws.
3. The Parliament reviews the proposals and passes decisions together with the Council of Ministers.
4. The Council of Ministers and Parliament approve the laws together.
5. The Commission ensures that decisions are followed in all Member States.
6. The European Court of Justice settles disagreements that may come up.

A standard decision-making procedure used in the EU (unless the treaties specifically state that one of the special legislative procedures is to be applied to a particular subject) is the *Ordinary Legislative Procedure* (EU Monitor, 2019). According to the ordinary legislative procedure, legislation is adopted jointly and on an equal footing by the Parliament and the Council, starting with a proposal from the Commission. The procedure comprises up to three readings, with the possibility to agree and conclude at any stage as shown in Fig. 5.3.

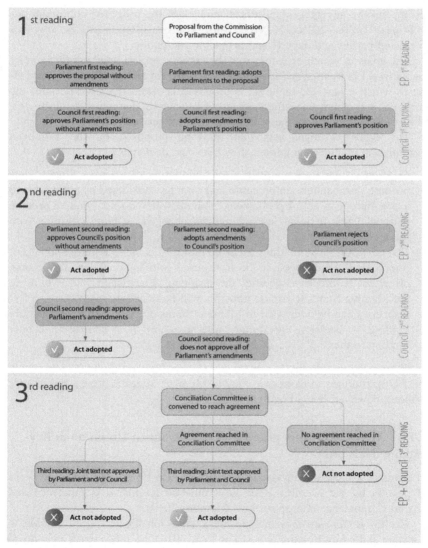

FIGURE 5.3   The three phases of the ordinary legislative procedure. *From http://www.europarl.europa.eu/ordinary-legislative-procedure/en/ordinary-legislative-procedure.html.*

In cases in which treaties state otherwise, an *extraordinary decision-making procedure* may be followed (European Parliament, 2017).

5.1.3 Types of legal acts proposed by the European Commission

Before proposing new initiatives, their potential economic, social and environmental consequences are assessed and presented in an impact assessment, setting out the advantages and disadvantages of the proposed policy options (European Union, 2019a, 2019b, 2019c). The consultation process involves interested parties and experts and is open to the public.

The areas in which decisions may be taken at an EU level are dictated by the various EU treaties and are limited to them. An article of a treaty according to which a new EU legal act is proposed is called the *legal basis* of the proposal and determines the legislative procedure that must be followed. Most of the cases follow the ordinary legislative procedure.

The types of legal acts that may be proposed by the European Commission include regulations, directives and decisions.

- *Regulations* are laws applicable and binding to all Member States. They become immediately enforceable and may be considered as equivalent to a pan-European act of parliament. Although they do not need to become national laws, national laws should be changed to avoid conflicts with the regulation.
- *Directives* are laws binding Member States to achieve a particular objective. Usually they need to be transposed into national law to become effective. A directive specifies the result to be achieved, and it is up to the Member States to decide how this will be done.
- *Decisions* can be addressed to Member States or even individuals and are binding. A decision specifying those to whom it is addressed is only binding to them.

Other instruments include *recommendations* and *opinions, which* enable the EU institutions to express a view to Member States and even individuals without, however, being legally binding.

5.1.4 Types of powers granted to the European Union on policy-making decisions

In terms of policy-making decisions, the EU may be granted two core types of powers by the Member State governments: Exclusive Competence and Shared Competence (European Law Monitor, 2019).

Exclusive Competences include areas in which the EU alone is able to legislate and adopt binding acts (EUR-Lex, 2016). Member states may do so themselves only if empowered by the EU to implement these acts. Policy areas in which the EU has exclusive competence are the following: customs union; establishing the competition rules necessary for the functioning of the internal market; monetary policy for the Member States whose currency is the euro; conservation of marine biological resources under the common fisheries policy; common commercial policy; concluding international agreements when their conclusion is required by a legislative act of the EU, or when their conclusion is necessary to enable the EU to exercise its internal competence, or in so far as their conclusion may affect common rules or later their scope.

Shared Competences include areas in which both the EU and its Member States may adopt legally binding acts. The Member States can do so only where the EU has not exercised its competence or has explicitly ceased to do so. Shared competences apply to the following policy areas: internal market; social policy, limited to the aspects defined in the TFEU; economic, social and territorial cohesion; agriculture and fisheries, excluding the conservation of marine biological resources; environment; consumer protection; transport; trans-European networks; energy; area of freedom, security and justice; common safety concerns in public health matters, limited to the aspects defined in the TFEU; research, technological development and space; development cooperation and humanitarian aid.

According to the Treaty of Lisbon, a third category in the division of competences between the EU and EU countries is the *Supporting Competences*. In this case the EU can only intervene to support, coordinate and complement the action of EU countries. The policy areas to which supporting competences relate include protection and improvement of human health; industry; culture; tourism; education, vocational training, youth and sport; civil protection; and administrative cooperation.

5.1.5 Financial support to European Union policy implementation: the multiannual financial framework

To support its policies, the EU produces the *multiannual financial framework*, which outlines long-term spending plans over a 5-year (or longer) period. The framework for the 2014−20 period allocates €1 trillion to the five main areas of EU activities: sustainable growth - natural resources; security and citizenship; global Europe; economic, social and territorial cohesion; and competitiveness for growth and jobs (European Union, 2017). The annual budget in 2017 was around €158 billion (European Union, 2019a, 2019b, 2019c) and is allocated as shown in Fig. 5.4.

Fig. 5.5 shows the areas and subareas financed over the 5-year period 2014−20 and their respective budget shares.

Sustainable growth: natural resources accounts for 39% of the budget, while economic, social and territorial cohesion accounts for 34%. The other areas, namely competitiveness for growth and jobs, global Europe, and security and citizenship, account for 13%, 6%, and 2%, respectively.

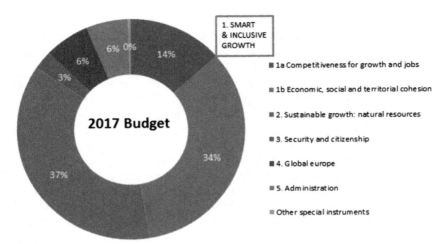

FIGURE 5.4 EU budget in 2017 (total €157.9 billion). *EU*, European Union. *From https://europa.eu/european-union/about-eu/eu-budget/expenditure_en.*

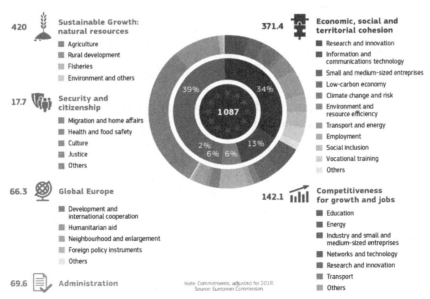

FIGURE 5.5 Areas financed by the EU budget (2014−20) (€billion). *EU*, European Union. *From European Union. (2017). The European Union—What it is and what it does. Retrieved from <https://publications.europa.eu/en/publication-detail/-/publication/715cfcc8-fa70-11e7-b8f5-01aa75ed71a1/language-en>.*

Transport policy—related activities are mainly covered under the areas of competitiveness for growth and jobs and economic, social and territorial cohesion, although, indirectly, a positive impact for transport is also derived through support allocated to other relevant areas and subareas.

5.2   Internal and external trade policy developments and impacts on the transportation system

5.2.1   Evolution of the European Union trade policy

The *Common Commercial Policy* is a keystone of the functioning of the European integration, since the establishment of the EC in 1957 by the Treaty of Rome.

The removal of tariffs and nontariff barriers to trade among the initial six signatories of the treaty required the formation of a *customs union*, with a common external commercial policy and common tariff applied to all their external trade partners. The common commercial policy came into effect in 1968 following a period of alignment of the trade policies of these Member States.

Decisions on trade in merchandise and agricultural products were conferred to the EC. Trade in services, intellectual property rights, government procurements or some investment issues could follow mixed agreements (agreements between the EU and a third country that touch both on powers, or competencies, exclusive to the EU and on other competencies exclusive to EU Member States, requiring approval by both), exercising shared external competencies between EC and Member States. Such agreements included the Member States as signatories. With the TFEU (Lisbon Treaty), the common commercial policy was further clarified as an exclusive competence and these competencies were conferred to the EU by all members. Nevertheless, certain aspects of the decision process are yet to be clarified (Štěrbová, 2010). It is noted (Schutze, 2012) that international transport agreements are specifically excluded from the scope of the common commercial policy and that Article 207 states that the exercise of the common commercial policy competence "shall not affect the delimitation of competences between the Union and the Member States."

According to Article 207 of the TFEU:

The common commercial policy shall be based on uniform principles, particularly with regard to changes in tariff rates, the conclusion of tariff and trade agreements relating to trade in goods and services, and the commercial aspects of intellectual property, foreign direct investment, the achievement of uniformity in measures of liberalisation, export policy and measures to protect trade such as those to be taken in the event of dumping or subsidies. The common commercial policy shall be conducted in the context of the principles and objectives of the Union's external action.

The EU negotiates international trade agreements, enhancing regulatory cooperation with major trade partners and increasing market access. EU countries are benefiting from increased negotiation power with other countries, growth in the economy, job creation and access to wider choice of products at lower prices. Besides contributing to job creation and the gross domestic product (GDP), trade agreements uphold European standards (European Council, 2018a, 2018b). Every EU trade agreement is transparent and has legally binding commitments on workers' rights and the environment. The EU trade policy, aiming at concluding ambitious free trade agreements (FTAs), enhancing regulatory cooperation with major trade partners and increasing market access, is a core component of the EU's 2020 strategy.

5.2.2 Types of European Union trade agreements

The EU may enter into international agreements on all the policy areas in which it has competence, with the aim to achieve results set out in the EU policies (EU Monitor, n.d.). In the trade policy area, trade agreements detail the terms of trade between countries, determining the tariffs and duties they impose on imports and exports. Depending on their content, trade agreements may be classified as economic partnership agreements (EPAs), FTAs, association agreements, and partnership and cooperation agreements.

EPAs eliminate barriers to the free movement of goods, services and investment between countries. Economic partnerships may be described as high standard variants of FTAs and are considered an intermediate step in the economic integration process, between a free trade area and single market. The EPAs between the EU and African, Caribbean, and Pacific (ACP) countries aim at fostering the smooth and gradual integration of the ACP countries into the world economy and ultimately contribute to sustainable development and poverty reduction (European Commission, 2018). The majority of ACP countries are either implementing an EPA or have concluded EPA negotiations with the EU.

FTAs aim to establish a free-trade area among cooperating countries. They determine tariffs and duties imposed on imports and exports, to reduce or eliminate trade barriers. They differ from customs unions mainly in their approach to third parties. A customs union requires all parties to establish identical external tariffs in trading with nonparties. A free trade area is not subject to such requirement (Krueger, 1995).

Association agreements are legally binding agreements between the EU and third-party countries, aiming to foster close relationships between the EU and countries on a wide variety of policy areas, especially economic cooperation (EU Monitor, n.d.). The EU has more than 20 association agreements. Their legal basis is defined in Article 217 of the Treaty of the Functioning of the EU, which provides for "an association involving reciprocal rights and obligations, common action and special procedures." Special types of association agreements include *stabilization and association agreements (SAAs)* (the EU has such agreements with Western Balkan countries) and *deep and comprehensive free trade area* (DCFTA) with Ukraine, Georgia and Moldova (Institute for Government, 2018).

Partnership and cooperation agreements provide a general framework for bilateral economic relations that are nonpreferential, leaving customs tariffs as they are. They are legally binding long-term agreements, aiming to support the democratic and economic development of a country, encouraging trade and investment (EUR-Lex, 2010).

The agreements govern trade with third countries and may concern areas such as tariffs, trade subsidies, import quotas, voluntary export restraints, and restriction on the establishment of foreign-owned businesses, regulation of trade in services and other barriers to international trade. The EU has concluded FTAs with many countries and is negotiating with many others, aiming to eliminate customs duties or quotas on EU exports and reduce bureaucracy in the export process, while upholding environmental and health and safety standards.

FTAs may be classified as unilateral, bilateral and multilateral (Amadeo, 2019).

Unilateral trade agreements occur when a country adopts a trade policy that isn't reciprocated. It may take the form of a trade restriction, such as a tariff, on all imports, or the lifting of a tariff on imports from a country.

Bilateral trade agreements occur between two nations promoting trade and investment by reducing or eliminating tariffs and other trade barriers such as import quotas and export restraints.

Multilateral trade agreements occur among three or more nations. They are generally more difficult to negotiate compared to bilateral agreements but have a bigger impact on economic growth.

In the case of other trade-related matters the EU has the right to negotiate and enter into trade agreements, but the European Commission has to be granted permission by the Member States prior to starting negotiations. The process is detailed next.

5.2.3   European Union trade agreement negotiation process

The decision-making process for the implementation of the EU Common Commercial Policy follows the ordinary legislative procedure. In a trade agreement negotiation process the European institutions have specific roles. The European Commission's role is to prepare, negotiate, and propose the EU's international trade agreements. The main role of the Council of the EU (Council) and the European Parliament is to jointly decide on the approval of the trade agreements (European Commission, 2012). The two institutions, acting by means of regulations in accordance with the ordinary legislative procedure, shall adopt the measures defining the framework for implementing the common commercial policy. Any actions taken within this policy require the European Commission to table a legislative proposal to the European Parliament and the Council, which have the powers to amend it prior to agreeing on a common final text. A trade agreement negotiation process involves numerous stages and may take several years.

In this step-by-step approach, the Council first authorizes the European Commission to negotiate a trade agreement with a partner country (European Parliament, 2016). The Council's authorization includes directives, often referred to as *mandates*, which set out what the Commission should achieve in the agreement.

The Commission negotiates with the trade partner on behalf of the EU, in consultation with the Council's trade policy committee, keeping the Council and the European Parliament informed. Meetings with interested parties and public consultations are held, and various position papers, reports on the negotiation process, impact assessments, factsheets and proposed texts on the agreement are produced during the process.

Once an agreement is reached, the trade negotiation text is translated and published into all official languages, and the European Commission submits a formal proposal for adoption to the Council. A review is carried out, and the Council adopts it provisionally. The European Parliament gives its consent. Upon approval the EU signs the agreement, the partner ratifies the signed agreement and the Council declares it concluded. In the case of a mixed agreement, EU Member State governments also ratify the agreement before it is applied in full.

5.2.4 Transport policy and trade

The Union has become deeply integrated into global markets and thus it is essential for the EU to have strong transport connections. Transportation infrastructure is also at the heart of EU's integration milestone, and it is linked with the completion of the internal market and improvement of trade. The core of supply chains is the transport network, enabling the efficient distribution of goods and making places more accessible. Thanks to the ease of modern transport and communications, it is now easier to produce, buy, and sell goods around the world, giving the European companies of every size the potential to trade outside Europe.

Over the past 60 years EU transport has made incredible progress. Without functional transport connections and networks trade would not be efficient, which would result in significant loss of income. EU is concerned with the creation of a Single European Transport area with fair competition conditions for all the different means of transport: road, rail, air and maritime. An objective has been set for the development of a safe and high-quality transportation system, including all modes, by upgrading the existing infrastructure and investing in new transportation infrastructure. The cost for the planned transportation infrastructure in the EU is estimated at €1.5 trillion for the period 2010—30. In 2017 the Commission agreed to invest €2.7 billion in 152 key projects concerning the transport system that promote competitive, clean and connected mobility throughout Europe (European Commission, 2017). Infrastructure investments have been noticeably low since the crisis of 2008. The OECD (2019) data on 2015 indicates that investment in most countries remain low, and most countries have a share of total transport infrastructure investment below 1%. Given the fact that public funds are limited, investment from the private sector is deemed important.

As transport is essential for most activities, it is being dealt with in policies at all levels, from the global level (United Nations, 2018) to the city councils. The EU has set a goal to solve the dilemma between growth-oriented policies that generate more transport and environmental policies that call for emissions reduction. At a European level, the main guiding document for this purpose is the "EU Common Transport Policy," which was published in 2001 and reviewed in 2006, and that sets priorities for action on transport matters, including aspects about the environment.

Many political decisions that influence the environmental damage caused by transport are taken at European level. These involve getting transport prices right, setting vehicle emissions limits, introducing fuel quality standards and taxes, and providing funding for infrastructure development. For this reason, the European Federation of Transport and Environment was formed in 1999 as the main organization that handles issues related to transport and the environment. A series of green papers on transport have been published by the European Commission, covering a number of transport- and environment-related issues. Green papers are policy documents issued by the EC, with the aim to open public debate and stimulate discussion on specific topics at the European level, contribute in setting new agendas on the topic within the Member States, and give rise to legislative developments. They constitute an important component of a transport policy strategy and may lead to the development and adoption of specific action plans.

In 2009 the green paper on "TEN-T: A Policy Review, Towards an Integrated Trans- European Transport Network at the Service of the Common Transport Policy," which emphasized the integration of trans-European transport network at the service of the common transport policy, was presented by the European Commission. It aimed to provide the infrastructure needed for the proper function of the internal market. TEN-T development constitutes an important EU policy and will be detailed in a subsequent chapter.

5.2.5 Today's context

During its 20-plus years of establishment, the single market has grown from 345 million consumers in 1992 to over 500 million in 2014. The intra-EU trade has also grown significantly from 800 billion in 1992 to 2.8 trillion in 2013 and to over 3 trillion in 2015 (in terms of the value of goods exchanged). Also, it is noticeable that at the same period (1992–2013), the trade between EU members with the rest of the world tripled from €500 billion in 1992 to €1.7 trillion in 2013 (Thirion, 2017).

The last decade was a challenging period for the future of the EU. The global economic crisis affected directly the finances of the EU, causing economic contraction and resulting in over a quarter of young people being unemployed. The evolution of the Single Market has gone a long way since its establishment, although there are still some gaps to be closed, concerning the areas of services, digital, and energy. The European Commission is continuously promoting ideas of partnerships in order to unlock further potential. The crisis has also affected EU Member States directly and made it essential to establish a so-called Banking Union, an institution set up to help the Member States recover from the crisis. The EU's leaders agreed to reduce harmful emissions with climate change still high on the agenda. Other difficulties that torment the cohesion of the Union are the increasing migration from the Middle East, the United Kingdom's withdrawal from the EU and the rise of terrorism.

5.3 European Union trade agreements, shaping trade relations with non-European Union countries

The EU has already concluded or has ongoing negotiations on trade agreements with countries all over the world. The state of EU trade for 2018 (European Council, 2018a, 2018b) is shown in Fig. 5.6.

FIGURE 5.6 State of EU trade. *EU*, European Union. *From https://www.consilium.europa.eu/ en/policies/trade-policy/trade-agreements/.*

The EU has a solid network of trade negotiations of different forms with strategic partners of world regions. The map in Fig. 5.6 highlights the EU and Customs Union (Andorra, Monaco, San Marino, Turkey), the European Economic Area (EEA) (Norway, Iceland, Liechtenstein), preferential trade agreements (PTAs) in place including FTAs, EPAs and *DCFTAs* (providing Georgia, Moldova, and Ukraine access to EU's internal market in selected sectors), preferential agreements awaiting adoption/ratification, PTAs being negotiated, potential for free trade partnerships, stand-alone investment agreements being negotiated and preferential agreements in the process of modernization.

The 2016–20 Strategic Plan for the EU's trade negotiations focuses on shaping globalization by reenergizing multilateral negotiations and designing an open approach to bilateral and regional agreements.

5.3.1 Customs union, the internal market and free trade areas in Europe

The Treaty of Rome that came into effect in 1958 had the objective to bring about economic integration, creating a *common market* and *customs union* among its six founding members. The aim was to eliminate trade barriers among Member States. The customs union was achieved in 1968.

The Single European Act that came into force in 1987 aimed at establishing the *internal market* (single market or common market) in the EEC. A deadline of December 31, 1992 was set for the adoption of the legislative acts. The single market was created in 1993.

A new strategy from 2003 to 2010 made substantial progress in opening up transport, telecommunications, electricity, gas, and postal services. A communication entitled "Towards a Single Market Act" was published by the Commission in 2010 [COM(2010)0608, n.d.], followed by a Communication on Single Market Act II [COM(2012)0573, n.d.] in 2012. The Single Market Act II aimed at a better integrated single market with emphasis on business mobility, the digital economy and consumer confidence.

Today's single market, created in 1993, is perhaps the most ambitious type of trade cooperation, eliminating tariffs, quotas, and taxes on trade and allowing the free movement of goods, people, services, and capital. The internal market made a significant contribution to the prosperity and integration of the EU economy (European Parliament, 2019a, 2019b). It is an ongoing process with the integration of the service industry still containing gaps.

The single market is the trading area in the EU in which most trade barriers are removed. The EU is not only a single market, it is also *a customs union*, meaning a group of countries that have removed customs from goods, apply the same import duties to nonmember countries and join together to negotiate trade deals involving customs. Goods clearing customs in one country may be shipped to other countries in the union without further tariffs being imposed. A country may be in the EU's single market, but not the customs union. In this case, the *rules of origin* apply, which may determine whether goods legally originating from this country qualify for duty-free entry into the EU.

The rules of origin (World Trade Organization, n.d.) are criteria needed to determine the national source of a product, depending on which duties and restrictions may apply on imports. They demonstrate where goods have legally originated and whether they contain parts and components above a certain level that have originated elsewhere.

The EU is the largest and most productive customs union. Like the single market, non-EU Member States can also be part of the customs union by agreement. The single market encompasses the 28 EU Member States and it has been extended to Iceland, Liechtenstein, and Norway (through the *EEA Agreement*) and Switzerland (through bilateral treaties) (Wikipedia, 2019a, 2019b). Switzerland no longer participates in the EEA. Croatia has submitted an application to join. The members maintain a common customs policy with respect to nonmember nations. Other countries have limited participation in selected sectors of the single market. Compliance with EU regulation is required. Non-EU Member States that are part of the customs union include Andorra, Monaco, San Marino, and Turkey. It is also possible for a country, such as the EEA countries (Iceland, Liechtenstein, and Norway), to trade in the single market without being members of the customs union.

Outside of the single market and the customs union, a country may still negotiate a free trade deal with the EU. A *free trade area* is one in which there are no tariffs, taxes or quotas on goods and services moving from one country to another. Every customs union, common market, economic union, customs and monetary union, and economic and monetary union is also a free trade area. Establishment of a free trade area requires time-consuming negotiations and may contain exceptions. For example, some products may be exempted, others protected and others not covered (Bloom, 2017).

5.3.2 Multilateral free trade areas in Europe

In addition to the EU with the single market and the customs union as previously described, within Europe there are three other multilateral free trade areas: European Free Trade Association (EFTA), Central European Free Trade Agreement (CEFTA), and Commonwealth of Independent States Free Trade Area (CISFTA).

The *EFTA* was founded by the Stockholm Convention in 1960 to promote free trade and economic integration between its Member States (now including Iceland, Liechtenstein, Norway, and Switzerland), within Europe, and globally. The EFTA secretariat has assisted Iceland, Liechtenstein and Norway in the management of the EEA Agreement, which incorporates the

EU Member States with the three EEA EFTA states into the internal market. The EFTA states have 29 FTAs in force or awaiting ratification, covering 40 partner countries outside Europe (European Free Trade Association, 2019).

The *CEFTA* was originally founded in 1994 by Poland, Hungary, and Czechoslovakia with the aim to mobilize efforts to integrate into Western European institutions. It expanded to include several Southeast European countries. Once a participating country joins the EU, its CEFTA membership ends (Central European Free Trade Agreement, 2016). Currently, parties of the CEFTA agreement include Albania, Bosnia, and Herzegovina, Moldova, Montenegro, North Macedonia, Serbia and the United Nations Interim Administration Mission in Kosovo on behalf of Kosovo. All former participating countries had previously signed association agreements with the EU, so CEFTA had served as a preparation for EU membership (Wikipedia, 2019a, 2019b).

The *CISFTA* is a free trade area among Russia, Ukraine, Belarus, Uzbekistan, Moldova, Armenia, Kyrgyzstan, Kazakhstan, and Tajikistan, which was proposed in 1991 and was signed by its initial members in 2011. It replaces existing bilateral and multilateral FTAs between the countries. Belarus, Kyrgyzstan, Kazakhstan, Armenia, and Russia form the Eurasian Economic Union, including a customs union and a single market.

5.3.3 Bi-lateral European Union free trade agreements

According to the European Commissioner for Trade (Malmström, 2019) the EU in early 2019 had 41 trade agreements with 72 countries. There are numerous bilateral trade agreements with countries, customs territories, trade blocks, or groups of countries.

The EU has an interest to support regional integration with the world's regions especially within those that are not fully industrialized. Also, the Union along with other powerful actors like China and the United States are engaged more and more frequently in negotiations with single countries. The EU turned from interregional negotiations to a bilateral mode of conducting external trade relations towards the same region over time, with single countries of several regional organizations. The EU has detailed trade policies in place for all its partners and abides by the global instructions on international trade set out by the World Trade Organization (WTO). Several EU trade agreements, by regions of the world, as presented by the European Commission (2019a, 2019b) are summarized below.

- *EU—West Africa* (EPA): The EU has initiated an Economic Partnership with 16 states of West Africa: the Economic Community of West African States and the West African Economic and Monetary Union. Until the adoption of the full regional EPA with West Africa, stepping-stone EPAs with Côte d'Ivoire and Ghana entered into provisional application in 2016.

- *EU−Central Africa* (EPA): The EU and Cameroon signed an interim EPA in 2009 and are currently implementing it. The agreement is open to any country or group of countries from the Central African region that is interested in joining. It is considered as a stepping-stone agreement for EU and Central African regional organizations (CEMAC and ECCAS) to reach a comprehensive EPA. Congo trades with the EU under the EU's generalized system of preferences (GSP). Gabon has not been eligible since 2014, as it has been classified as an upper-middle-income country. Chad, the Central African Republic, the Democratic Republic of Congo, São Tomé and Principe and Equatorial Guinea are least developed countries (LDCs), so they benefit under the EU's Everything but Arms (EBA) scheme.
- *EU−Eastern and Southern Africa (ESA)* (EPA): The six countries in the ESA region (Comoros, Madagascar, Mauritius, Seychelles, Zambia, and Zimbabwe) concluded an interim EPA with the EU in 2007. In 2009 four countries (Madagascar, Mauritius, Seychelles, and Zimbabwe) signed the agreement, which has been provisionally applied since 2012. In 2013 the European Parliament gave its consent to the agreement. Comoros signed it in 2017 and started applying it in 2019.
- *EU−East African Community (EAC)* (EPA): Negotiations for an EPA were finalized in 2014 with the EAC (Burundi, Kenya, Rwanda, Tanzania, Uganda, and South Sudan, which joined in 2016). Kenya and Rwanda signed the EPA in 2016, and Kenya has endorsed it. It will enter into force once the remaining countries sign and ratify it. The EC submitted a proposal for signature and provisional application of the full EPA with the EAC to the council in February 2016. Burundi, Rwanda, Tanzania, and Uganda are on the UN's list of LDCs.
- *EU−Southern African Development Community (SADC)* (EPA): On June 2016 the EU signed an EPA with an SADC group comprising Botswana, Lesotho, Mozambique, Namibia, South Africa, and Eswatini. Angola has an option to join the agreement in the future. The agreement is the first regional EPA in Africa to be fully operational in 2018. The other six members of the SADC region (the Democratic Republic of the Congo, Madagascar, Malawi, Mauritius, Zambia and Zimbabwe) are negotiating EPAs with the EU as part of other regional groups. Lesotho and Mozambique are LDCs. Botswana, Lesotho, Namibia, South Africa and Eswatini form the Southern Africa Customs Union.
- *EU−Caribbean (CARIFORUM)* (EPA): In October 2008 Antigua and Barbuda, the Bahamas, Barbados, Belize, Dominica, Grenada, Guyana, Jamaica, Saint Lucia, Saint Vincent, and the Grenadines, Saint Kitts, and Nevis, Suriname, Trinidad and Tobago, and the Dominican Republic signed with EU the CARIFORUM-EU EPA. Haiti signed the agreement in December 2009 but has not ratified it yet.
- *EU−Pacific* (EPA): The EPA with the Pacific states of Papua New Guinea, Fiji and Samoa was ratified by the European Parliament in

January 2011 and by Papua New Guinea in May 2011. Fiji started applying it in 2014 and Samoa in 2018. The agreement is open for the other 12 ACP Pacific countries (Cook Islands, Kiribati, Marshall Islands, Federal State of Micronesia, Nauru, Niue, Palau, Solomon Islands, Timor Leste, Tonga, Tuvalu, and Vanuatu) to join. The Solomon Islands and Tonga have expressed their wish to join the EPA.

- *EU−Andean Community (Colombia, Peru)* (Comprehensive Trade Agreement): The EU has a CTA with Colombian and Peru since 2013, which was joined by Ecuador in 2017. Bolivia, a member of the Andean Community can also seek accession to the trade agreement. Bolivia benefits from the preferential access that EU grants under the GSP scheme.
- *EU−Association of South East Asian Nations (ASEAN)* (Bilateral FTA): Bilateral agreement negotiations with Singapore and Vietnam were completed in 2014 and 2015, respectively. Negotiations with Indonesia are still ongoing while negotiations with Thailand, Malaysia and the Philippines are currently on hold. The bilateral agreements will serve as building blocks towards a future EU−ASEAN agreement, which is EU's ultimate objective, given the fact that this group of countries is EU's largest trading partner outside Europe, after the United States and China.
- *EU−Central America* (Association Agreement): The EU and the Central American region concluded a new association agreement, which was signed in 2012. The trade pillar of the Association Agreement has been provisionally applied with Honduras, Nicaragua, Panama, Costa Rica, El Salvador, and Guatemala since 2013. The EU's trade policy objective for Central America is to strengthen regional integration between the region's countries, with the creation of a customs union and economic integration in Central America. The trade part of the association agreement will replace the unilateral preferential access granted to Central America under the EU's GSP.
- *EU−Central Asia* (Generalized Scheme of Preferences): Kyrgyzstan, Tajikistan and Uzbekistan have favorable access to EU's markets through the GSP. They EU has bilateral trade relations with these countries, governed by a Partnership and Cooperation Agreement. Kyrgyzstan benefits also from the GSP + scheme, which grants additional preferences. Kazakhstan and Turkmenistan can no longer benefit from the GSP scheme, as upper-middle-income-level economies. The EU has bilateral trade relations, through an Enhanced Partnership and Cooperation Agreement, with Kazakhstan, signed in 2015. The EU is in the process of updating the Central Asia Strategy of 2007 with the new one expected to be adopted in summer 2019. The EU concluded a PCA with Turkmenistan in 1998 which is pending ratification by all EU Member States. Meanwhile, an interim agreement entered into force in 2010. Enhanced Partnership and Cooperation Agreements are currently negotiated with Kyrgyzstan and Uzbekistan.

- *EU−Euro-Mediterranean Partnership* (Association Agreement): Euro-Mediterranean Association Agreements are in force with most of the partners (with the exception of Syria and Libya, for which negotiations have been suspended), with the aim of creating a Euro-Mediterranean Free Trade Area removing trade and investment barriers between the EU and Southern Mediterranean countries (Algeria, Egypt, Israel, Jordan, Lebanon, Libya, Morocco, Palestine, Syria, Tunisia, and Turkey), as well as among the Southern Mediterranean countries themselves. Deepening South−South economic integration is a key goal of the Euro-Mediterranean trade partnership. Regional economic integration, however, between Southern Mediterranean countries is limited.
- *EU−Gulf region* (Cooperation Agreement): The six member countries of the Gulf Cooperation Council (GCC) are Bahrain, Kuwait, Oman, Qatar, Saudi Arabia, and the United Arab Emirates. They represent an essential region for the global trade, and they were EU's fourth largest export market in 2016. The GCC countries have formed a custom unions and are working towards the establishment of an internal market. They cooperate with the EU based on the EU−GCC cooperation agreement. The GCC countries are all classified as high-income economies by the World Bank and as such they do not benefit under the EU's GSP scheme.
- *EU−Mercosur* (Association Agreement): The EU concluded a trade agreement with the four founding members of Mercosur (Argentina, Brazil, Paraguay, and Uruguay) as part of a biregional association agreement. Current trade relations are based on an interregional Framework Cooperation Agreement that entered into force in 1999. EU−Mercosur negotiations for a trade agreement started in 2000 and experienced different phases over the last years. The negotiation process was relaunched in 2016 with the aim of concluding an ambitious, comprehensive and balanced agreement covering several issues. The EU and individual Mercosur countries have bilateral framework cooperation agreements, also dealing with trade-related matters.
- *EU−Western Balkans* (Stabilization and Association Process): EU policy in the Western Balkans is integrated into the Stabilization and Association Process, which gives all Western Balkan countries (Albania, Bosnia, and Herzegovina, FYROM, Montenegro, Serbia, Kosovo) a common future as EU Member States. Since the launch of the Stabilization and Association Process the EU has concluded bilateral FTAs (referred to as SAAs) with each of the Western Balkan countries. SAAs constitute the legal instrument for alignment to the EU acquis and progressive integration into the EU market.

The countries that EU has bilateral trade agreements with are shown in Fig. 5.7 (Wikipedia, 2011).

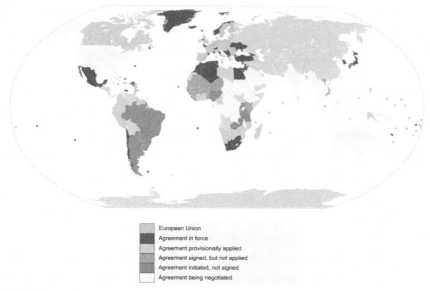

FIGURE 5.7 EU bilateral free trade agreements. *EU*, European Union. *From https://en.wikipe-dia.org/wiki/File:EU_FTAs.svg (this file is licensed under the Creative Commons Attribution-Share Alike 4.0 International license).*

A full list of EU's bilateral trade agreements and negotiations with countries, based on European Commission (2019a, 2019b) data is presented in Tables 5.2–5.6. Several of these agreements are in place or are being negotiated, within the context of regional agreements, as previously noted.

Table 5.2 presents a list of the countries with which the EU has bilateral trade agreements in place. The table lists 38 countries along with the type of agreement that each has with the EU and the year during which the agreement went into force. Table 5.3 lists the countries with which the EU has trade agreements that are partly in place. The agreements will be fully applied when all parties have ratified them. The table lists 46 countries. Table 5.4 lists the EU's pending agreements with 24 countries. Table 5.5 presents a list of the existing five agreements that are currently being updated. Table 5.6 presents the 21 countries with which agreements are currently being negotiated. These include the United States and China, which are the EU's first and second biggest trading partners, respectively. Trade between these countries is presented in a subsequent chapter.

5.3.4   Unilateral trade agreements

As previously noted, unilateral trade agreements are commerce treaties imposed by a nation without regard to others. *PTAs* in the WTO are

TABLE 5.2 European Union's bilateral trade agreements in place.

Country	Type of agreement	Entry into force	Country	Type of agreement	Entry into force
Albania	SAA	2009	Mexico	GA	2000
Algeria	AA	2005	Moldova	AA	2016
Andorra	CU	1991	Montenegro	SAA	2010
Armenia	PCA	1999	Morocco	AA	2000
Bosnia and Herzegovina	SAA	2015	Mozambique	EPA	2018
Botswana	EPA	2018	Namibia	EPA	2018
Chile	AA	2005	North Macedonia	SAA	2004
Egypt	AA	2004	Norway	EEA	1994
Eswatini	EPA	2018	Pakistan	CA	2004
Faroe Islands	A	1997	Palestinian Authority	IAA	1997
Georgia	AA	2016	San Marino	CU	2002
Iceland	EAA	1994	Serbia	SAA	2013
Israel	AA	2000	South Africa	EPA	2018
Japan	EPA	2019	South Korea	FTA	2016
Jordan	AA	2002	Sri Lanka	CPA	1995
Kosovo	SAA	2016	Switzerland	A	1873
Lebanon	AA	2006	Syria	CA	1977
Liechtenstein	EAA	1995	Tunisia	AA	1998
Lesotho	EPA	2018	Turkey	CU	1995

A, Agreement; *AA*, Association Agreement; *CPA*, Cooperation and Partnership Agreement; *CU*, Customs Union; *EAA*, Economic Area Agreement; *EEA*, European Economic Area; *EPA*, Economic Partnership Agreement; *GA*, Global Agreement; *IAA*, Interim Association Agreement; *PCA*, Partnership and Cooperation Agreement; *SAA*, Stabilization and Association Agreement.

unilateral trade preferences (World Trade Organization, 2019). They include *Generalized System of Preferences* scheme, under which preferential arrangements are offered by developed countries to developing countries, providing them with better access to their market without requiring a reciprocal treatment. The aim is to provide developing countries with an instrument for expanding their export capacities and taking part in the multilateral trading

TABLE 5.3 European Union's trade agreements partly in place (not all parties have ratified the agreement).

Country	Type of agreement	Provisionally applied since	Country	Type of agreement	Provisionally applied since
Antigua and Barbuda	EPA	2008	Honduras	AA	2013
Armenia	UPCA	2018	Iraq	PCA	2012
Bahamas	EPA	2008	Jamaica	EPA	2008
Barbados	EPA	2008	Kazakhstan	EPCA	2016
Belize	EPA	2008	Madagascar	EPA	2012
Botswana	EPA	2016	Mauritius	EPA	2012
Cameroon	IEPA	2014	Namibia	EPA	2016
Canada	CETA	2017	Nicaragua	AA	2013
Colombia	TA	2013	Panama	AA	2013
Côte d'Ivoire	EPA	2016	Papua New Guinea	IPA	2011
Comoros	IEPA	2019	Peru	TA	2013
Costa Rica	AA	2013	Samoa	EPA	2018
Cuba	CA	2017	Seychelles	EPA	2012
Dominica	EPA	2008	South Africa	EPA	2016
Dominican Republic	EPA	2008	St. Kitts and Nevis	EPA	2008

(Continued)

TABLE 5.3 (Continued)

Country	Type of agreement	Provisionally applied since	Country	Type of agreement	Provisionally applied since
Ecuador	TA	2013	St. Lucia	EPA	2008
El Salvador	AA	2013	St. Vincent and Grenadines	EPA	2008
Ethiopia	EPA	Pending	Sudan	EPA	Pending
Fiji	IPA	2011	Suriname	EPA	2008
China	EPA	2016	Trinidad and Tobago	EPA	2008
Grenada	EPA	2008	Ukraine	DCFTA	Pending
Guatemala	AA	2013	Zambia	EPA	Pending
Guyana	EPA	2008	Zimbabwe	EPA	2012

AA, Association Agreement; CA, Cooperation Agreement; CETA, Comprehensive Economic and Trade Agreement; DCFTA, deep and comprehensive free trade area; EPA, Economic Partnership Agreement; EPCA, Economic Partnership and Cooperation Agreement; FTA, Free Trade Agreement; IEPA, Interim Economic Partnership Agreement; IPA, Interim Partnership Agreement; PCA, Partnership and Cooperation Agreement; TA, Trade Agreement; UPCA, Updated Partnership and Cooperation Agreement.

TABLE 5.4 European Union's pending agreements (negotiations have finished; no part of the agreement is in place yet).

Country	Type of agreement		Country	Type of agreement	
Benin	EPA	—	Mali	EPA	—
Burkina Faso	EPA	—	Niger	EPA	—
Burundi	EPA	—	Nigeria	EPA	—
Cabo Verde	EPA	—	Rwanda	EPA	—
Djibouti	EPA	—	Senegal	EPA	—
Eritrea	EPA	—	Sierra Leone	EPA	—
Ethiopia	EPA	—	Singapore	FTA	—
Gambia	EPA	—	Tanzania	EPA	—
Guinea	EPA	—	Togo	EPA	—
Haiti	EPA	—	Mauritania	EPA	—
Kenya	EPA	—	Uganda	EPA	—
Liberia	EPA	—	Vietnam	FTA	—

EPA, Economic Partnership Agreement; *FTA*, Free Trade Agreement.

system, avoiding costs not compatible with their development needs (Gamberoni, 2007).

- The *Generalized System of Preference (GSP)* is the traditional unilateral trade preference program and it is one of the EU's tools to promote human rights in third countries. It grants certain developing countries preferential trade access to the EU market, while including a human rights conditionality, meaning that preferences may be withdrawn in cases of violation of human or labor rights (although the number of cases in which the suspension of preferences has been applied is limited). Special cases of GSP are the standard GSP, EBA, and GSP + (European Parliament, 2018).
- *Standard GSP* grants customs duty reductions for around 66% of all EU tariff lines to developing countries classified by the World Bank as low-income or lower-middle-income economies.
- *EBA* grants full duty-free, quota-free access for all products except arms and ammunition to countries classified by the United Nations as LDCs.

TABLE 5.5 European Union's agreements being updated (updates are negotiated on an existing trade agreement).

Country	Type of agreement	Negotiations began	Country	Type of agreement	Negotiations began
Azerbaijan	CPA	Began 2017	Morocco	AA to DCFTA	On hold since 2014
Chile	AA	Began 2017	Tunisia	AA to DCFTA	Began 2013
Mexico	GA	Agreement in part 2018			

AA, Association Agreement; CPA, Cooperation and Partnership Agreement; DCFTA, deep and comprehensive free trade area; GA, Global Agreement.

TABLE 5.6 European Union's agreements being negotiated.

Country	Type of agreement	Negotiations	Country	Type of agreement	Negotiations
Argentina	AA	Resumed 2010	Oman	FTA	Suspended 2008
Australia	A	Launched 2018	Paraguay	AA	Resumed 2010
Bahrain	FTA	Suspended 2008	Philippines	FTA	Started 2015
Brazil	AA	Resumed 2010	Qatar	FTA	Suspended 2008
China	IA	Started 2013	Saudi Arabia	FTA	Suspended 2008
India	FTA	Last round 2013	Thailand	FTA	Started 2013
Indonesia	FTA	Started 2016	United Arab Emirates	FTA	Suspended 2008
Kuwait	FTA	Suspended 2008	United States	TTIP	Paused 2016
Malaysia	FTA	Paused 2012	Uruguay	AA	Resumed 2010
Myanmar	IA	Started 2015	Venezuela	FTA	Suspended
New Zealand	A	Launched 2018			

A, Agreement; AA, Association Agreement; IA, Investment Agreement; TTIP, Transatlantic Trade and Investment Partnership.

- *GSP +* grants duty-free access for essentially the same 66% of tariff lines as standard GSP, to countries which are considered especially vulnerable because of a lack of economic diversification and insufficient integration within the international trading system.

The EU preferential trade arrangements are shown in Fig. 5.8. The figure shows the EU as the provider and the number of agreements by beneficiary country and territory concerned.

WTO's PTA database (World Trade Organization, 2018), reports GSP agreements with 88 countries (based on the most recent data as of June 29, 2017), as shown in Fig. 5.9. Of them, 49 are under the EBA scheme, and eight are under the GSP + .

FIGURE 5.8 EU preferential trade arrangements. *EU*, European Union. *From http://ptadb.wto. org/SearchByCountry.aspx.*

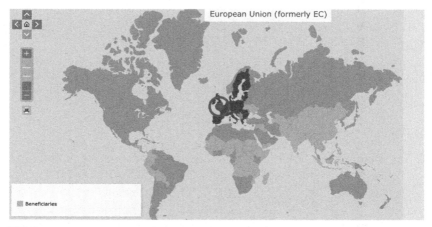

FIGURE 5.9 EU generalized system of preferences: all subschemes. *EU*, European Union. *From http://ptadb.wto.org/ptaBeneficiaries.aspx.*

The 88 countries under GSP agreements are: Afghanistan, Angola, Armenia, Bangladesh, Benin, Bhutan, Bolivia, Burkina Faso, Burundi, Cabo Verde, Cambodia, Central African Republic, Chad, China, Colombia, Comoros, Congo, Cook Islands, Costa Rica, Democratic Republic of the Congo, Djibouti, Ecuador, El Salvador, Equatorial Guinea, Eritrea, Ethiopia, Georgia, Guatemala, Guinea, Guinea-Bissau, Haiti, Honduras, India, Indonesia, Iraq, Kiribati, Kyrgyz Republic, Lao People's Democratic Republic, Lesotho, Liberia, Madagascar, Malawi, Maldives, Mali, Marshall Islands, Mauritania, Micronesia, Mongolia, Mozambique, Myanmar, Nauru, Nepal, Nicaragua, Niger, Nigeria, Niue, Pakistan, Panama, Paraguay, Peru, Philippines, Rwanda, Samoa, Sao Tome and Principe, Senegal, Sierra Leone, Solomon Islands, Somalia, South Sudan, Sri Lanka, Sudan, Syrian Arab Republic, Tajikistan, Tanzania, Thailand, The Gambia, Timor-Leste, Togo, Tonga, Turkmenistan, Tuvalu, Uganda, Ukraine, Uzbekistan, Vanuatu, Viet Nam, Yemen, Zambia (Fig. 5.10).

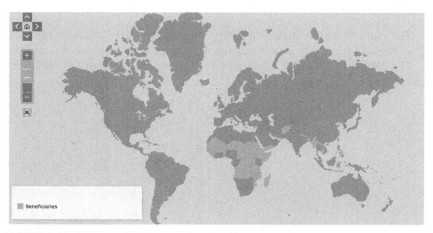

FIGURE 5.10 EU generalized system of preferences: everything but arms (LDCs) subscheme. *EU*, European Union; *LDCs*, least developed countries. *From http://ptadb.wto.org/ ptaBeneficiaries.aspx.*

The 49 countries under EBA subscheme include Afghanistan, Angola, Bangladesh, Benin, Bhutan, Burkina Faso, Burundi, Cambodia, Central African Republic, Chad, Comoros, Democratic Republic of the Congo, Djibouti, Equatorial Guinea, Eritrea, Ethiopia, Guinea, Guinea-Bissau, Haiti, Kiribati, Lao People's Democratic Republic, Lesotho, Liberia, Madagascar, Malawi, Mali, Mauritania, Mozambique, Myanmar, Nepal, Niger, Rwanda, Samoa, Sao Tome and Principe, Senegal, Sierra Leone, Solomon Islands, Somalia, South Sudan, Sudan, Tanzania, The Gambia, Timor-Leste, Togo, Tuvalu, Uganda, Vanuatu, Yemen, Zambia (Fig. 5.11).

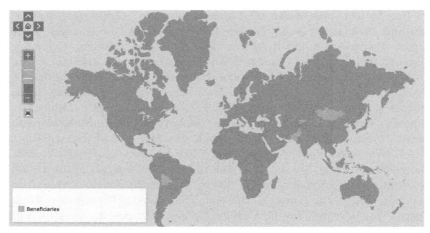

FIGURE 5.11 Generalized system of preferences: GSP + subscheme. *GSP*, Generalized system of preferences. *From http://ptadb.wto.org/ptaBeneficiaries.aspx.*

The eight countries under the GSP + subscheme are Armenia, Bolivia, Cabo Verde, Kyrgyz Republic, Mongolia, Pakistan, Philippines, and Sri Lanka.

The EU also has other trade preferences for countries of the Western Balkans, as shown in Fig. 5.12.

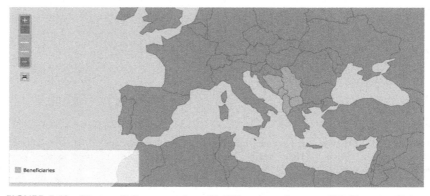

FIGURE 5.12 Western Balkan countries with EU trade preferences. *EU*, European Union. *From http://ptadb.wto.org/ptaBeneficiaries.aspx.*

Trade preferences in the Western Balkans are relevant to Albania, Bosnia and Herzegovina, Montenegro, North Macedonia, Serbia, and UNMIK/Kosovo.

References

Amadeo, K. (2019). *Free trade agreements, their impact, types and examples—How trade agreements lower prices.* Retrieved from <https://www.thebalance.com/free-trade-agreement-types-and-examples-3305897>

Bloom, J. (2017, August 14). Free trade area, single market, customs union — What's the difference? *BBC News.*

Central European Free Trade Agreement. (2016). *CEFTA parties.* Retrieved from <https://cefta.int/cefta-parties-2/>

COM(2010)0608. (n.d.). *Communication from the Commission to the European Parliament, the Council, the Economic and Social Committee and the Committee of the Regions Towards a Single Market Act for a highly competitive social market economy 50 proposals for improving our work, b.* Brussels: European Commission.

COM(2012)0573. (n.d.). *Communication from the Commission to the European Parliament, the Council, the European Economic and Social Committee and the Committee of the Regions Single Market Act II Together for new growth.* Brussels: European Commission.

EU Monitor. (2019). *Ordinary legislative procedure.* Retrieved from <https://www.eumonitor.eu/9353000/1/j9vvik7m1c3gyxp/vga3bya9max9>

EU Monitor. (n.d.). *International agreement.* Retrieved from <https://www.eumonitor.eu/9353000/1/j9vvik7m1c3gyxp/vh7dpnxrt5re>

EUR-Lex. (2010). *Partnership and cooperation agreements (PCAs): Russia, Eastern Europe, the Southern Caucasus and Central Asia.* Retrieved from <https://eur-lex.europa.eu/legal-content/EN/TXT/?uri = LEGISSUM%3Ar17002>

EUR-Lex. (2016). *Division of competences within the European Union.* Retrieved from <https://eur-lex.europa.eu/legal-content/EN/>

European Commission. (2012). *Negotiating EU trade agreements.* Retrieved from <https://trade.ec.europa.eu/doclib/docs/2012/june/tradoc_149616.pdf>

European Commission. (2017). *Investments in EU transport.* Retrieved from <https://europa.eu/rapid/press-release_IP-17-1729_en.htm>

European Commission. (2018). *Economic partnership agreements (EPAs).* Retrieved from <https://trade.ec.europa.eu/doclib/docs/2017/february/tradoc_155300.pdf>

European Commission. (2019a). *Trade—Policy—Countries and regions—Regions.* Retrieved from <https://ec.europa.eu/trade/policy/countries-and-regions/regions/>

European Commission. (2019b). *Negotiations and agreements.* Retrieved from <https://ec.europa.eu/trade/policy/countries-and-regions/negotiations-and-agreements/index_en.htm#_in-place>

European Council. (2018a). *EU trade agreements.* Retrieved from <https://www.consilium.europa.eu/en/policies/trade-policy/trade-agreements/>

European Council. (2018b). *EU trade policy.* Retrieved from <https://www.consilium.europa.eu/en/policies/trade-policy/>

European Free Trade Association. (2019). *About EFTA.* Retrieved from <https://www.efta.int/about-efta>

European Law Monitor. (2019). *EU policy areas.* Retrieved from <https://www.europeanlawmonitor.org/eu-policy-areas/in-what-areas-can-the-eu-legislate.html>

European Parliament. (2016). *A guide to EU procedures for the conclusion of international trade agreements.* Retrieved from <http://www.europarl.europa.eu/thinktank/en/document.html?reference = EPRS_BRI(2016)593489>

European Parliament. (2017). *Handbook on the ordinary legislative procedure.* Retrieved from <http://www.europarl.europa.eu/ordinary-legislative-procedure/en/ordinary-legislative-procedure.html>

European Parliament. (2018). *Human rights in EU trade policy.* Retrieved from <http://www.europarl.europa.eu/thinktank/en/document.html?reference = EPRS_BRI(2018)621905>

European Parliament. (2019a). *Decision-making in the EU.* Retrieved from <https://europarlamentti.info/en/decision-making/>

European Parliament. (2019b). *The internal market: General principles.* Retrieved from Fact Sheets on the European Union <http://www.europarl.europa.eu/factsheets/en/sheet/33/the-internal-market-general-principles>

European Union. (2017). *The European Union—What it is and what it does.* Retrieved from <https://publications.europa.eu/en/publication-detail/-/publication/715cfcc8-fa70-11e7-b8f5-01aa75ed71a1/language-en>

European Union. (2018). Retrieved from institutions and bodies <https://europa.eu/european-union/about-eu/institutions-bodies_en>

European Union. (2019a). *How the EU budget is spent.* Retrieved from <https://europa.eu/european-union/about-eu/eu-budget/expenditure_en>

European Union. (2019b). *How EU decisions are made.* Retrieved from <https://europa.eu/european-union/eu-law/decision-making/procedures_en>

European Union. (2019c). Retrieved from the EU in brief <https://europa.eu/european-union/about-eu/eu-in-brief_en#from-economic-to-political-union>

Gamberoni, E. (2007). *Do unilateral trade preferences help export diversification?* Geneva: Graduate Institute of International Studies, HEI Working Paper No: 17/2007.

Institute for Government. (2018). *Association agreements.* Retrieved from <https://www.instituteforgovernment.org.uk/explainers/association-agreements>

Krueger, A. (1995). *Free trade agreements versus customs unions—Working paper no. 5084.* Cambridge, MA: National Bureau of Economic Research.

Malmström, C. (2019). *The evolution of EU trade policy.* Retrieved from <https://www.theparliamentmagazine.eu>

OECD. (2019). *Infrastructure investment.* Retrieved from <https://data.oecd.org/transport/infrastructure-investment.htm>

Official Journal of the European Union. (2016). *eur-lex.* Retrieved from Article 13 <https://eur-lex.europa.eu/legal-content/EN/TXT/HTML/>

Schutze, R. (2012). *European constitutional law.* New York: Cambridge University Press.

Štěrbová, L. (2010). *Impacts of the lisbon treaty on the EU trade policy identification of possible new problems related to the EU competences, to the EU membership in international organizations and to hte role of the European parliament. University of economics, prague faculty of international relations Czech Republic.* Budapest: E-Leader.

Thirion, E. (2017). *European parliamentary research service.* Retrieved from European Added Value Unit <http://www.europarl.europa.eu/RegData/etudes/BRIE/2017/611009/EPRS_BRI%282017%2961109_EN.pdf>

United Nations. (2018). *Unilateral trade practices, measures harm most vulnerable nations, speakers say, as second committee takes up macroeconomic policy.* Retrieved from <https://www.un.org/press/en/2018/gaef3498.doc.htm>

Wikipedia. (2011). *List of bilateral free-trade agreements.* Retrieved from <https://en.wikipedia.org/wiki/List_of_bilateral_free-trade_agreements#European_Union>

Wikipedia. (2019a). *Central European free trade agreement.* Retrieved from <https://en.wikipedia.org/wiki/Central_European_Free_Trade_Agreement>

Wikipedia. (2019b). *European single market.* Retrieved from <https://en.wikipedia.org/wiki/European_Single_Market>

World Trade Organization. (2018). *Preferential trade agreements.* Retrieved from <http://ptadb.wto.org/ptaHistoryExplorer.aspx>

World Trade Organization. (2019). *Regional trade agreements and preferential trade arrangements.* Retrieved from <https://www.wto.org/english/tratop_e/region_e/rta_pta_e.htm>

World Trade Organization. (n.d.). *Technical information on rules of origin.* Retrieved from <https://www.wto.org/english/tratop_e/roi_e/roi_e.htm>

Chapter 6

Trade demand in the European Union

6.1 Introduction

The European Union (EU) is the world's largest economy. Its gross domestic product (GDP) was worth about US$13,669 billion in 2018, representing over 22% of the world economy. The Euro Area GDP is expected to reach US$14,000 billion by the end of 2019 and escalate to US$14,500 billion in 2020, as shown in Fig. 6.1.

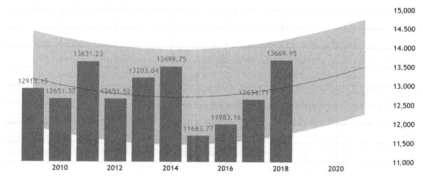

FIGURE 6.1 Euro area gross domestic product (US$billion). *From <https://tradingeconomics.com/euro-area/gdp>.*

In 2018, the EU exports represented 15.2% of global exports, and EU imports represented 15.1% of global imports.

The EU has played a leading role in shaping the global trading system and promoting trade, both by removing trade barriers and by encouraging other countries to trade with the EU. It is one of the most open economies in the world and has become deeply integrated into global markets. It is the largest trader of manufactured goods and services and the biggest export market for around 80 countries. Both in the World Trade Organization and with individual trading partners, EU Member States speak and negotiate collectively. Negotiations of trade agreements between the EU and third countries or international organizations are negotiated and conducted according

International Trade and Transportation Infrastructure Development.
DOI: https://doi.org/10.1016/B978-0-12-815741-1.00006-1
© 2020 Elsevier Inc. All rights reserved.

to the procedures noted in Article 218 of the Treaty of the Functioning of the EU.

As noted in the previous chapter, the EU's single, or internal, market is a market where goods, services, capital, and people can flow freely. This required the removal of national barriers to the free movement of goods within the EU. Articles 34–36 of the Treaty of the functioning of the EU prohibit measurable restrictions on imports, exports, or goods in transit and all similar restraining measures among member countries. The 28 Member States of the EU share a single market and a single external border, and they have a single trade policy.

This chapter presents trade demand and trends in the EU for both internal (intra-EU-28) and external (extra-EU-28) trade. The analysis is conducted on the basis of imports and exports, by major trading partner, commodity, and mode of transport, based on reports and data published by Eurostat, the statistical office of the EU.

6.2 Internal and external European Union trade

Statistics on external trade and intra-EU trade are compiled on the basis of Community regulations. Statistics on trade among the Member States are based on regulation (EC) No. 638/2004 of the European Parliament and of the council and Commission Regulation (EC) No. 1982/2004. Intra-EU exports of goods are declared free-on-board[1]-type value, while intra-EU imports of goods are declared as cost, insurance, and freight[2]-type value. As export statistics are considered to provide a more reliable measure of total intra-EU trade in goods with better coverage than the total intra-EU imports of goods, they are typically used for reporting purposes.

External trade statistics are usually recorded on the basis of customs declarations submitted by traders when clearing customs. The same regulations are generally the basis for the compilation of statistics published nationally by each Member State. Nevertheless, due to methodological differences, Community statistics and national statistics do not match exactly.

The transactions of a specific Member State are split into two parts: on the one hand, with the countries outside the EU (extra-EU), and on the other hand, with the 27 other Member States (intra-EU). Intra-EU trade refers to transactions occurring within the EU (Eurostat, 2019).

In most EU member states, traditionally, the proportion of intra-EU trade in goods is higher than that of extra-EU trade in goods, a fact that underlines the importance of the EU's internal market. Between 2002 and 2016, the

---

1. Free-on-board: the values associated with those incidental costs (freight and insurance) that relate, for intra-EU exports, to the journey within the territory of the Member State from which the goods are exported.

2. Cost, insurance, and freight: the values associated with those incidental costs (freight and insurance) that relate, for intra-EU imports, to the journey outside the territory of the Member State into which the goods are imported/enter.

proportion of trade with EU-28 partners decreased from 68% to 64%. In 2016, with the exception of Malta, the United Kingdom, and Cyprus, all Member States exported more goods to partners within the EU than outside the EU. There was a relatively large variation among Member States in this proportion, ranging from almost 85% of Slovakia's total exports of goods going to other EU Member States to under 42% of Malta's total goods exports. Two Member States saw a decrease in this proportion of over 10% points, with the largest decreases for Ireland followed by the United Kingdom. In 2018 (Fig. 6.2), Slovakia remained the country with the highest percentage of its exports (over 85%) going to EU Member States, with Cyprus on the other end as the country with the highest share (over 70%) of its trade in goods going to nonmember countries.

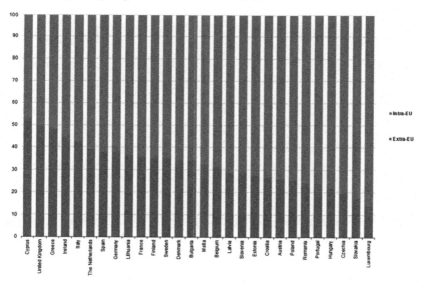

FIGURE 6.2 Extra- and intra-EU-28 trade in goods (2018) (imports plus exports, %share of total trade). *EU*, European Union. *From <https://ec.europa.eu/eurostat/statistics-explained/index.php/International_trade_in_goods_for_the_EU_-_an_overview>.*

Prior to the crisis, intra-EU trade was established even faster than world trade, pointing toward the strong integration among European countries. After a rapid decline in 2009, EU trade in goods recovered in both imports and exports.

The value of exports among EU Member States quadrupled between 1994 and 2016, while trade between the EU and the rest of the world tripled over the same period. However, it must be noted that the composition of the EU grew from 12 to 28 countries over this same period. In 2018, the value of export trade in goods within the EU ranged from €911 billion for Germany (23% of total intra-EU exports) to €3 billion for Malta (0.07% of total intra-EU exports). The evolution of exports of goods to other Member States for the years 2002, 2010, and 2018 is shown in Fig. 6.3.

	2002	2010	2018	Annual average growth rate
Belgium	114	175	244	4.9%
Bulgaria	6	14	21	8.5%
Czechia	18	40	64	9.0%
Denmark	32	44	62	4.5%
Germany	417	672	911	5.4%
Estonia	2	5	9	9.1%
Ireland	50	54	103	4.9%
Greece	19	32	42	5.3%
Spain	89	163	238	6.8%
France	233	302	380	3.3%
Croatia	5	10	10	4.8%
Italy	202	309	379	4.3%
Cyprus	2	2	7	9.1%
Latvia	2	5	9	12.4%
Lithuania	5	14	22	9.8%
Luxembourg	4	6	5	2.0%
Hungary	19	37	46	5.8%
Malta	2	3	3	1.7%
The Netherlands	156	307	457	7.4%
Austria	36	59	82	5.7%
Poland	26	65	114	10.2%
Portugal	14	23	33	5.8%
Romania	10	23	37	9.0%
Slovenia	5	11	21	10.4%
Slovakia	6	21	27	10.2%
Finland	30	43	47	3.0%
Sweden	57	89	101	3.9%
United Kingdom	280	377	490	3.8%

FIGURE 6.3   Exports of goods to other Member States (2002, 2010, 2018) (€billion). *From <https://ec.europa.eu/eurostat/statistics-explained/index.php?title = Intra-EU_trade_in_goods_-_main_features&oldid = 452727>.*

The first estimate for extra-EU-28 exports of goods in May 2018 was €160.9 billion, down by 2.7% compared with May 2017 (€165.4 billion). Imports from the rest of the world stood at €160.7 billion, down by 1.4% compared with May 2017 (€163.0 billion). As a result, the EU-28 recorded a €0.2 billion surplus in trade in goods with the rest of the world in May 2018, compared with + €2.3 billion in May 2017. Intra-EU-28 trade rose to €294.7 billion in May 2018, +1.6% compared with May 2017. The main extra-EU trade partners are shown in Fig. 6.4 (Eurostat, 2019).

In terms of exports of goods, the EU's largest partners from January to August 2019 were the United States (€259.9 billion), China (€145.3 billion), and Switzerland (€105.6 billion). During this period, the EU imported the most from China (€272.7 billion), followed by the United States (€193.2 billion) and Russia (€105.0 billion).

Since the financial crisis in 2008, the EU and the United States have experienced similar trade patterns in terms of exports and imports. Exports from emerging economies declined in 2015. In particular, Argentina, Brazil, Bulgaria, Chile, China, Colombia, Hungary, India, Indonesia, Latvia, Lithuania, Malaysia, Mexico, Pakistan, Peru, Philippines, Poland, Romania,

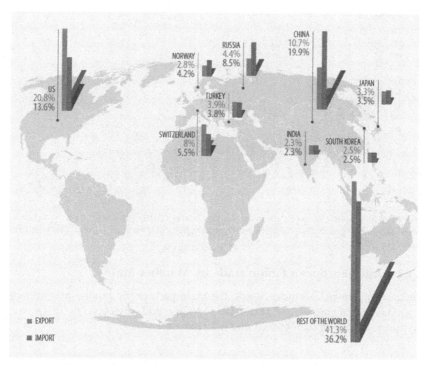

FIGURE 6.4   EU import and export of goods (2018). *EU*, European Union. *From <https://www. europarl.europa.eu/news/en/headlines/economy/20180703STO07132/the-eu-s-position-in-world-trade-in-figures-infographic>*.

Russia, South Africa, Thailand, Turkey, Ukraine, and Venezuela experienced significant declines. Total exports from this group of countries fell by 11% in 2015, bringing the total value of exports to about US$5 trillion, representing 30% of the world total. The largest among this group were Russia (32%), India (17%), and Brazil (15%) (European Union, 2012).

6.3   Intra-European Union trade

The value of intra-EU export trade in goods by Member State varies significantly. As noted in the previous section, in 2018 the highest value was for Germany (€911 billion), and the lowest was for Malta (€3 billion). This variation is shown in Fig. 6.5, which presents the value of intra-EU exports by Member State. According to this information, the value of goods exported by 10 Member States (Germany, the United Kingdom, the Netherlands, France, Italy, Belgium, Spain, Poland, Ireland, and Sweden) to partners in the EU accounted for 86% of the total intra-EU goods exports value (Eurostat, 2019).

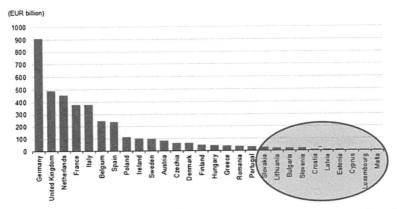

FIGURE 6.5 Exports of goods to other Member States (2018) (€billion). *From <https://ec. europa.eu/eurostat/statistics-explained/index.php?title = Intra-EU_trade_in_goods_-_main_features &oldid = 452727>.*

6.3.1 Intra-European Union trade by Member State

For most of the EU Member States, the main partner for exports and imports of goods (total intra- and extra-EU exports and imports) in 2018 was Germany, as shown in Figs. 6.6 and 6.7 (Eurostat, 2019).

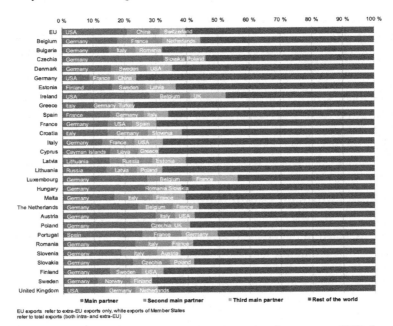

FIGURE 6.6 Exports of goods of the EU Member States (top three partners, 2018) (based on trade value). *EU*, European Union. *From <https://ec.europa.eu/eurostat/documents/2995521/ 9678910/6-20032019-AP-EN.pdf/0ebd7878-dad5-478e-a5f0-3ae2c91f7ea3>.*

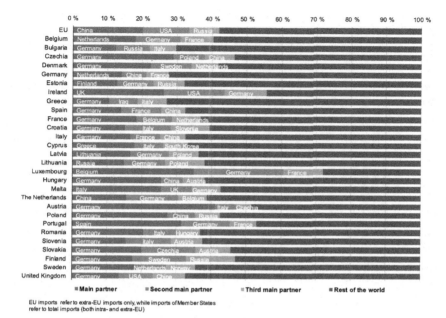

FIGURE 6.7 Imports of goods of 4the EU Member States (top three partners, 2018) (based on trade value). *EU*, European Union. *From <https://ec.europa.eu/eurostat/documents/2995521/ 9678910/6-20032019-AP-EN.pdf/0ebd7878-dad5-478e-a5f0-3ae2c91f7ea3>.*

Fig. 6.6 shows the top three trade partners for exports of goods (based on trade value) for each EU Member State, for both internal and external trade. Similarly, Fig. 6.7 shows the top three trade partners for imports of goods for each EU Member State (total for internal and external trade).

Considering only the internal EU-28 trade, the distribution of exports of goods from a Member State to other EU partners is shown in Fig. 6.8.

For the majority of Member States within the EU (19 Member States), the top three intra-EU trading partners account for over 50% of their intra-EU exports. For eight Member States the share of the top three intra-EU export partners is between 40% and 50%. In Germany, the top three partners accounted for only 36%.

6.3.2 Intra-European Union trade by product type

Intra-EU exports of goods by product type for the years 2002, 2010, and 2018 are shown in Fig. 6.9. The figure shows the intra-EU exports for primary products (food, drinks, and tobacco; energy products; and raw materials), manufactured goods (machinery and vehicles, and other manufactured goods), and chemicals.

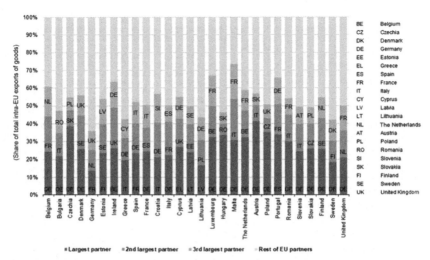

FIGURE 6.8 Distribution of exports of goods to other EU partners by Member State (2018). *EU*, European Union. *From <https://ec.europa.eu/eurostat/statistics-explained/index. php?title = Intra-EU_trade_in_goods_-_main_features&oldid = 452727#Intra-EU_trade_in_goods_ by_Member_State>.*

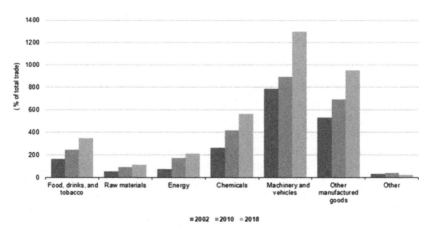

FIGURE 6.9 Intra-EU exports of goods by product group (2002, 2010, 2018) (€billion). *EU*, European Union. *From <https://ec.europa.eu/eurostat/statistics-explained/index.php? title = Intra-EU_trade_in_goods_-_main_features&oldid = 452727#Intra-EU_trade_in_goods_by_ Member_State>.*

The share of primary goods in total exports of goods in intra-EU exports increased from 15% in 2002 to 19% in 2018. The share of manufactured goods in total exports of goods decreased from 83% to 80%. Czechia had the highest share (91%) of goods exports of manufactured products in 2018, with Slovakia being a close second (90%). The EU average is 80%. In addition to Czechia and Slovakia, the share of manufactured goods in total exports of goods was above average for Germany, Ireland, France, Italy, Luxemburg, Hungary, Austria, Poland, Romania, and Slovenia. Greece and Cyprus were the countries with the highest share of primary goods in total intra-EU exports, with 44% and 40%, respectively, followed by Denmark, Latvia, Lithuania, and the Netherlands, which had a share of primary goods above 30%.

According to the statistical Classification of Products by Activity (CPA), the most exported products in intra-EU trade are shown in Table 6.1.

TABLE 6.1 Shares of exports of goods by product type and Member State (2002−18) (%).

Shares of exports of goods by product type and Member State, 2002-2018
(%)

	Primary goods				Manufactured goods				Other goods			
	2002	2010	2018	Trend	2002	2010	2018	Trend	2002	2010	2018	Trend
EU-28	15	20	19		83	78	80		2	2	1	
Belgium	17	22	22		83	77	77		0	1	0	
Bulgaria	21	30	26		77	70	74		2	0	1	
Czechia	9	12	9		91	88	91		0	0	0	
Denmark	30	38	31		65	60	67		4	2	1	
Germany	9	12	12		88	86	87		3	2	1	
Estonia	21	29	29		79	71	70		0	1	1	
Ireland	10	16	17		85	83	82		5	1	1	
Greece	34	41	44		64	56	54		2	3	2	
Spain	21	24	27		79	75	72		0	1	1	
France	16	20	19		84	77	80		1	3	1	
Croatia	20	24	27		79	76	73		0	0	0	
Italy	10	15	14		88	84	85		2	1	1	
Cyprus	42	41	40		58	58	58		0	1	2	
Latvia	39	39	37		61	60	63		0	0	0	
Lithuania	38	48	36		61	52	64		0	0	0	
Luxembourg	9	9	12		90	89	86		1	1	2	
Hungary	9	13	13		89	87	87		1	0	0	
Malta	2	15	27		98	83	71		0	2	2	
Netherlands	30	34	30		67	64	70		2	2	0	
Austria	12	16	14		88	83	86		0	2	1	
Poland	14	18	18		86	82	82		0	0	0	
Portugal	12	20	20		88	78	79		0	1	0	
Romania	12	14	12		88	86	88		0	0	0	
Slovenia	5	13	14		95	87	86		0	0	0	
Slovakia	13	13	10		86	87	90		1	0	0	
Finland	13	20	23		86	74	76		1	6	1	
Sweden	14	22	25		79	76	73		6	2	1	
United Kingdom	16	27	24		83	72	75		1	0	1	

Source: From <https://ec.europa.eu/eurostat/statistics-explained/index.php?title = Intra-EU_trade_in_goods_-_main_features&oldid = 452727#Intra-EU_trade_in_goods_by_Member_State>.

During the period from 2014 to 2018, intra-EU exports increased by €586 billion, which is equivalent to a 4.7% annual growth rate. This increase for the five most exported types of goods, which include motor vehicles, trailers, and semitrailers (cars); chemicals and chemical products (chemicals); machinery and equipment n.e.c. (machines); computer, electronic, and optical products (computers); and food products (food), was €326 billion, equivalent to a 4.5% annual growth rate (Eurostat, 2019).

Among the top intra-EU exported products, 20 recorded their highest exports in 2018.

The evolution of intra-EU trade of the five most exported products is shown in Table 6.2. For cars, exports grew from €343 billion to €460 billion. For chemicals, exports amounted to €330 billion, machines €308 billion, computers €304 billion, and food €244 billion. The shares of intra-EU exports of these products, for each Member State, are shown in Fig. 6.10.

TABLE 6.2 Evolution of intra-EU exports (2014−18) (€billion).

CPA code	CPA label	2014	2015	2016	2017	2018	Trend
TOTAL	Total	2 932.5	3 069.1	3 115.9	3 352.7	3 518.3	
29	Motor vehicles, trailers and semi-trailers	342.8	394.0	428.3	449.2	460.1	
20	Chemicals and chemical products	278.4	283.1	282.0	305.8	329.8	
28	Machinery and equipment n.e.c.	244.1	261.5	273.9	292.5	308.3	
26	Computer, electronic and optical products	240.8	263.4	268.8	295.1	303.6	
10	Food products	214.4	220.7	227.7	243.0	244.3	
24	Basic metals	160.3	162.1	157.6	187.3	198.3	
21	Basic pharmaceutical products and pharmaceutical preparations	156.4	166.4	168.3	175.5	190.2	
27	Electrical equipment	136.8	147.7	155.5	168.7	178.8	
22	Rubber and plastics products	106.3	112.7	117.3	124.1	129.1	
25	Fabricated metal products, except machinery and equipment	94.9	99.6	103.4	111.1	116.5	
19	Coke and refined petroleum products	122.3	93.5	80.9	96.6	113.7	
30	Other transport equipment	80.0	88.7	94.4	94.8	92.5	
14	Wearing apparel	73.2	77.8	82.3	88.2	92.5	
1	Products of agriculture, hunting and related services	74.0	80.1	85.0	89.1	87.6	
32	Other manufactured goods	66.2	73.9	79.7	82.9	84.2	
17	Paper and paper products	63.7	65.9	65.4	67.3	71.5	
15	Leather and related products	40.0	43.3	46.3	49.6	51.2	
23	Other non-metallic mineral products	39.6	41.5	43.8	46.0	48.1	
31	Furniture	34.2	37.4	40.3	42.3	43.4	
13	Textiles	36.5	38.0	39.2	40.6	41.0	
6	Crude petroleum and natural gas	47.8	34.2	24.0	32.2	40.1	
16	Wood and of products of wood and cork, except furniture; articles of straw and plaiting materials	26.1	27.3	28.7	31.1	32.7	
11	Beverages	27.7	28.5	29.4	30.8	32.5	
38	Waste collection, treatment and disposal services; materials recovery services	26.8	24.6	23.4	27.9	29.4	
Other	Other	199.2	203.2	170.3	181.1	199.0	

Source: From <Eurostat (https://ec.europa.eu/eurostat/statistics-explained/index.php?title = File:Intra-EU_exports_of_main_CPA_groups,_2014-2018.png), https://ec.europa.eu/eurostat/statistics-explained/index.php?title = Intra-EU_-_most_traded_goods>.

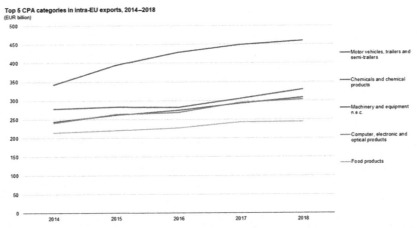

Top 5 CPA categories in intra-EU exports, 2014–2018
(EUR billion)

FIGURE 6.10 Shares of top 5 CPA categories in intra-EU Exports (2014−18) (€billion). *CPA,* Classification of Products by Activity; EU, European Union. *From <https://ec.europa.eu/euro-stat/statistics-explained/index.php?title = Intra-EU_-_most_traded_goods>.*

Table 6.3 shows the share of motor vehicles, trailers, and semitrailers by individual Member State. Germany was the largest exporter of cars to other EU Member States with exports amounting to €119 billion, 25.9% of the total intra-EU car exports and over 15% of all German intra-EU exports. Germany's share in EU-28 for cars is followed by France (9.1%), Spain (8.9%), Belgium (8%), and Czechia (6.8%). The top five car exporters represent 58.7% of total intra-EU car exports.

TABLE 6.3 Intra-EU Exports of Motor Vehicles, Trailers and Semitrailers (2018) (€million and %).

Intra-EU exports of motor vehicles, trailers and semi-trailers, 2018
(EUR billion and %)

	Total trade (EUR million)	Motor vehicles, trailers and semi-trailers (EUR million)	Member States' share in EU-28 for motor vehicles, trailers and semi-trailers (%)	Motor vehicles, trailers and semi-trailers share in Member States' total trade
EU-28	3 518 278	460 111	100.0	13.1
Germany	778 747	119 207	25.9	15.3
France	290 715	41 921	9.1	14.4
Spain	193 288	40 946	8.9	21.2
Belgium	287 689	36 670	8.0	12.7
Czechia	144 098	31 421	6.8	21.8
Poland	177 218	24 946	5.4	14.1
Italy	260 620	24 301	5.3	9.3
United Kingdom	193 831	20 303	4.4	10.5
Slovakia	68 375	19 238	4.2	28.1
Netherlands	455 972	19 070	4.1	4.2
Hungary	87 208	18 797	4.1	21.6
Sweden	83 624	13 473	2.9	16.1
Austria	111 602	13 269	2.9	11.9
Romania	51 975	12 552	2.7	24.2
Portugal	44 062	7 213	1.6	16.4
Slovenia	28 532	6 553	1.4	23.0
Finland	38 070	3 457	0.8	9.1
Denmark	56 287	1 999	0.4	3.6
Lithuania	16 599	993	0.2	6.0
Luxembourg	11 531	913	0.2	7.9
Estonia	9 791	696	0.2	7.1
Bulgaria	19 296	655	0.1	3.4
Croatia	9 969	567	0.1	5.7
Latvia	8 850	540	0.1	6.1
Ireland	70 011	307	0.1	0.4
Greece	17 659	99	0.0	0.6
Cyprus	1 186	6	0.0	0.5
Malta	1 471	2	0.0	0.1

Source: From <https://ec.europa.eu/eurostat/statistics-explained/index.php?title = Intra-EU_-_most_traded_goods>.

Exports of cars made up more than 20% of the total intra-EU exports of Spain (21.2%), Czechia (21.8%), Slovakia (28.1%), Hungary (21.6%), Romania (24.2%), and Slovenia (23%).

Table 6.4 shows the share of chemicals and chemical products by individual Member State. Germany was the largest exporter of chemicals to other EU Member States with exports amounting to €66 billion, 20.1% of the total intra-EU chemical exports and over 8.5% of all German intra-EU exports.

TABLE 6.4 Intra-European Union exports of chemicals and chemical products (2018) (€million and %).

Intra-EU exports of chemicals and chemical products, 2018
(EUR billion and %)

	Total trade (EUR million)	Chemicals and chemical products (EUR million)	Member States' share in EU-28 for chemicals and chemical products (%)	Chemicals and chemical products share in Member States' total trade
EU-28	3 518 278	329 842	100.0	9.4
Germany	778 747	66 353	20.1	8.5
Belgium	287 689	59 749	18.1	20.8
Netherlands	455 972	52 108	15.8	11.4
France	290 715	31 907	9.7	11.0
United Kingdom	193 831	18 588	5.6	9.6
Italy	260 620	17 815	5.4	6.8
Spain	193 288	17 096	5.2	8.8
Ireland	70 011	16 058	4.9	22.9
Poland	177 218	10 454	3.2	5.9
Czechia	144 098	5 540	1.7	3.8
Hungary	87 208	5 173	1.6	5.9
Austria	111 602	5 060	1.5	4.5
Sweden	83 624	4 818	1.5	5.8
Denmark	56 287	3 054	0.9	5.4
Slovakia	68 375	2 366	0.7	3.5
Portugal	44 062	2 346	0.7	5.3
Finland	38 070	1 965	0.6	5.2
Lithuania	16 599	1 835	0.6	11.1
Slovenia	28 532	1 683	0.5	5.9
Romania	51 975	1 277	0.4	2.5
Greece	17 659	1 030	0.3	5.8
Bulgaria	19 296	1 023	0.3	5.3
Luxembourg	11 531	817	0.2	7.1
Estonia	9 791	657	0.2	6.7
Croatia	9 969	489	0.1	4.9
Latvia	8 850	442	0.1	5.0
Malta	1 471	89	0.0	6.1
Cyprus	1 186	51	0.0	4.3

Source: From <https://ec.europa.eu/eurostat/statistics-explained/index.php?title = Intra-EU_-_most_traded_goods>.

Germany's share in EU-28 for chemicals is followed by Belgium (18.1%), Netherlands (15.8%), France (9.7%), and United Kingdom (5.6%). The top five chemical exporters represent over 69% of total intra-EU chemical exports.

Exports of chemicals made up more than 20% of the total intra-EU exports of Belgium (20.8%) and Ireland (22.9%), as well as more than 10% of total intra-EU exports of Netherlands (11.4%), France (11%), and Lithuania (11.1%).

Table 6.5 shows the share of other machinery and equipment n.e.c. products by individual Member State. Germany was the largest exporter of machines to other EU Member States with exports amounting to €94 billion, 30.6% of the total intra-EU car exports and over 12.1% of all German intra-EU exports. Germany's share in EU-28 for machines is followed by Italy (12.5%), Netherlands (8.7%), France (7.1%), and Belgium (5.2%). The top five machine exporters represent over 64% of total intra-EU machine exports.

TABLE 6.5 Intra-European Union Exports of Other Machinery and
Equipment (2018) (€million and %).

Intra-EU exports of machinery and equipment n.e.c., 2018
(EUR billion and %)

	Total trade (EUR million)	Machinery and equipment n.e.c. (EUR million)	Member States' share in EU-28 for machinery and equipment n.e.c. (%)	Machinery and equipment n.e.c. share in Member States' total trade
EU-28	3 518 278	308 315	100.0	8.8
Germany	778 747	94 327	30.6	12.1
Italy	260 620	38 491	12.5	14.8
Netherlands	455 972	26 927	8.7	5.9
France	290 715	22 011	7.1	7.6
Belgium	287 689	16 038	5.2	5.6
Czechia	144 098	15 927	5.2	11.1
United Kingdom	193 831	15 107	4.9	7.8
Austria	111 602	12 855	4.2	11.5
Poland	177 218	11 103	3.6	6.3
Spain	193 288	8 333	2.7	4.3
Sweden	83 624	7 484	2.4	8.9
Hungary	87 208	7 092	2.3	8.1
Denmark	56 287	6 919	2.2	12.3
Slovakia	68 375	5 812	1.9	8.5
Romania	51 975	4 543	1.5	8.7
Finland	38 070	3 768	1.2	9.9
Slovenia	28 532	2 373	0.8	8.3
Ireland	70 011	2 071	0.7	3.0
Portugal	44 062	1 853	0.6	4.2
Bulgaria	19 296	1 562	0.5	8.1
Luxembourg	11 531	1 151	0.4	10.0
Croatia	9 969	666	0.2	6.7
Lithuania	16 599	595	0.2	3.6
Estonia	9 791	570	0.2	5.8
Greece	17 659	406	0.1	2.3
Latvia	8 850	269	0.1	3.0
Malta	1 471	42	0.0	2.9
Cyprus	1 186	20	0.0	1.7

From <https://ec.europa.eu/eurostat/statistics-explained/index.php?title = Intra-EU_-_most_traded_goods>.

Exports of machines made up more than 10% of the total intra-EU
exports of Germany (12.1%), Italy (14.8%), Czechia (11.1%), Austria
(11.5%), Denmark (12.3%), and Luxembourg (10%).

Table 6.6 shows the share of computer, electronic, and optical products
by individual Member State. Netherlands was the largest exporter of computers to other EU Member States with exports amounting to €88 billion,
29.1% of the total intra-EU car exports, and over 19.4% of all intra-EU
Dutch exports. The share of the Netherlands in EU-28 for computers is followed by Germany (21.5%), Czechia (7.9%), France (5.8%), and Poland
(5.2%). The top five computer exporters represent over 69% of total intra-
EU computer exports.

Exports of computers made up more than 10% of the total intra-EU
exports of the Netherlands (19.4%), Czechia (16.7%), Hungary (13.4%),
Slovakia (16%), Malta (12.5%), and Cyprus (11.8%).

TABLE 6.6 Intra- European Union exports of computer, electronic and optical products (2018) (€million and %).

Intra-EU exports of computer, electronic and optical products, 2018
(EUR billion and %)

	Total trade (EUR million)	Computer, electronic and optical products (EUR million)	Member States' share in EU-28 for computer, electronic and optical products (%)	Computer, electronic and optical products share in Member States' total trade
EU-28	3 518 278	303 844	100.0	8.6
Netherlands	455 972	88 373	29.1	19.4
Germany	778 747	65 378	21.5	8.4
Czechia	144 098	24 015	7.9	16.7
France	290 715	17 739	5.8	6.1
Poland	177 218	15 908	5.2	9.0
United Kingdom	193 831	13 552	4.5	7.0
Hungary	87 208	11 671	3.8	13.4
Slovakia	68 375	10 953	3.6	16.0
Austria	111 602	8 943	2.9	8.0
Italy	260 620	8 236	2.7	3.2
Belgium	287 689	7 909	2.6	2.7
Sweden	83 624	5 484	1.8	6.6
Ireland	70 011	4 445	1.5	6.3
Spain	193 288	4 123	1.4	2.1
Romania	51 975	3 613	1.2	7.0
Denmark	56 287	3 261	1.1	5.8
Portugal	44 062	2 358	0.8	5.4
Finland	38 070	1 259	0.4	3.3
Greece	17 659	1 024	0.3	5.8
Slovenia	28 532	929	0.3	3.3
Estonia	9 791	805	0.3	8.2
Lithuania	16 599	795	0.3	4.8
Latvia	8 850	783	0.3	8.8
Bulgaria	19 296	771	0.3	4.0
Luxembourg	11 531	634	0.2	5.5
Croatia	9 969	361	0.1	3.6
Malta	1 471	184	0.1	12.5
Cyprus	1 186	140	0.0	11.8

From <https://ec.europa.eu/eurostat/statistics-explained/index.php?title = Intra-EU_-_most_traded_goods>.

Table 6.7 shows the share of food products by individual Member State. Germany was the largest exporter of food products to other EU Member States, with exports amounting to €43 billion, 17.8% of the total intra-EU food products exports, and 5.6% of all intra-EU German exports, with Netherlands being a close second with €40 billion in exports, 16.8% of the total intra-EU food products exports, and 9% of all intra-EU Dutch exports. The share of Germany and the Netherlands in EU-28 for food products is followed by Belgium (9.5%), France (9%), and Spain (7.4%). The top five food products exporters represent over 60% of total intra-EU food products exports.

Exports of food products made up more than 10% of the total intra-EU exports of Poland (10%), Denmark (14.7%), Ireland (11.4%), Greece (15.8%), Lithuania (12.5%), and Cyprus (17.1%).

TABLE 6.7 Intra- European Union exports of food products (2018) (€million and %).

Intra-EU exports of food products, 2018
(EUR billion and %)

	Total trade (EUR million)	Food products (EUR million)	Member States' share in EU-28 for food products	Food products share in Member States' total trade
EU-28	3 518 278	244 265	100.0	6.9
Germany	778 747	43 508	17.8	5.6
Netherlands	455 972	40 978	16.8	9.0
Belgium	287 689	23 141	9.5	8.0
France	290 715	21 880	9.0	7.5
Spain	193 288	18 132	7.4	9.4
Poland	177 218	17 787	7.3	10.0
Italy	260 620	17 234	7.1	6.6
United Kingdom	193 831	10 783	4.4	5.6
Denmark	56 287	8 284	3.4	14.7
Ireland	70 011	8 014	3.3	11.4
Austria	111 602	6 335	2.6	5.7
Hungary	87 208	4 199	1.7	4.8
Czechia	144 098	4 027	1.6	2.8
Sweden	83 624	2 952	1.2	3.5
Greece	17 659	2 794	1.1	15.8
Portugal	44 062	2 703	1.1	6.1
Lithuania	16 599	2 076	0.8	12.5
Slovakia	68 375	1 636	0.7	2.4
Bulgaria	19 296	1 452	0.6	7.5
Romania	51 975	1 405	0.6	2.7
Slovenia	28 532	1 018	0.4	3.6
Latvia	8 850	853	0.3	9.6
Luxembourg	11 531	832	0.3	7.2
Finland	38 070	725	0.3	1.9
Croatia	9 969	671	0.3	6.7
Estonia	9 791	636	0.3	6.5
Cyprus	1 186	202	0.1	17.1
Malta	1 471	6	0.0	0.4

From <https://ec.europa.eu/eurostat/statistics-explained/index.php?title = Intra-EU_-_most_traded_goods>.

6.4 Extra-European Union trade

EU is among the three largest global players in international trade. In 2018, extra-EU trade in goods (both imports and exports) was €3935 billion, about €16 billion lower than the respective value for China and €341 billion higher than for the United States. These data are shown in Fig. 6.11.

Following a significant decrease in 2009 as a result of the financial crisis, the extra-EU trade in goods recovered in subsequent years (Fig. 6.12). From 2008 to 2012, imports were higher than exports resulting in a negative trade balance (Eurostat, 2019). Between 2012 and 2016, imports fell while exports grew, resulting in a positive trade balance between 2013 and 2017. In 2018, imports grew more than exports, resulting in a trade deficit of €25 billion.

The evolution of extra-EU trade with its main trading partners between the years 2000 and 2018 is shown in Fig. 6.13. In 2018, one-third of the EU trade was with the United States and China (Eurostat, 2019). More specifically, trade with the United States totaled €674 billion while trade with

Main players for international trade in goods, 2018
(billion EUR)

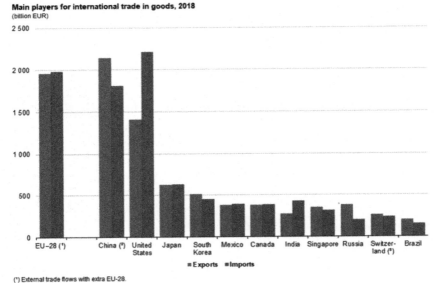

(¹) External trade flows with extra EU-28.
(²) Excluding Hong Kong, estimated data.
(³) Including Liechtenstein.

FIGURE 6.11 Main players for international trade in goods (2018) (€billion). *From <https:// ec.europa.eu/eurostat/statistics-explained/index.php/International_trade_in_goods>.*

Evolution of extra EU-28 trade, 2008–2018
(EUR billion)

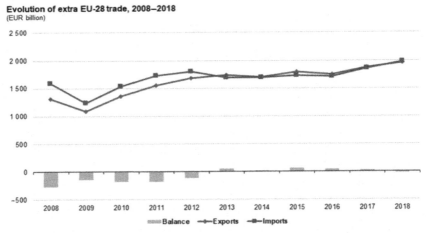

FIGURE 6.12 Evolution of extra-EU-28 Trade (2008–18) (€billion). *EU*, European Union. *From <https://ec.europa.eu/eurostat/statistics-explained/index.php/Extra-EU_trade_in_goods>.*

China totaled €605 billion. Other key EU trade partners include Switzerland (6.7%), Russia (6.4%), Turkey (3.9%), and Japan (3.4%).

The main trading partners for exports and imports of extra-EU trade are shown in Fig. 6.14. The major export partner for extra-EU trade is the

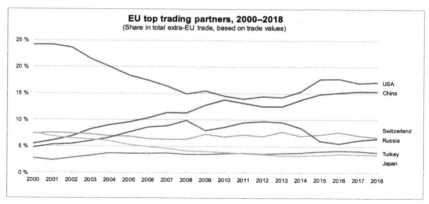

FIGURE 6.13   EU top trading partners (2000−18) (share in total extra-EU trade, based on trade values). *EU*, European Union. *From <https://ec.europa.eu/eurostat/documents/2995521/9678910/6-20032019-AP-EN.pdf/0ebd7878-dad5-478e-a5f0-3ae2c91f7ea3>.*

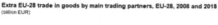

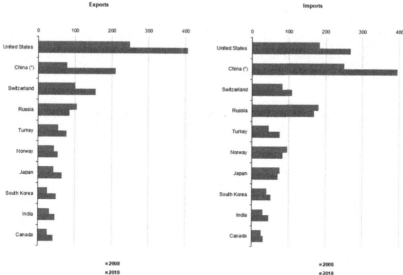

FIGURE 6.14   Extra-EU trade in goods by main trading partners (2008−18) (€billion). *EU*, European Union. *From <https://ec.europa.eu/eurostat/statistics-explained/index.php/International_trade_in_goods>.*

United States, followed by China, Switzerland, Russia, and Turkey. Between 2008 and 2018, the largest increase in exports was with China. Export trade to Russia was the only trade with the main EU trading partners that decreased during this period.

In terms of imports, China is the largest extra-EU trading partner, followed by the United States, Russia, Switzerland, and Norway. Import trade from Russia, Norway, and Japan decreased during the period from 2008 to 2018.

The evolution of extra-EU trade with EU's main export partner, the United States, between 2008 and 2018 is shown in Fig. 6.15. In 2018, the United States was the largest partner for EU exports of goods (21%) and the second largest partner for EU imports of goods (13%).

The evolution of extra-EU trade with EU's main import partner, China, between 2008 and 2018 is shown in Fig. 6.16. In 2018, China was the largest partner for EU imports of goods (20%) and the second largest partner for EU exports of goods (11%) (Eurostat, 2019).

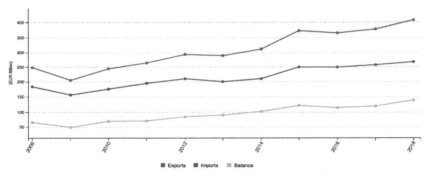

FIGURE 6.15 Evolution of extra-EU trade with the United States (2008–18) (€billion). *EU*, European Union. *From <https://ec.europa.eu/eurostat/statistics-explained/index.php/USA-EU_-_international_trade_in_goods_statistics>.*

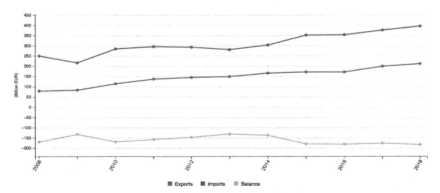

FIGURE 6.16 Evolution of extra-EU trade with China (2008–18) (€billion). *EU*, European Union. *From <https://ec.europa.eu/eurostat/statistics-explained/index.php/China-EU_-_international_trade_in_goods_statistics>.*

6.4.1 Extra-European Union trade by Member State

In 2018, Germany had the highest share of extra-EU trade, accounting for 28% of EU exports and 18.6% of imports (Fig. 6.17). Among the largest exporters were also the United Kingdom (11%), Italy (10.5%), and France (10.4%). Among the largest importers were the Netherlands (14.9%), the United Kingdom (14.2%), France (8.9%), and Italy (8.7%) (Eurostat, 2019).

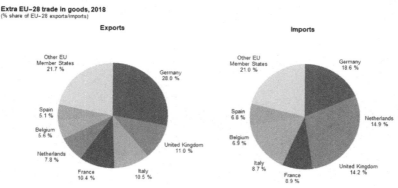

FIGURE 6.17 Extra-EU trade in goods (2018) (% share of EU-28 exports/imports). *EU,* European Union. *From <https://ec.europa.eu/eurostat/statistics-explained/index.php/International_trade_in_goods>.*

Trade with the EU's major export partner by Member State is shown in Table 6.8 and Table 6.9 for EU imports from and for EU exports to the United States, respectively (Eurostat, 2019).

The major importers from the United States include the United Kingdom (€55 billion), Germany (€48 billion), and the Netherlands (€39 billion). Ireland, Luxemburg, and the United Kingdom have a high share of their extra-EU imports with the United States, 49.4%, 32.5%, and 20.6%, respectively.

Major EU exporters to the United States include Germany (€114 billion), the United Kingdom (€54.8 billion), and Italy (€42.4 billion). Ireland has a high share (56.1%) of its extra-EU exports with the United States. Other countries with over 20% of their extra-EU exports with the United States include Germany (21.1%), the United Kingdom (25.2%), Ireland (21%), Austria (22.2%), Denmark (20.9%), Portugal (20.8%), Slovakia (22.7%), and Estonia (20.1%).

Trade with the EU's major import partner by Member State is shown in Table 6.10 and Table 6.11 for EU imports from and for EU exports to China, respectively (Eurostat, 2019).

TABLE 6.8 European Union imports of goods from the United States by Member State (2018).

EU-28 imports of goods from the United States by Member State, 2018		
	EUR million	% of the United States in extra-EU-28 imports
United Kingdom	55 426	20.6
Germany	48 547	13.3
Netherlands	39 047	13.1
France	28 558	16.2
Belgium	26 262	19.4
Italy	15 964	9.2
Ireland	15 639	49.4
Spain	11 017	8.1
Poland	4 508	6.5
Sweden	3 910	9.0
Austria	3 872	10.5
Czechia	2 994	8.1
Denmark	2 510	9.6
Hungary	1 427	5.5
Finland	1 388	7.0
Portugal	1 384	7.6
Romania	898	4.3
Luxembourg	810	32.5
Greece	690	2.6
Slovenia	559	4.8
Lithuania	410	4.2
Slovakia	346	2.2
Bulgaria	291	3.3
Latvia	267	6.5
Croatia	180	3.4
Estonia	168	4.4
Malta	115	7.7
Cyprus	87	2.2

TABLE 6.9 European Union exports of goods to the United States by Member State (2018).

EU-28 exports of goods to the United States by Member State, 2018		
	EUR million	% of the United States in extra-EU-28 exports
Germany	114 524	21.1
United Kingdom	54 848	25.2
Italy	42 449	21.0
Ireland	38 967	56.1
France	38 665	19.1
Netherlands	26 900	17.2
Belgium	20 574	19.2
Spain	12 783	12.9
Austria	9 939	22.2
Sweden	9 555	16.8
Denmark	7 529	20.9
Poland	6 143	14.1
Finland	4 453	16.9
Czechia	3 530	13.0
Portugal	2 878	20.8
Slovakia	2 594	22.7
Hungary	2 501	12.9
Lithuania	1 461	12.5
Greece	1 371	8.7
Romania	1 312	8.5
Estonia	929	20.1
Slovenia	580	6.5
Bulgaria	475	5.4
Latvia	467	10.6
Luxembourg	373	17.1
Croatia	341	7.2
Malta	146	13.5
Cyprus	84	2.8

TABLE 6.10 European Union imports of goods from China by Member State (2018).

EU-28 imports of goods from China by Member State, 2018

	EUR million	% of China in extra-EU-28 imports	
Netherlands	85 280	28.7	
Germany	75 467	20.6	
United Kingdom	53 320	19.8	
Italy	30 780	17.7	
France	29 374	16.7	
Spain	22 551	16.5	
Poland	17 972	26.0	
Belgium	15 126	11.2	
Czechia	13 175	35.5	
Sweden	7 672	17.6	
Hungary	6 450	24.9	
Denmark	6 119	23.5	
Austria	5 450	14.8	
Romania	4 406	21.0	
Ireland	3 599	11.4	
Greece	3 593	13.4	
Slovakia	2 867	17.9	
Portugal	2 350	12.9	
Finland	2 131	10.7	
Slovenia	1 778	15.2	
Bulgaria	1 317	15.0	
Lithuania	864	8.8	
Croatia	816	15.3	
Estonia	691	18.2	
Latvia	491	11.9	
Luxembourg	464	18.6	
Cyprus	388	10.1	
Malta	207	13.9	

Source: From <https://ec.europa.eu/eurostat/statistics-explained/index.php/China-EU_-_international_trade_in_goods_statistics>.

TABLE 6.11 European Union Exports of Goods from China by Member State (2018).

EU-28 exports of goods to China by Member State, 2018

	EUR million	% of China in extra-EU-28 exports	
Germany	93 715	17.3	
United Kingdom	23 365	10.7	
France	20 850	10.3	
Italy	13 169	6.5	
Netherlands	11 123	7.1	
Belgium	6 989	6.5	
Sweden	6 556	11.5	
Spain	6 275	6.4	
Ireland	4 612	6.6	
Austria	4 260	9.5	
Denmark	3 798	10.5	
Finland	3 579	13.6	
Czechia	2 188	8.1	
Poland	2 115	4.9	
Hungary	1 501	7.8	
Slovakia	1 352	11.8	
Greece	901	5.7	
Bulgaria	748	8.5	
Portugal	658	4.7	
Romania	645	4.2	
Slovenia	531	6.0	
Luxembourg	222	10.2	
Lithuania	189	1.6	
Estonia	185	4.0	
Latvia	152	3.4	
Croatia	133	2.8	
Cyprus	64	2.1	
Malta	32	3.0	

Source: From <https://ec.europa.eu/eurostat/statistics-explained/index.php/China-EU_-_international_trade_in_goods_statistics>.

The major importers from China include the Netherlands (€85 billion), Germany (€75 billion), and the United Kingdom (€53 billion). Member States with over 20% their extra-EU imports with China include the Netherlands (28.7%), Germany (20.6%), Poland (26%), Czechia (35.5%), Hungary (24.9%), Denmark (23.5%), and Romania (21%).

Major EU exporters to China include Germany (€93.7 billion), United Kingdom (€23.3 billion), and France (€20.8 billion).

6.4.2 Extra-European Union trade by product type

In terms of trade by product group, in 2018, machinery and transport equipment had the highest share in total extra-EU exports and imports, as shown in Fig. 6.18. This product group accounted for 41% of total extra-EU exports and 31% of total extra-EU imports (Eurostat, 2019). Machinery and transport equipment is followed by other manufactured goods (22% of extra-EU exports and 25% of extra-EU imports), chemicals (18% of extra-EU exports and 10% of extra-EU imports), and energy (6% of extra-EU exports and 21% of extra-EU imports).

The share of extra-EU export trade by product category is shown in Fig. 6.19. The share of exports for machinery and vehicles, other

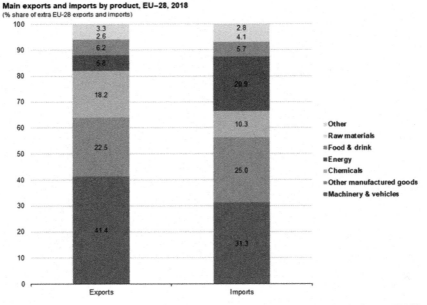

FIGURE 6.18 Extra-European Union trade by product group (2018) (% share of extra EU-28 exports/imports). *EU*, European Union. *From <https://ec.europa.eu/eurostat/statistics-explained/index.php/International_trade_in_goods>.*

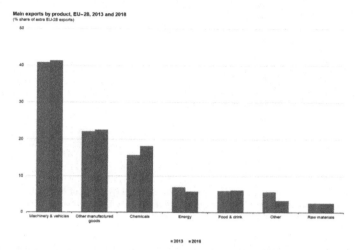

FIGURE 6.19   Main EU-28 exports by product (2013, 2018) (% share of extra EU-28 exports). *EU*, European Union. *From <https://ec.europa.eu/eurostat/statistics-explained/index.php/ International_trade_in_goods>.*

manufactured products, chemicals, and food and drink products increased during the period from 2013 to 2018. In 2018, machinery and vehicles made up 41% of the total exports, other manufactured goods accounted for 22%, and chemical products for 18%. Primary products (food and drink, raw materials, and energy) accounted for 15% of total exports.

The share of extra-EU import trade by product category is shown in Fig. 6.20. The share of imports for machinery and vehicles, chemicals, energy, food and drink, and raw materials increased during the period from 2013 to 2018, while the share of imports of other manufactured goods was reduced (Eurostat, 2019). The majority of import products are manufactured goods (machinery and vehicles, other manufactured goods, and chemical products), which account for over 75% of EU-28 imports. Primary products (food and drink, raw materials, and energy) accounted for about 18% of total imports.

Trade with the United States, EU's major import partner, by product group is shown in Fig. 6.21.

In terms of its trade with the United States, in 2018, the EU had a trade surplus in food and drink, machinery and vehicles, raw materials, other manufactured goods, and other goods. It had trade deficit in raw materials, energy, and other goods.

Trade with China, EU's major export partner, by product group is shown in Fig. 6.22.

In terms of its trade with China, in 2018, the EU had a trade surplus in food and drink, raw materials, energy, chemicals, and other products. It had a trade deficit in machinery and vehicles and other manufactured products.

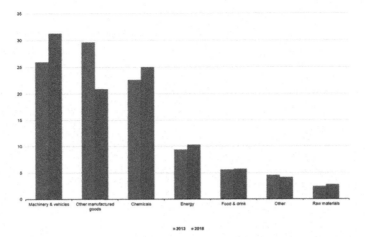

FIGURE 6.20 Main EU-28 imports by product (2013, 2018) (% share of extra EU-28 imports). *EU*, European Union. *From <https://ec.europa.eu/eurostat/statistics-explained/index.php/ International_trade_in_goods>.*

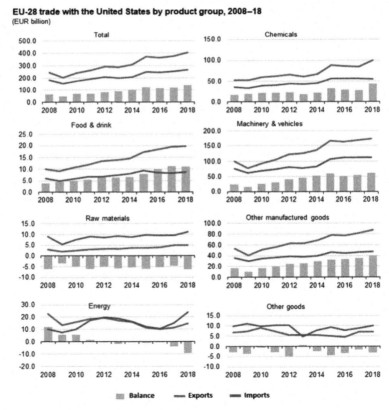

FIGURE 6.21 EU trade with the United States by product group (2008, 2018) (€billion). *EU*, European Union. *From <https://ec.europa.eu/eurostat/statistics-explained/index.php/USA-EU_- _international_trade_in_goods_statistics>.*

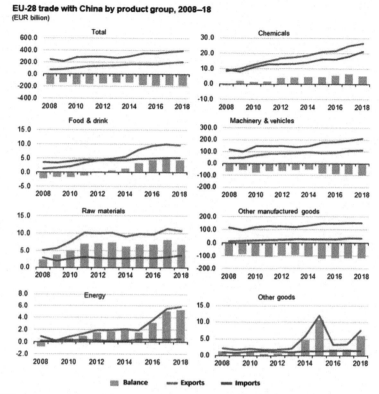

FIGURE 6.22 EU trade with China by product group (2008, 2018) (€billion). *EU*, European Union. *From <https://ec.europa.eu/eurostat/statistics-explained/index.php/China-EU_-_international_trade_in_goods_statistics>.*

6.5 European Union trade by mode of transport

6.5.1 Extra-European Union trade by mode

In 2018, sea transport accounted for almost 47% of the extra-EU goods exports (an increase from 43.4% in 2002) and for 55% of the extra-EU goods imports (an increase from 43.4% in 2002), by value. The total value of EU goods transported by sea to non-EU countries was €2006 billion. The value of extra-EU trade in goods transported by air was €999 billion, while for goods transported by road, it was €618 billion. The share of both exported and imported goods by sea increased between 2002 and 2018. For air transport, the share of exported goods increased, while the share of imported goods decreased (Eurostat, 2019). The share by mode of the value of extra-EU goods trade for both exports and imports is shown in Fig. 6.23.

A similar analysis is shown in Fig. 6.24. This figure presents the share in terms of quantity instead of value.

Value of extra-EU trade in goods, by mode of transport, EU-28, 2002 and 2018
(% of total)

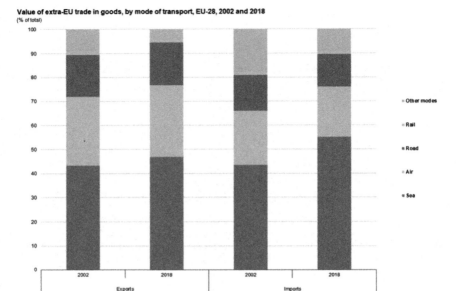

FIGURE 6.23 Value of extra-EU trade in goods by mode of transport (2002, 2018) (% of total, based on €). *EU*, European Union.

Quantity of extra-EU trade in goods, by mode of transport, EU-28, 2002 and 2018
(% of total, based on tonnes)

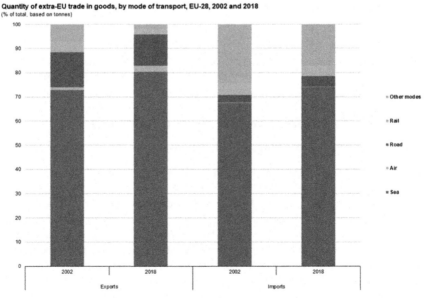

FIGURE 6.24 Quantity of extra-EU trade in goods, by mode of transport (2002, 2018) (% of total based on tonnes). *EU*, European Union. *From <https://ec.europa.eu/eurostat/statistics-explained/index.php?title = International_trade_in_goods_by_mode_of_transport&oldid = 451571>.*

In 2018, sea transport accounted for over 80% of extra-EU exports and almost 74% of extra-EU imports in terms of quantity (in tonnes). Air transport accounted for only 2.6% of extra-EU exports and 0.3% of extra-EU imports. Comparison of the relative data between the two figures indicates that air transport is mainly used for higher-value products.

The modal share of extra-EU exports and imports by Member State is shown in Figs. 6.25 and 6.26, respectively. Fig. 6.25 shows the value of extra-EU exports by mode for each Member State, while Fig. 6.26 shows the respective values for extra-EU imports (Eurostat, 2019).

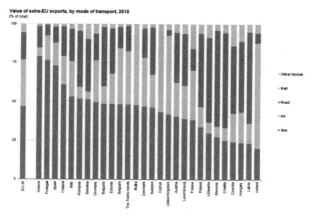

FIGURE 6.25 Value of extra-EU exports, by mode of transport, by Member State (2018) (% of total). *EU*, European Union. *From <https://ec.europa.eu/eurostat/statistics-explained/index.php?title = International_trade_in_goods_by_mode_of_transport&oldid = 451571>.*

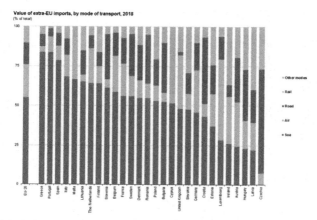

FIGURE 6.26 Value of extra-EU imports, by mode of transport, by Member State (2018) (% of total). *EU*, European Union. *From <https://ec.europa.eu/eurostat/statistics-explained/index.php?title = International_trade_in_goods_by_mode_of_transport&oldid = 451571>.*

The preferred mode of transport carrying over 25% of extra-EU exports by value for each of 24 Member States, with the exceptions of Czechia, Hungary, Latvia, and Ireland, is sea transport. Poland, Lithuania, Slovenia, Croatia, Czechia, Hungary, and Latvia relied mainly on road transport for their extra-EU exports. Air transport accounted for over 68% of the total value of exports from Ireland to non-EU countries. This share was about 51% each for the United Kingdom and Malta.

The share of sea transport in extra-EU imports is significantly higher compared to exports. It accounted for over 50% of the extra-EU imports for 17 Member States and for over 25% for 24 Member States. For Greece, Portugal, and Spain, sea accounted for more than three-quarters of total value of exports to nonmember states (83.8% for Greece, 83.6% for Portugal, and 78.7% for Spain). Sea was the preferred mode of transport for 22 states. Road transport was the preferred mode of transport in Czechia, Hungary, and Austria, air transport in Luxembourg, and other modes of transport in Ireland and Latvia.

6.5.2 Inland European Union freight transport

In terms of inland freight transport in the EU, road transport carries almost three-quarters of freight in tonne-kilometers. Fig. 6.27 shows the evolution of the modal split of inland freight transport from 2012 to 2017. In 2017, road accounted for 76.7%, with rail and inland waterways accounting for 17.3% and 6%, respectively.

Fig. 6.28 shows the modal split of land freight transport for the year 2017 by Member State.

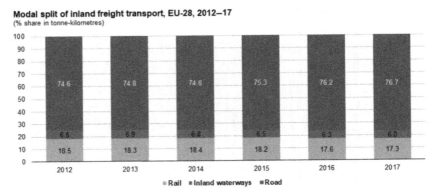

Modal split of inland freight transport, EU-28, 2012—17
(% share in tonne-kilometres)

FIGURE 6.27 Modal split of inland freight Transport (2012—17) (% share in tonne-kilometers). *From* <*https://ec.europa.eu/eurostat/statistics-explained/index.php/Freight_transport_statistics_-_modal_split*>.

Modal split of inland freight transport, 2017
(% share in tonne-kilometres)

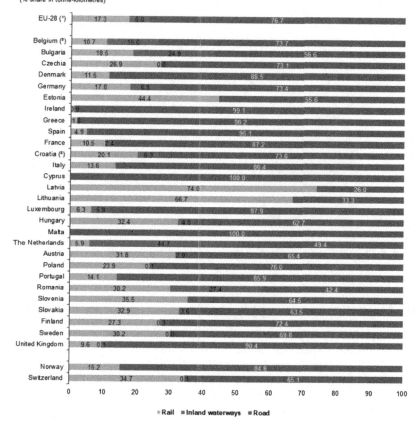

■ Rail   ■ Inland waterways   ■ Road

(¹) EU-28 includes rail transport estimates for Belgium, road freight transport for Malta and inland waterways trasnport for Finland. Figures may not add up to 100% due to rounding.
(²) Estimated values.

FIGURE 6.28   Modal split of land freight transport by Member State (2017) (% share in tonne-kilomete)   *From https://ec.europa.eu/eurostat/statistics-explained/index.php/Freight_transport_statistics_-_modal_split*

As shown in Fig. 6.28, only 18 Member States report data on inland waterways, as this mode is not available in every Member State. In addition, Malta and Cyprus report data only on road, as it is the only freight mode available in these Member States.

Rail transport is very important for the Baltic countries, while inland waterways have a high share in Belgium, Bulgaria, Romania, and the Netherlands. In the Netherlands, inland transport is a close second to road transport, with shares of 44.7% and 49.4%, respectively.

Considering the modal split of intra-EU trade on the basis of five transport modes, as shown in Fig. 6.29, road is still the main mode. It accounts for about 50% of total intra-EU trade. Maritime has the second highest share (about 32%), followed by rail (about 12%).

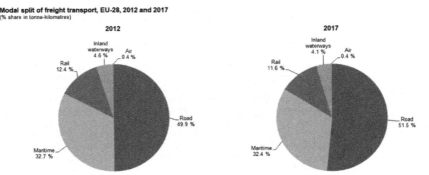

FIGURE 6.29 Modal split of freight transport (2012, 2017) (% share in tonne-kilometers). *From <https://ec.europa.eu/eurostat/statistics-explained/index.php/Freight_transport_statistics_-_modal_split>.*

6.6 Major European supply chains

The Europe-based supply chain organizations exhibit a strong performance and demonstrate exemplary demand-diven leadership and corporate social responsibility, as reported by Gartner (Gartner, 2019).

However, and despite the solid economic growth in Europe, uncertainty and the lack of clarity on Brexit as well as trade conflicts, especially between the United States and China have (Gartner, 2019) an impact on European as well as on international supply chains (Supply Chain Movement, 2018).

According to Gartner, the top 15 European Supply Chain companies for 2019 include Inditex, Nestle, Schneider Electric, Diageo, L'Oreal, H&M, Novo Nordisk, BASF, Adidas, AkzoNobel, BMW, British American Tobacco, Nokia, Roche Holding, and Danone. Fig. 6.30 shows key production facilities of the world's top 100 brands, in Europe (Supply Chain Movement, 2015). Each company logo indicates the company's choice of locating close to its consumer market.

In addition to the proximity of companies to their consumer markets, the map shows the location of existing distribution hubs, as well as emerging and potential distribution hubs in 2020. It also shows the key rail, motorways of the sea, and inland waterways transportation networks; main current, fastest growing, and other important container seaports; and top five and other important cargo airports. Furthermore, the map shows the location of major industries, including car, chemical, high tech, and aerospace.

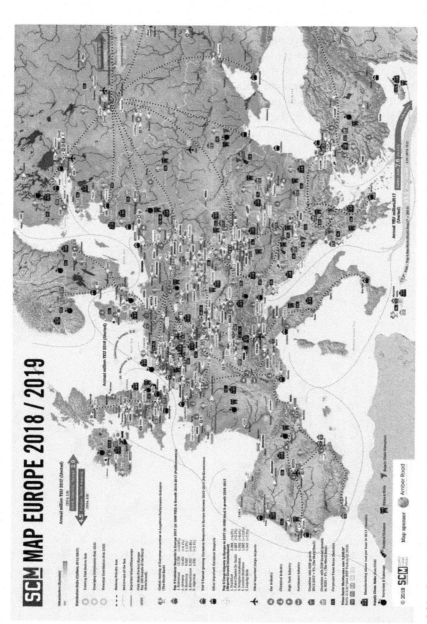

FIGURE 6.30 Supply chain map (Europe 2018/19). *From <https://www.supplychainmovement.com/scm-map-europe-european-location-decisions-remain-complex/>.*

In terms of tonne-kilometer-based performance, the top five European countries include Germany, France, Poland, Spain, and Italy. Out of the 4000 billion tonne-kilometers of goods transported in Europe every year, 10% are related to the agriculture sector, 20% to the mining industry, and 70% to the manufacture sector.

Many of the existing distribution hubs are located in the so-called Blue Banana corridor, which represents the key sales market for many brands in Europe. The corridor region comprises the northwest of England, Benelux, northern Italy, the Ruhr and the Rhine region, southern Germany, Switzerland and the Tirol, as shown in Fig. 6.31.

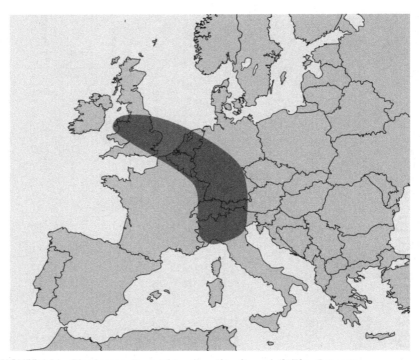

FIGURE 6.31   Blue banana. *From <https://en.wikipedia.org/wiki/Blue_Banana>*.

The new emerging and potential distribution hubs, however, as shown in Fig. 6.30, are located toward the east, reshaping the European industrial geography into a circle. The circle is centered on southern Germany and is reaching into Poland, Hungary, the Czech Republic, Slovakia, Austria, and Romania on the east. There has been significant relocation into a central European manufacturing core, with Eastern European countries becoming the extended production line of German industry. The region comprising Germany, the Netherlands, the Czech Republic, Slovakia, and Romania increased its intra-EU trade share by 5.3% points between 2004 and 2013, while the region comprising the UK, France, Ireland, Spain, and Portugal lost about 4.4% points in intra-EU market share (Taylor, 2015).

Data sources

The sources for the statistics in this article are from Eurostat. Statistical data have been reported to Eurostat by EU Member States in the framework of various EU legal acts. The essential legal acts are the following:

- *Road.* Regulation (EU) No. 70/2012 on statistical returns in respect of the carriage of goods by road (recast);
- *Rail.* Regulation (EC) No. 91/2003 on rail transport statistics;
- *Inland waterways.* Regulation (EC) No. 1365/2006 on statistics of goods transport by inland waterways;
- *Air.* Regulation (EC) No. 437/2003 on statistical returns in respect of the carriage of passengers, freight, and mail by air;
- *Maritime.* Directive 2009/42/EC on statistical returns in respect of carriage of goods and passengers by sea.

References

European Union. *Regulation (EU) No 1219/2012 of hte European Parliament and of the Council.* (2012). Retrieved from <https://eur-lex.europa.eu/LexUriServ/LexUriServ.do?uri = OJ:L:2012:351:0040:0046:EN:PDF>

Eurostat. *USA-EU - international trade in goods statistics.* (2019). Retrieved from <https://ec.europa.eu/eurostat/statistics-explained/index.php/USA-EU_-_international_trade_in_goods_statistics>

Gartner. *Gartner announces rankings of the 2019 supply chain top 15 for Europe.* (2019). Retrieved from <https://www.gartner.com/en/newsroom/press-releases/2019-06-19-gartner-announces-rankings-of-the-2019-supply-chain-t>

Supply Chain Movement. *SCM map Europe: European location decisions remain complex.* (2015). Retrieved from <https://www.supplychainmovement.com/scm-map-europe-european-location-decisions-remain-complex/>

Supply Chain Movement. *SCM map Europe 2018–2019.* (2018). Retrieved from <https://www.supplychainmovement.com/scm-map-europe-2018-2019/>

Taylor, P. *No more Blue Banana, Europe's industrial heart moves east.* (2015). Retrieved from Reuters: <https://www.reuters.com/article/us-eu-industry-analysis/no-more-blue-banana-europes-industrial-heart-moves-east-idUSKBN0MB0AC20150315>

Chapter 7

Transportation corridor infrastructure planning and funding in the European Union

7.1 Transport network development in Europe

The Treaty of Rome, or Treaty on the Functioning of the European Union (EU), led to the establishment of a common market and customs union and promoted the free movement of goods, services, people, and capital in the EU. Transport networks have been essential in the European integration process and in the completion of the internal market, supporting the facilitation of free movement. They are also essential in supporting the increasing Union's integration into global markets.

Transport networks in Europe have been originally designed and developed from a national point of view. In the postwar period, the European transport system had several shortcomings related mainly to missing links and lack of interoperability between national networks. In the 1970s, the United Nations' Economic Commission for Europe (UNECE) carried out a project on Trans-European-Motorways (UNECE, 2011), which was later extended to rail transport trans-European railway project (TER) as well. The project presented the concept of corridors and networks on a European level.

To connect all the regions and to facilitate the effective and efficient movement of goods and people among Member States, as well as external trade, missing links had to be developed and bottlenecks had to be removed in the European transport infrastructure.

An EU infrastructure policy at the Community level was decided at the beginning of the 1990s, aiming to develop continuous and efficient transport networks (European Commission, 2019a). The Trans-European Transport Network (TEN-T) entered EU policies with the Maastricht Treaty in 1992. The Maastricht Treaty gave the task to the EU to develop the TEN-Ts, along with the telecommunications and energy networks, with the aim to strengthen social, economic, and territorial cohesion in the EU. The legal basis for the functioning of the Trans-European Networks was provided by the Treaty on the Functioning of the European Union (European Union, 2012a, 2012b) (Articles 170, 171, 172, 194).

International Trade and Transportation Infrastructure Development.
DOI: https://doi.org/10.1016/B978-0-12-815741-1.00007-3

The first "Community Guidelines" for the development of a Trans-European Network in the transport sector was adopted by the European Parliament and the Council in 1996 (European Commission, 1996) with the aim to connect national networks of all transport modes and to serve as a reference framework for the Member States' infrastructure policy. The guidelines established the characteristics of the modal networks and identified projects of common interest. Emphasis was placed mainly on rail projects, with rail considered as an environmentally friendly mode of transport.

In 2001 the TEN-T guidelines were amended (European Commission, 2001) to further consider seaports, inland ports, and intermodal terminals, resulting in a Community "transport development plan" for all modes of transport. Further revisions were necessitated by the 2004 and 2007 enlargements. The revised guidelines included an increased number of projects and introduced the concept of Motorways of the Sea (MoS) with the aim to improve the efficiency of sea routes and to integrate short sea shipping with rail transport.

An executive agency, the TEN-T Executive Agency (TEN-T EA), was set up in 2006 to facilitate contacts with national authorities, transport operators, and users and to undertake the technical preparation and monitoring of decisions on projects managed by the Commission.

An important policy review in 2009, with a view to the 2014−20 financial framework, placed emphasis on the areas of governance at the European level, a strong legal form, and a genuine network approach. A new legislative framework was introduced in 2013 for the financing period 2014−20, the Union guidelines for the development of the TEN-T (TEN-T Regulation or TEN-T Guidelines) (European Union, 2013a). The legislative framework was accompanied by the 2011 Transport White Paper, "Roadmap to a Single European Transport Area—Towards a Competitive and Resource-Efficient Transport System" (European Commission, 2011). The document presented the Commission's vision for the future of the EU transport system as a competitive and sustainable transport system and for the strategy to develop it, including several initiatives on TEN-T.

The revisions of the TEN-T Guidelines changed the perspective of TEN-T development. The revisions aimed at further enhancing modal networks integrating them into a coherent transport infrastructure supported by innovative technological solutions. The new policy introduced a dual-layer structure, comprising a comprehensive network and a core network. Furthermore, the policy revisions introduced nine major multimodal corridors, as an instrument to facilitate the coordinated implementation of core network projects, pulling together public and private sector resources. The European transport networks and corridors are detailed in subsequent sections. The new policy also supports the development of the Motorways of the Sea, as well as the European Railway Transport Management System (ERTMS). European coordinators have been appointed to lead the development process and harmonization of each corridor as well as the MoS and ERTMS actions.

The TEN-T EA was renamed Infrastructure and Networks Executive Agency in 2014. The agency is responsible for the technical and financial management of programs aimed at financing TEN-T development. Following an evaluation of the progress of the TEN-T development in 2018, a revision of the TEN-T policy will take place in 2023 (European Parliament, 2019b).

7.2 The Trans-European Transport Networks

The TEN-T include infrastructure comprising roads, railway lines, inland waterways, railroad terminals, airports, ports, and their subcomponents throughout the 28 Member States. Furthermore, TEN-Ts comprise telematic applications as well as measures promoting the efficient management and use of the infrastructure and the provision of sustainable and efficient transport services. Selected core infrastructure comprises the Core Network layer, while the remaining infrastructure forms the comprehensive network layer.

The comprehensive network covers all European regions and consists of all existing and planned infrastructure that needs to be in place to meet the requirements of the TEN-T Guidelines. The network aims to ensure effective connections to all the EU regions. The total length of the comprehensive network amounts to 138,072 km of railway lines, 136,706 km of roads, and 23,506 km of inland waterways (European Commission, 2019e), while it also includes 328 maritime ports. It comprises the basic layer of the TEN-T, and it is planned to be fully in place by the end of 2050. Priorities for the development of the TEN-T are outlined in the TEN-T Regulation (EU) No. 1315/2013 document. The document also details the infrastructure components, infrastructure requirements, and infrastructure development priorities for each mode and multimodal transport component.

The Core Network overlays the comprehensive network and mainly connects its strategically most important elements. It consists of the parts of the comprehensive network that are of highest strategic importance for achieving the objectives of the TEN-T policy. The idea of the Core Network was to establish European priorities with reference to the comprehensive network. The total length of the Core Network amounts to 50,762 km of rail lines, 34,401 km of roads, and 12,880 km of inland waterways (European Commission, 2019e). The Core Network shall be interconnected at nodes and provide for transport infrastructure connections between Member States and with neighboring countries. It is planned to be in place by the end of 2030.

By the year 2020, the TEN-T network is anticipated to comprise 89,500 km of roads, 94,000 km of rail lines, 11,250 km of inland waterways, 210 inland ports, 294 seaports, and 366 airports (Trans-European Transport Networks, 2019).

The key TEN-T infrastructure is shown in the following figures. Fig. 7.1 shows freight railways, ports, and railroad terminals; Fig. 7.2 shows inland waterways and port infrastructure, while Fig. 7.3 shows the roadways, along with ports, railroad terminals and airports, for both the Comprehensive and the Core Networks.

In addition to the physical infrastructure development, the TEN-T policy supports the implementation of new technologies and advanced digital solutions to all modes of transport, aiming to close technical gaps and eliminate barriers, as well as to improve operational, environmental, and energy efficiency, to increase infrastructure utilization, and to reduce accidents.

The requirements to be met by the TEN-T infrastructure for each mode and multimodal component are detailed in the TEN-T regulation document [Regulation (EU) No. 1315/2013]. Additional requirements are to be met by the Core Network infrastructure. These include full electrification of the line tracks, at least 22.5-t axle load, 100-km/h line speed, 740-m train length, full deployment of ERTMS and 1435-mm track gauge for the rail transport infrastructure; availability of alternative clean fuels for inland waterway and maritime transport infrastructure; development of rest areas about every 100 km and availability of clean fuels for road transport infrastructure.

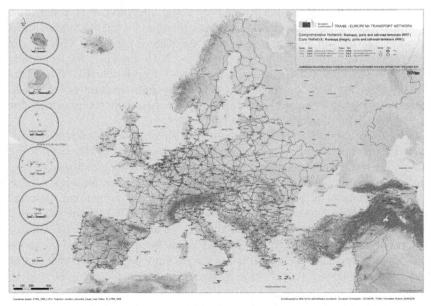

FIGURE 7.1 TEN-T comprehensive and core network freight railway, port, and railroad terminal infrastructure. *TEN-T*, Trans-European Transport Network. *From <https://ec.europa.eu/transport/infrastructure/tentec/tentec-portal/site/maps_upload/tent_modes/EU_A0Landscape2019_freight.png>.*

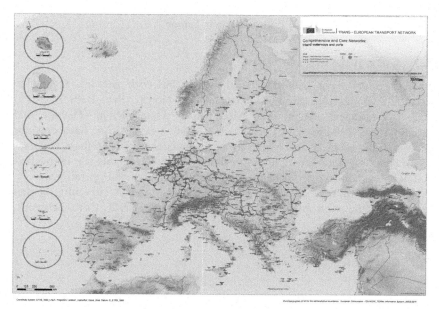

FIGURE 7.2 TEN-T comprehensive and core network inland waterways and ports. *TEN-T*, Trans-European Transport Network. *From <https://ec.europa.eu/transport/infrastructure/tentec/ tentec-portal/site/maps_upload/tent_modes/EU_A0Landscape2019_iwws.png>.*

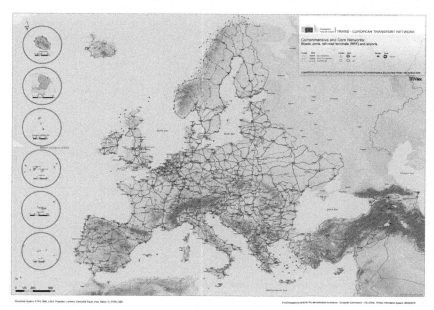

FIGURE 7.3 TEN-T comprehensive and core network roads, ports, railroad terminals, and airports. *TEN-T*, Trans-European Transport Network. *From <https://ec.europa.eu/transport/infrastructure/tentec/tentec-portal/site/maps_upload/tent_modes/EU_A0Landscape2019_roads.png>.*

7.3   Core network corridors

Nine corridors have been identified within the core network layer: the Atlantic, Baltic−Adriatic, Mediterranean, North Sea−Baltic, North Sea−Mediterranean, Orient−East Med, Rhine−Alpine, Rhine−Danube, and Scandinavian−Mediterranean corridors, as shown in Fig. 7.4. Each corridor embraces all modes of transport and the connections between them, enhancing modal integration and interoperability. They also embrace innovation and new technologies to further support freight services and operations.

The development of the nine corridors is aimed at streamlining and facilitating the coordinated development of the TEN-T Core Network.

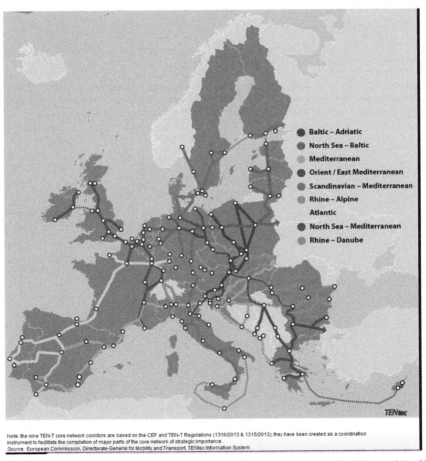

Note: the nine TEN-T core network corridors are based on the CEF and TEN-T Regulations (1316/2013 & 1315/2013); they have been created as a coordination instrument to facilitate the completion of major parts of the core network of strategic importance.
Source: European Commission, Directorate-General for Mobility and Transport, TENtec Information System

FIGURE 7.4   Core network corridors. *From <https://ec.europa.eu/eurostat/statistics-explained/index.php?title = File:TEN-T_Core_Network_Corridors_(Freight_and_Passenger)_RYB17.png&oldid = 338850>.*

The corridors are complemented by the two horizontal priorities, the ERTMS and the MoS.

Subsequent sections present brief overviews of the core transportation infrastructure elements for each of the nine corridors. Relevant information is mainly gathered from the Corridor Work Plan documents, which present views of the European Coordinators.

7.3.1 Atlantic corridor

The Atlantic Corridor connects the Iberian Peninsula to Northern France at the port of Le Havre and with the cities of Strasbourg and Mannheim on the French—German border. The corridor's infrastructure components, including rail, road, inland waterway, and maritime transport nodes, are shown in Fig. 7.5.

The Atlantic Corridor connects with the Mediterranean Corridor in Madrid and Zaragoza, with the North Sea—Mediterranean Corridor through Paris, Metz, and Strasbourg, and with the Rhine—Alpine and the Rhine—Danube Corridors through its recent extension to Mannheim in Germany, as shown in Fig. 7.5.

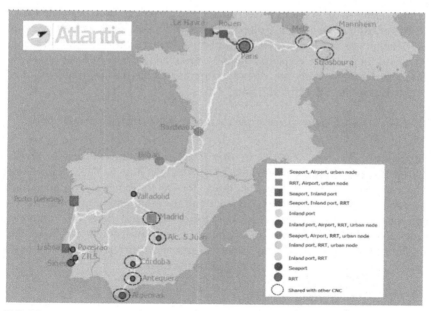

FIGURE 7.5 Atlantic corridor and its nodes. *From <https://ec.europa.eu/transport/sites/transport/files/atlworkplaniiiweb.pdf>.*

The Atlantic Corridor transportation infrastructure, by mode, and the level of compliance with the Regulation requirements are presented next, based on information available in the Corridor Work Plan (Secchi, 2018).

7.3.1.1 Atlantic corridor railway network

The corridor consists of about 6200 km of railway lines in operation and covers an extension of 7616 km in total. Currently, only 56% of the Atlantic Core Railways consist of a standard European gauge (Secchi, 2018). Future development will extend this coverage to about 74% by 2030, connecting all border crossings in International Union of Railways (UIC) gauge. Only 12% of the rail network meets the ERTMS criteria. The corridor is fully compliant in all its extensions (on its freight component) with minimum axle road of 22.5 t. The compliance rate with the 740-m train length on rail freight lines is 57%. This is a clear restraining factor for freight operations in the Iberian Peninsula, particularly in Spain and the sections connecting the core ports in Portugal, where the maximum freight train length is 550 m.

7.3.1.2 Atlantic inland waterway network and inland ports

The only inland waterway infrastructure in the Atlantic Corridor is the Seine River, comprising the whole section Le Havre—Paris. The Corridor will be connected with the North Sea—Mediterranean corridor through the planned Seine—Scheldt canal.

The Seine River section in the Atlantic includes three core network ports: Le Havre, Rouen, and Paris, grouped as HaRoPa ports. Other inland ports in the Atlantic are Bordeaux (both sea and inland ports), Strasbourg, Metz, and Manheim. In total, the corridor counts seven inland core ports with regard to inland waterways. Ports are already compliant with the minimum criteria established in the TEN-T regulation.

7.3.1.3 Atlantic maritime infrastructure and motorways of the sea

There are eight core seaports in the Atlantic Corridor: Algeciras, Sines, Lisboa, Leixoes, Bilbaio, Bordeaux, Le Havre, and Roueu. Their connection with rail and inland waterways is critical for freight movement to and from the economic regions along the Corridor and for promoting port competitiveness and strengthening hinterland connections. Several ports are operating near capacity and are in need of upgrades of their infrastructure to meet the anticipated requirements due to growth in demand. Bigger ships will impose new standards to both equipment and infrastructure.

7.3.1.4 Atlantic road infrastructure

The Atlantic Corridor roadway infrastructure is of high quality, and to a large extent (99.8%), it fulfills the TEN-T class requirements for motorways or express roads. The compliance rate for liquefied natural gas (LNG) is currently at about 12% and for electric charging at about 18%. These rates are expected to increase, as deployment has started in 2018 and is anticipated to be accomplished by 2025. Interoperability of tolling systems has not been achieved at corridor level.

7.3.2   Baltic—Adriatic corridor

The Baltic—Adriatic Corridor connects the Baltic seaports of Gdansk, Gdynia, Szczecin, and Swinoujscie in the north to the ports of Koper, Trieste, Venice, and Ravenna on the Adriatic Sea in the south. The Corridor is one of the most important trans-European road and rail axes in Central Europe, connecting industrial regions in Central Europe from Poland, Czech Republic, Slovakia, and Austria to Italy and Slovenia in the south. The main transport infrastructure components of the Corridor are shown in Fig. 7.6.

The Baltic—Adriatic Corridor connects with five other corridors. It crosses the North Sea—Baltic Corridor in Poland in the west—east direction; it crosses the Orient—East Med and the Rhine—Danube Corridors in the Czech Republic, Austria, and Slovakia; in Italy and Slovenia, the Corridor runs parallel to the Mediterranean Corridor; between Bologna and Faenza along the Bologna—Ravenna rail line, it intersects with the Scandinavian—Mediterranean Corridor.

The Baltic—Adriatic Corridor transportation infrastructure, by mode, and the level of compliance with the Regulation requirements are presented next, based on information available in the Corridor Work Plan (Bodewig, 2018).

7.3.2.1   Baltic—Adriatic railway network

The Baltic—Adriatic railway network consists of 4285 km of 1435 mm standard gauge railway infrastructure. Compliance limitations include differences in electrification and power systems, with three different power systems in use; small sections of the corridor (7% of the railway infrastructure) not compliant with the 22.5-t axle load requirement; 28% of the corridor not compliant with the 100-km/h line speed; several sections of the corridor shorter than the 740-m train length; and ERTMS-related technology available on only 17% of the corridor sections.

Issues with the technical standards occur mainly in Poland and Slovenia and at border crossings between the corridor countries.

7.3.2.2   Baltic Adriatic ports infrastructure

Ten core ports are in operation along the Baltic Adriatic Corridor. Five of them are classified as maritime and inland waterway ports (Szczecin, Świnoujście, Trieste, Venezia, and Ravenna); three are classified as maritime ports (Gdynia, Gdańsk, and Koper); and two are classified as inland

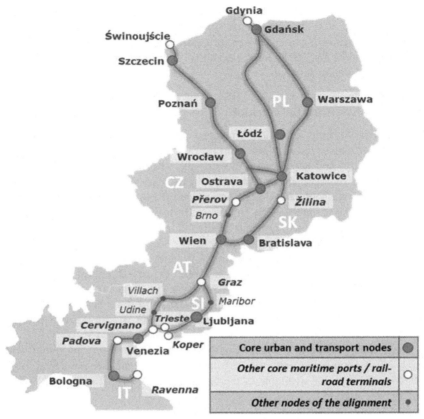

FIGURE 7.6 Main Baltic–Adriatic corridor transport infrastructure. *From Baltic Adriatic–Third Work Plan of the European Coordinator (2018).*

waterway ports (Wien and Bratislava). These ports are all interconnected to the road and rail links of the corridor, representing a basic infrastructure for intermodal transport. However, last mile road and/or rail connection limitations are present in all Baltic–Adriatic ports. Logistics platforms are in operation or under development to promote multimodal transport, and all ports have at least one terminal open to all operators in a nondiscriminatory way. Alternative clean fuels are not yet available for maritime transport operations at any of the corridor ports.

7.3.2.3   Baltic–Adriatic road infrastructure

The Baltic–Adriatic corridor comprises 3600 km of road infrastructure, not entirely compliant with the Regulation requirements, especially regarding the type of the infrastructure. This is the case mainly with the Polish road network, whereas the road network in Italy and Slovenia is fully compliant.

Currently, 16% of the corridor road infrastructure is not compliant with requirements. Issues with the technical required standards are also present at the Poland—Slovakia and Czech Republic—Austria cross-border sections.

7.3.3 Mediterranean corridor

The Mediterranean Corridor runs from the southwestern Mediterranean region of Spain to the Ukrainian border with Hungary. It follows the coastlines of Spain and France and crosses the Alps through Italy, Slovenia, and Croatia. It continues through Hungary to its eastern border with Ukraine (Radicova, 2018). The main transport infrastructure components of the Corridor are shown in Fig. 7.7.

The Mediterranean Corridor connects with the Atlantic Corridor in Spain, the North Sea—Mediterranean Corridor in France, the Rhine—Alpine Corridor in Italy, the Scandinavian—Mediterranean Corridor in Italy, the Baltic—Adriatic Corridor in Italy and Slovenia, the Rhine—Danube Corridor in Croatia and Hungary, and the Orient—East Med Corridor in Hungary.

The Mediterranean Corridor transportation infrastructure, by mode, and the level of compliance with the Regulation requirements are presented next, based on information available in the Corridor Work Plan (Brinkhorst, 2018).

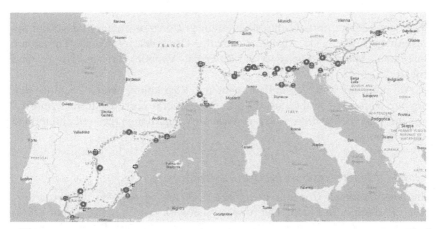

FIGURE 7.7 Mediterranean corridor transportation infrastructure. *From Mediterranean Third Work Plan of the European Coordinator.*

7.3.3.1 Mediterranean railway network

The railway network is already 92% compliant with electrification requirements, while interventions in the remaining parts, in Spain, are planned. Nevertheless, three different voltages are in use, raising interoperability issues. The main issue with the Corridor is the track gauge, with France, Italy, Slovenia, Croatia, and Hungary featuring 1435-mm standard UIC gauge and Spain featuring both standard as well as 1668-mm gauge. ERTMS is deployed in 89% of the Corridor lines in Slovenia, on high-speed lines in Spain and Italy and on some cross-border sections. Train length of 740 m is only allowed in France and parts of the Hungarian, Spanish, and Slovenian networks. Limitations of the 22.5-t axle load occur in some sections in Hungary and Slovenia. Some sections in Slovenia and Croatia do not allow for the 100-km/h speed limit.

7.3.3.2 Mediterranean inland waterway network

The Mediterranean Corridor inland waterway network consists of nine inland ports (Sevilla, Marseille/Fos-Sur-Mer, Lyon, Cremona, Mantua, Venice, Trieste, Ravenna, and Budapest), the Rhone River between Lyon and Fos-Sur-Mer, and the Po River connecting the inland ports of Cremona and Mantua to Ferrara/Porto Garibaldi and Venice/Porto Nogaro/Monfalcone. The Regulation requirement for the inland waterways is met by about 80% of the network.

7.3.3.3 Mediterranean ports infrastructure

There are 12 core ports in the Mediterranean Corridor, mainly located in the western part: Bahía de Algeciras, Sevilla, Cartagena, Valencia, Tarragona, Barcelona, Marseille/Fos-sur-Mer, Ravenna, Venetia, Trieste, Koper, and Rijeka.

All ports are fully compliant with the Regulation, which requires that they are connected to the railway network. Several ports are further improving the rail connection with a view to improving the rail hinterland connection.

7.3.3.4 Mediterranean road infrastructure

The Mediterranean Corridor comprises 5500 km of roadway infrastructure, 50% of which is in Spain. The roadway network is to a major extent (98%) compliant with the express road/motorway requirement. There are several liquefied petroleum gas (LPG) and compressed natural gas (CNG) refueling points along the corridor roadways. In terms of parking space requirements, France, Italy, and Slovenia are 100% compliant, while the compliance ratios in Spain, Hungary, and Croatia are 88%, 50%, and 34%, respectively.

7.3.4   North Sea—Baltic corridor

The North Sea—Baltic Corridor connects the ports of the east side of the Baltic Sea with the ports of the North Sea in Germany, Belgium, and the Netherlands. It comprises transport infrastructure in eight countries: Belgium, the Netherlands, Germany, Poland, Lithuania, Latvia, Estonia, and Finland. The Corridor starts in Helsinki, passes through the three Baltic States and northeastern Poland, and follows the east—west corridor through Lodz, Poznan, and Berlin, continuing to the North Sea coast ports of Hamburg, Bremen, and Bremerhaven, continuing to Amsterdam, Rotterdam, Moerdijk, and Antwerp. It has branches to Ventspils in Latvia, Klaipeda and Vilnius in Lithuania, and Terespol on the Polish - Belarussian border. The main transport infrastructure components of the Corridor are shown in Fig. 7.8.

The North Sea—Baltic Corridor connects with several other Corridors, including the Scandinavian—Mediterranean Corridor, the Baltic—Adriatic Corridor, the Orient—East Med Corridor, the Scandinavian—Mediterranean Corridor, the Rhine—Alpine Corridor, and the North Sea—Mediterranean Corridor.

The North Sea—Baltic Corridor transportation infrastructure, by mode, and the level of compliance with the Regulation requirements are presented

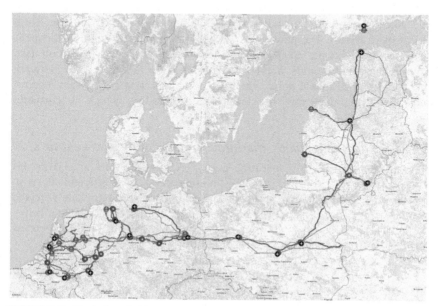

FIGURE 7.8 North Sea—Baltic corridor transportation infrastructure. *From North Sea—Baltic Third Work Plan of the European Coordinator.*

next, based on information available in the Corridor Work Plan (Trautmann, 2018).

7.3.4.1 North Sea–Baltic railway network

The network comprises 5986 km of rail lines. The majority of the network is electrified in five countries (100% in Belgium, the Netherlands, and Finland, and over 90% in Germany and Poland). Smaller sections of the network are electrified in Lithuania, Latvia, and Estonia (18%, 11%, and 17%, respectively). Different voltage systems exist across some Member States. There are three different track gauges. Belgium, Germany, Poland, and the Netherlands have the standard UIC gauge (1435 mm); Estonia, Latvia, and Lithuania have the 1520-mm gauge; and Finland has the 1524-mm gauge. The Baltic States and Finnish networks are exempt from the Regulation requirements, as isolated networks. These networks are also exempt from the minimum line speed requirement. All lines in the Netherlands and the majority of the lines in Germany and Belgium comply with the minimum speed requirement. With very minor exceptions, the North Sea Baltic rail network is compliant with the minimum axle load and train length requirements. Only 43% of the network in the Netherlands and 32% of the network in Belgium comply with the ERTMS requirement.

7.3.4.2 North Sea–Baltic inland waterway network and inland ports

The North Sea–Baltic inland waterway network stretches from the North Sea ports to Berlin. The network is almost fully compliant with all the technical requirements in all Member States, with only one exception (the requirement for minimum height under bridges) in Germany. The network also comprises 20 inland ports, which are compliant with all relevant requirements with the exception of clean fuel availability, which is currently limited.

7.3.4.3 North Sea–Baltic maritime infrastructure and seaports

The corridor has 12 core maritime ports. All core seaports are connected with rail and road; however, capacity in some cases is insufficient. Ports in Belgium, the Netherlands, Germany, and Lithuania are compliant with the alternative fuel requirement. The maritime ports of the corridor have a heavy impact on the corridor's development, as these are the main gateways between the EU market and the rest of the world.

7.3.4.4 North Sea–Baltic road infrastructure

The Corridor comprises 4092 km of roads that connect the capitals of all the Member States on the Corridor. Road infrastructure is fully compliant with the road class requirement in Belgium, the Netherlands, Germany, and Finland.

In Poland and Latvia, 56% and 55% of the roadways, respectively, are compliant, while in Latvia and Estonia this share is less than 10%. The network in the Netherlands, Belgium, and Germany is fully compliant with the parking area requirements. In Poland, compliance is at 56%, while for other Member States of the corridor, the requirement is not applicable as there are no roadways with motorway standard. The formal requirement for alternative fuels is fully met, although there are discrepancies with regard to the type of the alternative fuel provided.

7.3.5   North Sea−Mediterranean corridor

The North Sea−Mediterranean Corridor covers six Member States: Belgium, Ireland, France, Luxemburg, the Netherlands, and the United Kingdom. It connects Edinburgh, Scotland in the north with Marseille, France, in the south, passing through Ireland, England, the Low Countries, and the French capital before connecting to the French−German border (European Commission, 2019g). The main transport infrastructure components of the Corridor are shown in Fig. 7.9.

The North Sea−Mediterranean Corridor connects to the North Sea−Baltic Corridor, the Rhine−Alpine Corridor, the Mediterranean Corridor, and the Atlantic Corridor.

The main transportation infrastructure, by mode, and the level of compliance with the Regulation requirements are presented next, based on information available in the Corridor Work Plan (Balázs, 2018).

7.3.5.1   North Sea−Mediterranean railway network

The Irish railway network is considered an isolated network, and as such it is exempt from the interoperability requirements. The rest of the North Sea−Mediterranean Corridor railway network, with some exceptions, is compliant with the requirements, including train length, track gauge, electrification, line speed, and axle load. More specifically, in Belgium, the agreement of the infrastructure manager is needed for trains longer than 650 m, and trains are frequently limited to 650 m during peak hours. In the United Kingdom, 20% of the corridor sections are above standard, 50% are below standard, and the rest are unknown. In terms of electrification, only a few last mile connections are not electrified, although interoperability issues arise because of differences in voltage among several sections. Line speed limit on most corridor sections is above 100 km/h with the exception of sections in the United Kingdom, representing about 32% of the rail lines, which have a lower speed limit. In terms of ERTMS, Luxembourg, the Netherlands, and Belgium have high levels of implementation, while in other parts of the corridor, implementation is limited.

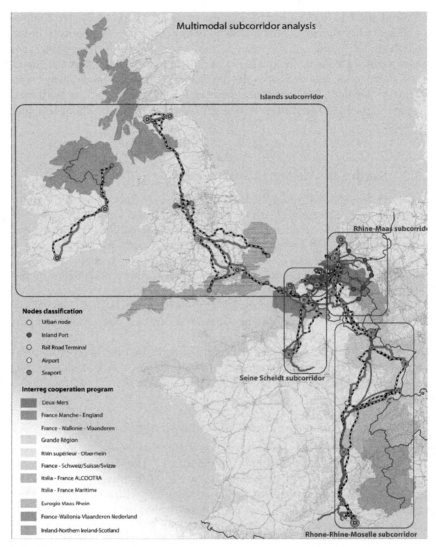

FIGURE 7.9 North Sea—Mediterranean corridor transportation infrastructure. *From North Sea—Mediterranean Third Work Plan of the European Coordinator.*

7.3.5.2 North Sea—Mediterranean inland waterway network

The inland waterway network in the four continental countries of the Corridor is well developed. Due to the high concentration of transport volumes in several parts of the network, further investment is planned in terms of developing waterway connections, expanding the lock system and upgrading multimodal transfer connections.

7.3.5.3 North Sea—Mediterranean maritime infrastructure and ports

Corridor seaports offer rail connections with very few exceptions in the United Kingdom. Several corridor ports in continental countries have waterway connections, and several ports in France, Belgium, and the Netherlands are developing LNG bunkering facilities.

7.3.5.4 North Sea—Mediterranean road infrastructure

In the North Sea—Mediterranean Corridor, virtually all of the core roadway links comply with the requirements. All corridor links comply with the motorway/expressway requirement with some last mile connections to seaports as exceptions. In terms of parking areas, the adequacy requirement is met at the majority of the roadways, while security measures are still to be implemented in some locations. Several clean fuel stations exist, and more are planned for construction.

7.3.6 Orient—East Med corridor

The Orient—East Med Corridor connects large parts of Central Europe with ports of the North, Baltic, Black, and Mediterranean Seas. The Corridor provides economic centers in central Europe with multimodal connections to Motorways of the Sea. It incorporates the Elbe River as a key inland waterway, providing multimodal connections between North Germany, the Czech Republic, the Pannonian region, and Southeastern Europe. It also provides an improved link to Cyprus (European Commission, 2019h). The main transport infrastructure components of the Corridor are shown in Fig. 7.10.

The Orient—East Med Corridor connects with the Mediterranean Corridor, the Rhine—Danube Corridor, the Baltic—Adriatic Corridor, the North Sea—Baltic Corridor, and the Scandinavian—Mediterranean Corridor.

The North Sea—Baltic Corridor transportation infrastructure, by mode, and the level of compliance with the Regulation requirements are presented next, based on information available in the Corridor Work Plan (Grosch, 2018).

7.3.6.1 Orient—East Med railway network

The Orient—East Med Corridor rail network comprises 5884 km of rail lines. By the end of 2016, the network is to a main extent not compliant with technical requirements relating to train length and control system (ERTMS). The noncompliance rate in terms of line speed, axle load, and electrification is around 20%. More specifically, the minimum line speed requirement is not

FIGURE 7.10 Orient–East Med corridor transportation infrastructure. *From Orient–East Med Work Plan of the European Coordinator.*

fulfilled in parts of Slovakia and in Bulgaria, amounting to 21% of the rail network; axle load is an issue mainly in Romania, adding up to 17% of the overall network; only 11% of the network is not electrified.

7.3.6.2 Orient–East Med inland waterway network and inland ports

The Orient–East Med corridor comprises 1659 km of inland waterways on the Elbe, Weser, and Vltava Rivers and several canals, as well as on the Danube River, which is assessed in the Rhine–Danube Corridor analysis. Overall, 98% of the network is compliant with the Regulation requirements. There are 10 core river ports in the network, which comply with the Regulation requirements regarding rail and road connections, availability of at least one terminal open to all operators in an nondiscriminatory manner, and application of transparent charges. None of the ports provides alternative fuels refueling points.

7.3.6.3 Orient–East Med maritime infrastructure and ports

The Orient–East Med Corridor comprises 12 core ports: the German ports of Hamburg, Bremerhaven, Bremen, Wilhelmshaven, and Rostock; the Greek Ports of Piraeus, Heraklion, Thessaloniki, Igoumenitsa, and Patra; and Burgas and Lemesos in Bulgaria and Cyprus, respectively. Some of these, namely Bremerhaven, Bremen, and Hamburg, are also inland ports. A Motorways of the Sea link in Eastern Mediterranean is also part of the Corridor, connecting the Greek port of Piraeus to the port of Lemesos in Cyprus via the port of Heraklion in Crete. All ports comply with the requirement to have at least one terminal open to all users; all ports provide connections with the road network and, with the exception of the ports of Igoumenitsa and Parta, all ports provide connections with the rail network. Most ports do not comply with the requirement for the provision of alternative fuel refueling stations.

7.3.6.4 Orient–East Med road infrastructure

The Orient–East Med Corridor comprises 5369 km of roadway links. The level of compliance with the motorway/expressway requirement is very high, at 88%. There are many alternative fuel refueling stations along the corridor roadways, covering the requirement for about 95% of the corridor length. Coverage of the parking availability and safety requirement is very low (7%), since, although there is an adequate number of facilities, not all of them provide the appropriate level of security.

7.3.7 Rhine–Alpine corridor

The Rhine–Alpine Corridor runs through five Member States (the Netherlands, Belgium, Germany, France and Italy) and Switzerland. It connects the North Sea ports of Belgium and the Netherlands with the Mediterranean port of Genoa. It runs through the so-called blue banana region (European Commission, 2019i). The main transport infrastructure components of the Corridor are shown in Fig. 7.11.

The Rhine–Alpine Corridor connects with the Mediterranean Corridor, the North Sea–Mediterranean Corridor, the Atlantic Corridor, the Rhine–Danube Corridor, and the North Sea–Baltic Corridor.

The Rhine–Alpine Corridor transportation infrastructure, by mode, and the level of compliance with the Regulation requirements are presented next, based on information available in the Corridor Work Plan (Wojciechowski, 2018).

7.3.7.1 Rhine–Alpine railway network

The 3,225 km of rail are the backbone of the corridor. The Rhine–Alpine rail freight corridor is one of the first European rail freight corridors to

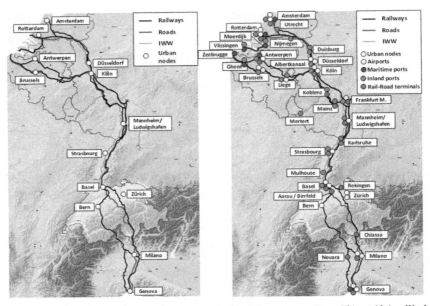

FIGURE 7.11 Rhine–Alpine corridor transportation infrastructure. *From Rhine–Alpine Work Plan of the European Coordinator.*

become operational. Most infrastructure characteristics of the Corridor are compliant with the TEN-T requirements in terms of electrification, line speed, axle load, and train length. More specifically, all sections are electrified and have the UIC standard track gauge of 1435 mm. Nevertheless, interoperability issues arise due to difference in electrification systems among participating countries. Different operation procedures in different countries, relating to the minimum train length of 740 m, present an obstacle to seamless international freight traffic flows. Individual sections of the Corridor require upgrades to improve the operational speed. In terms of ERTMS implementation, there is a gap, with only 12% of the rail sections currently being equipped.

7.3.7.2 Rhine–Alpine inland waterway network and inland ports

The corridor includes 22 inland ports and inland waterways of about 1600 km, including the Rhine River as the most important route. This part of the network complies with the Regulation requirements in terms of capacity, bridge clearance, good navigability, river information services (RIS), and intermodal connections, as well as availability of alternative fuel stations at the core ports. A compliance issue is related to the draught limitations along the Rhine in Germany and to inadequate lock capacity and mooring places at cross-border sections between the Netherlands and Germany.

7.3.7.3   Rhine−Alpine maritime infrastructure and motorways of the sea

There are eight core maritime ports along the corridor: Amsterdam, Rotterdam, Moerdijk, and Vissinger in the Netherlands and Antwerp, Ghent, and Zeebrugge in Belgium and the *port* of Genoa in Italy. These ports play a crucial role for the import of goods from outside the Corridor and serve as entry and exit points of the Corridor, connecting road, rail, and inland waterways. The maritime port infrastructure complies with almost all criteria set by the EU regulation.

7.3.7.4   Rhine−Alpine road infrastructure

The Rhine−Alpine Corridor roadway network comprises 1721 km of roads. It complies largely with the Regulation requirements, with minor exceptions. The availability of alternative fuels fueling station infrastructure is still under development in some parts, mainly in Switzerland and Italy. There is also a need for secure truck parking development, especially in border crossing sections and around important multimodal nodes and ports. A nighttime driving ban for trucks in Switzerland creates cross-border bottlenecks.

7.3.8   Rhine−Danube corridor

The Rhine−Danube corridor covers all modes of transport and provides the main east−west connection across Continental Europe. It connects nine Member States (Bulgaria, Croatia, Czech Republic, Germany, France, Hungary, Austria, Romania, Slovakia) and is divided into two main branches. The main route of the corridor follows the Danube River. It connects Strasburg and southern Germany with Central European cities (Vienna, Bratislava, Budapest), also passing through Bucharest. The second branch of the corridor crosses the city of Frankfurt to the Slovenian/Ukrainian border, connecting Munich, Prague, Zilina and Kosice (European Commission, 2019j). The main transport infrastructure components of the Corridor are shown in Fig. 7.12.

The Rhine−Danube Corridor has a number of overlapping and crossing sections with other corridors: the Orient−East Med, the Baltic−Adriatic, the Scandinavian−Mediterranean, the Rhine−Alpine and the Mediterranean Corridor.

The Corridor transportation infrastructure, by mode, and the level of compliance with the Regulation requirements are presented next, based on information available in the Corridor Work Plan (Peijs, 2018).

7.3.8.1   Rhine−Danube railway network

The Rhine−Danube corridor comprises 5,715 km or railway lines. The corridor complies largely with the Regulation's requirements. The compliance

FIGURE 7.12 Rhine Danube corridor map. *From <https://ec.europa.eu/transport/themes/ infrastructure/rhine-danube_en>.*

rate is 91% for the electrification requirement, 100% for the track gauge requirement of 1435 mm, 95% for line speed, 75% for axle load, and 47% for the train length requirement. Electrification gaps relate only to some sections in Germany and in Czech Republic. Line speed and axle load requirements are not fully met in some sections in Romania and in Hungary. Train length limitations exist mainly on the Czech–Slovak branch, in Romania, and on some sections in Austria. ERTMS compliance rate is low, at 7%.

7.3.8.2 Rhine–Danube inland waterway network and the inland ports

The corridor consists of 3650 km of inland waterways and 18 inland ports. The alignment of the inland waterways includes the Main river starting with the confluence with the Rhine, which is connected to the Danube by the Main–Danube Canal. The network complies with the *Conférence europénne des ministres des Transports* (CEMT) requirement for class IV at a rate of 85%, with the permissible draught requirement at a rate of 77%, the permissible height under bridges at a rate of 86%, RIS implementation at 95%, and targeted depth at 45%. More specifically, only the Sava River does not have a class IV waterway. Sections of the same river, as well as sections of the Upper Main and the Danube, do not meet the draught requirement. Information services are not available on the Tisza River. Inland ports have class IV waterway connection with 100% compliance rate, rail connection at 89%, availability of at least one freight terminal open to all operators in a nondiscriminatory way in all ports, and no availability of clean fuels infrastructure.

7.3.8.3 Rhine–Danube maritime infrastructure and motorways of the sea

The port of Constanta is the only seaport in the entire Rhine–Danube Core Network Corridor. The port has a key role in the development of the area, as it connects the routes of the TEN-T network to the markets of the Caucasus and Central Asia. The port is connected to rail and to inland waterways. It has at least one freight terminal open to all operators in a nondiscriminatory manner. It does not have alternative fuels refueling infrastructure.

7.3.8.4 Rhine–Danube road infrastructure

The Rhine–Danube roadway network consists of 4488 km in total. About 77% of the total length of roads is classified as motorway/expressway, while 23% comprises conventional roads. The majority of the conventional roads are in the eastern part of the corridor, in Czech Republic, Slovakia, and in Romania. Alternative fuel refueling stations are available in all Member States at different densities. There is ongoing investment on the development and provision of safe and secure parking areas for trucks.

7.3.9 Scandinavian–Mediterranean corridor

The Scandinavian–Mediterranean corridor comprises transport infrastructure in seven Member States (Finland, Sweden, Denmark, Germany, Austria, Italy, and Malta), stretching from Finland and Sweden in the North to the island of Malta in the South and taking in Denmark, Northern, Central and Southern Germany, the industrial heartlands of Northern Italy, and the southern Italian ports. The regions of this Corridor generate about 20% of the EU's gross domestic product (GDP). In terms of length, it is the largest of the corridors, with more than 9300 km of rail and more than 6300 km of roadways, also comprising 25 core ports. The main transport infrastructure components of the Corridor are shown in Fig. 7.13.

FIGURE 7.13 Scandinavian–Mediterranean corridor. *From <https://ec.europa.eu/transport/themes/infrastructure/scandinavian-mediterranean_en>.*

The Scandinavian–Mediterranean Corridor has a number of overlapping and crossing sections with other corridors, including the North Sea–Baltic, the Orient–East Med, the Rhine–Danube, and the Mediterranean Corridor.

The Corridor transportation infrastructure, by mode, and the level of compliance with the Regulation requirements are presented next, based on information available in the Corridor Work Plan (Cox, 2018).

7.3.9.1 Scandinavian–Mediterranean railway network

The Scandinavian–Mediterranean Railway network consist 9300 km of railways. With the exception of Finland, the network of which is exempt as an isolated network, the whole corridor is at a standard track gauge. Electrification is available along the entire network with the exception of some sections in Germany and one in Denmark. Interoperability constraints arise as are the result of different electrification standards. Technical characteristics that do not meet the Regulation requirements include train length in parts of Sweden and Italy and in axle load on 18% of the sections in Italy. With the exceptions of Austria and Denmark, ETRMS implementation is still rather low.

7.3.9.2 Scandinavian−Mediterranean inland waterway network and the inland ports

Inland waterways and inland ports are not part of the Scandinavian−Mediterranean Corridor.

7.3.9.3 Scandinavian−Mediterranean maritime infrastructure and ports

The Scandinavian−Mediterranean Corridor comprises 25 ports. The ports fulfill to a large extent the Regulation requirements in terms of maritime and hinterland transport infrastructure connections, with connection to rail available at 83% of the ports. All ports have at least one freight terminal open to all operators in a nondiscriminatory way. Availability of clean fuels infrastructure is limited, at a rate of 24%.

7.3.9.4 Scandinavian−Mediterranean road infrastructure

The corridor comprises 6300 km of road network. The minimum road standard requirement for expressway/motorway is met by all routes with minor exceptions in some sections in Finland, Italy, and Malta, which amount to just 1% of the total corridor. Safe parking and rest areas for trucks are available in all countries but at different densities. Alternative fuels facilities are widespread in some countries, and they practically do not exist in others.

7.4 European transportation infrastructure funding mechanisms

Article 171 of the Treaty on the Functioning of the European Union (European Union, 2012a, 2012b) stipulates that EU aid may be granted to projects of common interest that meet the requirements of the TEN-T guidelines. The general rules for the granting of Community financial aid for the Trans-European networks were presented in EC Regulation in 1995 (European Commission, 1995) and in subsequent amendments in 1999 (European Commission, 1999), 2004 (European Commission, 2004), and 2007 (European Commission, 2007).

Regulation (EC) No. 680/2007 introduced the first multiannual program for the financing period 2007−13. It presented specific requirements for future projects, which put emphasis on high-cost, complex cross-border projects with long implementation periods. Regulation (EC) No. 67/2010 defined the conditions and procedures for granting Community aid to TEN-T transport projects of common interest. Regulation EU No 913/2010 laid down the rules for the establishment and organization of international rail corridors for competitive rail freight with a view to the development of a European rail network for competitive freight. It set out the rules for the selection, organization, management, and the indicative investment planning of freight corridors.

Regulation (EU) No. 1316/2013 of the European Parliament and the Council of 21 December 2013 established the connecting Europe facility (CEF), amending Regulation EU No. 913/2010 and repealing Regulations (EC) No. 680/2007 and (EC) No. 67/2010. This Regulation determined the conditions, methods, and procedures for providing Union financial assistance to trans-European networks in order to support projects of common interest in the transport sector, along with telecommunications and energy sectors, and to exploit potential synergies among those sectors. It also established the breakdown of the resources to be made available under the multiannual financial framework for the years 2014−20.

The TEN-T Guidelines (2013) (European Union, 2013a, 2013b) and the CEF are the two main instruments through which the TEN-T policy is being implemented. The Guidelines present the objectives, priorities, and measures for the implementation of projects of common interest, while CEF is the funding instrument introduced to support TEN-T implementation.

The TEN-Ts are partly funded by the EU and partly by Member States, which are required to cover a major part of the financing. Complementary funds may be provided through the European Structural and Investment Funds, the European Fund for Strategic Investment, the European Investment Bank, and private sector contributions (European Union, 2019). The EU aims to bring together public and private sector funds for the financing of transportation infrastructure projects. Support from the CEF is concentrated on integrating transport corridors, promoting clean fuel and other innovative transport solutions, advancing telematics applications for efficient infrastructure use, integrating urban areas into the TEN-Ts, and enhancing safety (European Commission, 2019e).

7.4.1 Connecting Europe facility

The CEF program started in 2014 with the aim to provide financial support for strategic investment in transport, energy, and digital infrastructure, supporting the development of interconnected trans-European networks. In addition to grants, it offers financial support through other innovative financial instruments such as guarantees and project bonds. The total budget for CEF Transport for the period 2014−20 is €24.05 billion, including €11.3 billion that was transferred from the Cohesion Fund. Emphasis is placed on cross-border projects, bottleneck removal, and missing link development in the

Core and the comprehensive networks, as well as projects on traffic management systems. Funding by mode is shown in Fig. 7.14.

Regulation (EU) No. 1316/2013, upon which the current CEF program is based, was amended in 2017 and 2018. The 2017 amendment transferred part of the CEF's unspent budget and money from the revenue and repayments from the CEF Debt Instrument across to the European Fund for Strategic Investment (EFSI). The 2018 amendment created the option to establish CEF blending facilities (European Commission, 2019c). A provisional agreement on adapting the CEF program was reached by colegislators in March 2019; however, certain provisions, such as budget, remain open, pending decisions on the EU's overall long-term budget (European Commission, 2019c.

7.4.2 European fund for strategic investment

EFSI, also known as the Juncker Plan, was established to remedy the investment gap in Europe, which was an outcome of the recent financial crisis. It is a €21 billion guarantee program, an initiative of the European Investment Bank (EIB) and the European Commission. The program is built on a €5 billion guarantee from the EIB and a €16 billion guarantee from the EU budget. The aim was to utilize this €21 billion guarantee program (EFSI) to trigger €315 billion of additional investment by mid-2018.

The EFSI was established in 2015 through Regulation (EU) 2015/1017 of the European Parliament and of the Council of June 25, 2015 on the European Fund for Strategic Investments, the European Investment Advisory Hub, and the European Investment Project Portal and amending Regulations

FIGURE 7.14 CEF Funding by Mode (€billion). *CEF*, Connecting Europe facility. *From* <*https://ec.europa.eu/transport/themes/infrastructure/cef_en*>.

(EU) No. 1291/2013 and (EU) No. 1316/2013—the European Fund for Strategic Investments. The purpose of the EFSI is to support investments in the Union through the supply of risk-bearing capacity to the EIB. The EFSI is the core of the investment plan for Europe and aims to boost the economy by mobilizing private financing for strategic investments.

Upon its adoption in June 25, 2015, the regulation entered into force in July of the same year. In September 2016, the Council started working on amending the 2015 EFSI Regulation to extend the fund's activities and introduce technical changes. In December 2017, the Council extended the EFSI until December 2020, raised the investment target from €315 billion to €500 billion, increased the EU budget guarantee from €21 billion to €26 billion, and increased the EIB's contribution from €5 billion to €7.5 billion.

7.4.3 European structural and investment funds

The European Structural and Investment Funds include five different funds, covered by Regulation (EU) No. 1303/2013 of the European Parliament and the Council. The five funds include the European Regional Development Fund (ERDF), the European Social Fund (ESF), the Cohesion Fund (CF), the European Agricultural Fund for Rural Development (EAFRD), and the European Maritime and Fisheries Fund (EMFF). Transport is mainly covered by ERDF and CF. All ESIFs are managed by the Member States (MSs) and the Commission through Partnership Agreements.

7.4.3.1 European regional development fund

The European Regional Development Fund (ERDF) focuses investment on various key priority areas, with the aim to strengthen economic and social cohesion in the EU by correcting imbalances among its regions (European Commission, 2019d). It was developed in 1975 to assist the least developed regions, placing emphasis on infrastructure and SMEs development (Dall'Erba, 2003). ERDF funds are available to all EU regions; however, they are allocated to different regions based on their relative per capita GDP. Based on their GDP, the regions are classified in three different categories, the least developed regions with per capita GDP less than 75% of the EU 27 average GDP, transition regions (between 75% and 90% of the average), and most developed regions (higher than 90% of the average). These regions may receive cofinancing from 80% to 85% of the eligible costs for the least developed, up to 60% for the transition and up to 50% for the most developed regions. ERDF may support TEN-T projects and connections to TEN-T infrastructure, including multimodal nodes, low-carbon transport systems and interoperable railway systems. ERDF may also fund cross-border, interregional, and transnational projects (Vassalo & Garrido, 2019). The current budget for the period 2014−20 amounts to €199 billion (Sapala, 2016).

7.4.3.2   Cohesion fund

The Cohesion Fund (CF) was set up in 1994 with the aim to strengthen the economic, social, and territorial cohesion of the Union with the view to promoting sustainable development (Vassalo & Garrido, 2019). During the 2014−20 programming period, it has committed about €63.4 billion to activities related to the development of TEN-Ts and supports infrastructure projects under the CEF. The CF is aimed at Member States with gross national income per inhabitant less than 90% of the EU average and mainly concerns Bulgaria, Croatia, Cyprus, the Czech Republic, Estonia, Greece, Hungary, Latvia, Lithuania, Malta, Poland, Portugal, Romania, Slovakia, and Slovenia (European Commission, 2019b). The proposed budget for the next programming period (2021−27) is €41.3 billion. The CF will continue to support projects under the "investment for growth and jobs" goal with two specific objectives: a greener, low-carbon, and circular objective and a more connected Europe (European Parliament, 2019a).

7.4.4   Horizon 2020

Further financial support to projects implementing the TEN-T is made available through the Horizon 2020 Program, which provides funding for research and development projects with the aim of bringing research products and outcomes to the market. The Horizon 2020 program includes support for research in the field of smart, green, and integrated transport. The Transport Challenge is allocated a budget of €6.3 billion for the period 2014−20 (European Commission, 2019k).

7.5   Infrastructure connectivity with neighboring countries and key trade partners

The EU is building upon existing agreements with partner countries (e.g., partnership and cooperation agreements or association agreements as noted in Chapter 5: Trade and transportation evolution in the European Union) to develop joint bilateral action plans. A wide range of activities have been put in place that include all modes of transport. Although the activities vary depending on the country or region concerned, the main focus of the EU international transport cooperation is on extending internal market rules (European Commission, 2019f).

7.5.1   European neighborhood policy

Through its European Neighborhood Policy (ENP), the EU aims to foster stabilization, security, and prosperity with its neighboring regions, including its Southern and Eastern neighbors. The ENP was conceived after the 2004 enlargement of the EU to enhance integration with neighboring countries.

The policy was first outlined by the European Commission in March 2003. On May 2011, the Commission launched what is described as a new and ambitious European Neighborhood Policy (European Union, 2011). The EU is taking forward transport cooperation with its neighbors to the East (Eastern Partnership) and to the South (Euro-Mediterranean Partnership). The ENP countries are shown in Fig. 7.15.

In this regard, high-level agreements have been signed between the EU and six neighboring countries in the East: Armenia, Azerbaijan, Belarus, the Republic of Georgia, the Republic of Moldova, and Ukraine. The aim of this Eastern Partnership is to make border crossings more efficient and improve transport safety (European Commission, 2018).

Countries in the South covered within the ENP Euro-Mediterranean Transport Partnership include Algeria, Morocco, Egypt, Israel, Jordan,

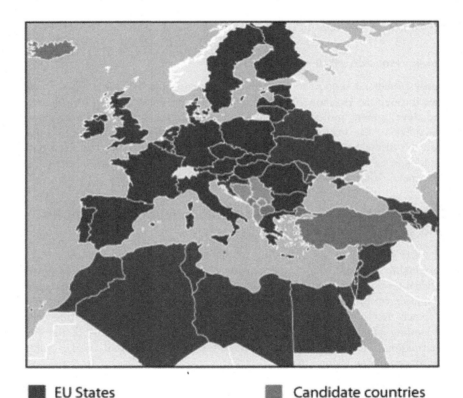

■ EU States   ■ Candidate countries

■ Potential candidate countries   ■ ENP countries

FIGURE 7.15 Immediate EU neighbors, including ENP countries. *ENP*, European Neighborhood Policy; EU, European Union. *From <https://ec.europa.eu/home-affairs/what-we-do/policies/international-affairs/european-neighbourhood-policy_en>.*

Lebanon, Libya, State of Palestine, Syria, and Tunisia. The main objective is to achieve sustainable, efficient, and safe transport in the Euro-Mediterranean area.

7.5.2   The EU–China connectivity platform

The Connectivity Platform was established in 2015 by the European Commission and the National Development and Reform Commission of China to improve transport connectivity between the EU and China. One of the main objectives of the Platform was to promote synergies between the EU's TEN-T development and China's Belt and Road Initiative and to develop a level playing field for businesses in the area of transport infrastructure development. Regular Expert Group meetings are held, during which planned transport infrastructure projects are presented by both the European and the Chinese sides, for possible cooperation.

References

Balázs, P. (2018). *North Sea—Mediterranean Third Work Plan of the European Coordinator.* European Commission—Mobility and Transport.

Bodewig, K. (2018). *Baltic Adriatic—Third Work Plan of the European Coordinator.* European Commission—Mobility and Transport.

Brinkhorst, L. (2018). *Mediterranean Third Work Plan of the European Coordinator.* European Commission.

Cox, P. (2018). *Scandinavian Mediterranean—Third Work Plan of the European Coordinator.* European Commission—Mobility and Transport.

Dall'Erba, S. (2003). European Regional Development Policies: History and current issues. In *EUC Working Paper* (Vol. 2, No. 4). University of Illinois.

European Commission. *Council Regulation (EC) No 2236/95 of 18 September 1995 laying down general rules for the granting of community financial aid in the field of Trans-European Networks.* (1995). Retrieved from <https://eur-lex.europa.eu/LexUriServ/LexUriServ.do?uri = CELEX:31995R2236:EN:HTML>.

European Commission. *Decision No 1692/96/EC of the European Parliament and of the Council of 23 July 1996 on community guidelines for the development of the Trans-European Transport Network.* (1996). Retrieved from <https://eur-lex.europa.eu/LexUriServ/LexUriServ.do?uri = CELEX:31996D1692:EN:HTML>.

European Commission. *Regulation (EC) No 1655/1999 of the European Parliament and of the Council of 19 July 1999 amending Regulation (EC) No 2236/95 laying down general rules for the granting of community financial aid in the field of Trans-European Networks.* (1999). Retrieved from <https://eur-lex.europa.eu/legal-content/GA/TXT/?uri = CELEX:31999R1655>.

European Commission. *Decision No 1346/2001/EC of the European Parliament and of the Council of 22 May 2001 amending Decision No 1692/96/EC as regards seaports, inland ports and intermodal terminals as well as project No 8 in Annex III.* (2001). Retrieved from <https://eur-lex.europa.eu/legal-content/EN/TXT/?uri = CELEX%3A32001D1346>.

European Commission. *Regulation (EC) No 807/2004 of the European Parliament and of the Council of 21 April 2004 amending Council Regulation (EC) No 2236/95 laying down general rules for the granting of community financial aid in the field of trans-European networks.* (2004). Retrieved from <https://eur-lex.europa.eu/legal-content/EN/TXT/?uri = CELEX%3A32004R0807>.

European Commission. *Regulation (EC) No 680/2007 of the European Parliament and of the Council of 20 June 2007 laying down general rules for the granting of community financial aid in the field of the trans-European transport and energy networks.* (2007). Retrieved from <https://eur-lex.europa.eu/legal-content/EN/ALL/?uri = CELEX%3A32007R0680>.

European Commission. (2011). *White Paper—Roadmap to a Single European Transport Area—Towards a competitive and resource efficient transport system.* Brussels: COM(2011) 144 final.

European Commission. *New Trans-European Network maps to improve connectivity with Eastern Partnership countries.* (2018). Retrieved from <https://ec.europa.eu/transport/themes/infrastructure/news/2018-11-09-ten-t-maps-eastern-partnership_en>.

European Commission. *Trans-European Transport Network (TEN-T).* (2019a). Retrieved from mobility and transport <https://ec.europa.eu/transport/themes/infrastructure/ten-t_en>.

European Commission. *Cohesion fund.* (2019b). Retrieved from EU regional and urban development <https://ec.europa.eu/regional_policy/en/funding/cohesion-fund/>.

European Commission. *Connecting Europe facility.* (2019c). Retrieved from mobility and transport <https://ec.europa.eu/transport/themes/infrastructure/cef_en>.

European Commission. *European Regional Development Fund.* (2019d). Retrieved from <https://ec.europa.eu/regional_policy/en/funding/erdf/>.

European Commission. *Infrastructure and Investment.* (2019e). Retrieved from mobility and transport <https://ec.europa.eu/transport/themes/infrastructure_en>.

European Commission. *International relations—External transport policy—What do we want to achieve?* (2019f). Retrieved from mobility and transport <https://ec.europa.eu/transport/themes/international_en>.

European Commission. *North Sea-Mediterranean.* (2019g). Retrieved from mobility and transport <https://ec.europa.eu/transport/themes/infrastructure/north-sea-mediterranean_en>.

European Commission. *Orient—East Med.* (2019h). Retrieved from mobility and transport <https://ec.europa.eu/transport/themes/infrastructure/orient-east-med_en>.

European Commission. *Rhine—Alpine.* (2019i). Retrieved from mobility and transport <https://ec.europa.eu/transport/themes/infrastructure/rhine-alpine_en>.

European Commission. *Rhine—Danube* (2019j). Retrieved from mobility and transport <https://ec.europa.eu/transport/themes/infrastructure/rhine-danube_en>.

European Commission. *Smart, green and integrated transport.* (2019k). Retrieved from <https://ec.europa.eu/programmes/horizon2020/en/h2020-section/smart-green-and-integrated-transport>.

European Parliament. *Cohesion fund.* (2019a). Retrieved from fact sheets on the European Union <https://www.europarl.europa.eu/factsheets/en/sheet/96/cohesion-fund>.

European Parliament *Trans-European Networks—guidelines.* (2019b). Retrieved from fact sheets on the European Union <https://www.europarl.europa.eu/factsheets/en/sheet/135/trans-european-networks-guidelines>.

European Union. *Communication from the Commission to the Council and the European Parliament the EU and its neighbouring regions: A renewed approach to transport cooperation COM/2011/0415 final.* (2011). Retrieved from <https://eur-lex.europa.eu/legal-content/EN/ALL/?uri = CELEX%3A52011DC0415>.

European Union. *Consolidated version of the treaty on functioning of the European Union C326|47.* (2012a). Retrieved from Official Journal of the European Union <https://eur-lex. europa.eu/legal-content/EN/TXT/?uri = celex%3A12012E%2FTXT>.

European Union *Consolidated version of the treaty on the functioning of the European Union.* (2012b). Retrieved from Official Journal of the European Union <https://eur-lex.europa.eu/ legal-content/EN/TXT/PDF/?uri = CELEX:12012E/TXT&from = EN>.

European Union. *Regulation (EU) No 1315/2013 of the European Parliament and of the Council of 11 December 2013 on Union guidelines for the development of the Trans-European Transport Network and repealing Decision No 661/2010/EU.* (2013a). Retrieved from <https://eur-lex.europa.eu/legal-content/EN/TXT/?uri = celex%3A32013R1315>.

European Union. *Regulation (EU) No 1316/2013 of the European Parliament and of The Council of 11 December 2013 establishing the Connecting Europe Facility, amending Regulation (EU) No 913/2010 and repealing Regulations (EC) No 680/2007 and (EC) No 67/2010).* (2013b). Retrieved from <https://eur-lex.europa.eu/legal-content/EN/TXT/? uri = CELEX%3A32013R1316>.

European Union. *European Parliament, Fact Sheets on the European Union. Financing the Trans-European Networks.* (2019). Retrieved from <http://www.europarl.europa.eu/fact-sheets/en/sheet/136/financing-the-trans-european-networks>.

Grosch, M. (2018). *Orient—East Med Third Work Plan of the European Coordinator.* European Commission—Mobility and Transport.

Peijs, K. (2018). *Rhine—Danube Third Work Plan of the European Coordinator.* European Commission—Mobility and Transport.

Radicova, I. *Mediterranean.* (2018). Retrieved from mobility and transport <https://ec.europa. eu/transport/themes/infrastructure/mediterranean_en>.

Sapala, M. (2016). *Briefing—How the EU budget is spent.* European Parliament.

Secchi, C. (2018). *Atlantic—Third Work Plan of the European Coordinator.* European Commission—Mobility and Transport. Retrieved from Europa: <https://ec.europa.eu/trans-port/themes/infrastructure/atlantic_en > (n.d.). Retrieved from Europa: <https://ec.europa. eu/transport/sites/transport/files/atlworkplaniiiweb.pdf > .

Trans-European Transport Networks. *Facts and figures.* (2019). Retrieved from <http://www. green-ten-t.eu/facts-figures/>.

Trautmann, C. (2018). *North Sea Baltic—Third Work Plan of the European Coordinator.* European Commission—Mobility and Transport.

UNECE. *About the Trans-European Motorways (TEM) Project* (2011). Retrieved from <http:// www.unece.org/trans/main/tem/tem.html>.

Vassalo, M. J., & Garrido, L. *Research for TRAN Committee—EU funding of transport projects* (2019). Directorate-general for internal policies, PE 629.199: Policy department for struc-tural and cohesion policies.

Wojciechowski, P. (2018). *Rhine—Alpine Third Work Plan of the European Coordinator.* European Commission—Mobility and Transport.

Further reading

EU. *Europa.* (2019). Retrieved from <https://ec.europa.eu/transport/themes/infrastructure_en>.

Part IV

Trade and Transportation Future Trends

Chapter 8

Future outlook

8.1 Introduction

The development of transportation infrastructure has been lagging behind that of trade. Trade flows have been growing at a very fast pace (trade grew more than five times in the 1999–2000 period, from US$3.5 trillion to US $18.2 trillion (Annual 202 Session of the Parliamentary Conference of the Two, 2012)), compared to the time it takes to develop transportation infrastructure to serve that trade (ports, railroads, roadways, warehouses, and other logistics infrastructure).

The gap between the paces of trade growth and of transportation infrastructure development is amplified by the 21st-century globalization in which emerging, disruptive technologies are revolutionizing trade. These new technologies are already transforming the typical international and domestic supply chains. Recent trade disputes and tariffs could also change trade patterns in a very short time, having important effects in the transportation infrastructure serving trade. Maritime and land ports of entry, roadway and rail infrastructure require substantial investment. These transportation infrastructure assets, key elements of international supply chains, require years to plan, finance and build, compared to the speed of the technological changes or changes in trade due to geopolitical developments. For example, at the US–Mexico border an international land port could take 15 years to develop due to the complicated binational process that requires many stakeholders from public and private sectors and two different countries to agree in funding, design, environmental standards, operations, and other factors.

The following sections present a brief description of the most recent disruptive technologies, and geopolitical developments, along with their related potential effects in transportation infrastructure development.

8.2 Disruptive technologies

The need to increase efficiencies and to remain competitive in the global environment has manufacturing, global logistics firms, carriers, and shippers, as well as government agencies searching and developing new technologies.

International Trade and Transportation Infrastructure Development.
DOI: https://doi.org/10.1016/B978-0-12-815741-1.00008-5

Some of the most recent developments in the international trade and supply chain environment are discussed in the following sections.

8.2.1 Blockchain

A *blockchain* is a digital record of transactions (a ledger) that is decentralized and distributed. Transactions are stored in a highly secure, verifiable and permanent way using various cryptographic techniques. As transactions are shared, verified, and validated on a peer-to-peer basis, blockchains can operate without the need for a central authority or trusted intermediaries. Information, once added to a blockchain, is time-stamped and cannot easily be modified. Blockchain therefore enables the creation of a shared, trusted ledger that all participants can access and check at any time, but that no single party can control (Ganne, 2019).

Given the number of stakeholders that participate in paper-intensive international trade transactions, blockchain has the potential of enhancing multiple processes that are part of the international trade supply chains, including trade finance, customs, and certification processes, insurance, merchandize distribution, logistics, and transportation. Blockchain is a tool that could make these processes more efficient, reducing costs and time.

One of the key features of blockchain that has the potential to impact international trade environment is *smart contracts*, which are computer programs that automatically enforce themselves without a participating third party. They follow a typical programing logic that, if a condition is met, then an action follows. For example, if an international shipment has reached its destination, then the instruction to transfer funds is approved by the smart contract.

Several blockchain proofs of concept are being tested in the international trade environment. One of the most advanced blockchain application is the Maersk and IBM—developed TradeLens, a trade platform for containerized shipping, connecting the entire supply chain ecosystem. It integrates trade data from industry partners onto a common, secure business network and provides real-time, secure access to end-to-end supply chain information for all actors involved in a global shipping transaction (TradeLens, 2019). As of May 2019, more than 100 organizations use TradeLens including 50 ports and terminals, logistics companies as well as railroads, trucking companies, and beneficial cargo owners. TradeLens has active pilots underway with eight customs agencies, including those in Canada, Australia, and Saudi Arabia (Dupin, 2019).

8.2.2 Internet of Things

The Internet of Things (IoT) is not a technology itself but rather a concept and is a network of connected devices embedded with sensors that capture data. The IoT system architecture enables these devices to communicate, aggregate, and analyze data to achieve specific results. IoT transforms conventional physical objects into smart ones through various sensing devices and analytic functionalities. While the enabling technologies and functionalities in IoT are not new, the architecture that connects devices and enables them to work together is. Connectivity across technologies is key to how IoT creates value.

IoT has the potential of transforming the supply chain from end to end, providing high visibility and information to make decisions during all aspects of an international trade transaction. IoT technologies allow for the better tracking and tracing of shipment as well as capturing data on the condition of the shipment. Information can be obtained from geographic positioning systems (GPS) as well as radio-frequency identification technology, determining with a higher level of accuracy the location of objects and even the state of that object in transit. The object could be a specific item in a shipment or a complete container. Some of the key variables that could be traced include, temperature, vibration, humidity, and the like, and the information can be transmitted to the cloud for real-time updates.

This advanced information results in better control of the supply chain, identifying potential issues, and minimizing losses. Detecting problems in real time allows supply chain managers more time to find solutions. Routes can be monitored and modified if needed, reducing travel time and costs. Warehousing space can be optimized because inventory can be better managed to avoid running out of stock.

8.2.3 Additive manufacturing (three-dimensional printing)

Three-dimensional (3D) printing or *additive manufacturing* can produce objects from a digital file and a printer that lays down successive layers of material until the object is complete. Each layer is a thinly sliced cross section of the actual object, and it uses less material than traditional manufacturing. Most of the materials used in 3D printing are thermoplastics (a type of plastic that becomes liquid when heated but solidify when cooled and not be weakened) (Marr, 2018).

Digital manufacturing is changing the typical manufacturing, supply chain and transportation models. 3D printing allows "on-demand" manufacturing to cut costs by significantly reducing or in some cases eliminating inventory requirements. The transportation system benefits by eliminating the need for trips to move parts from off-site or even offshore sites to manufacturers.

Manufacturers can use 3D printing to lower costs and to speed up production. Some of the key industries using 3D printing are the automotive and aerospace sectors, producing replacement machinery parts, as well as prototyping new products.

8.2.4 Automated vehicles/connected vehicles

Automated and connected vehicles (AVs and CVs) are distinct but symbiotic technologies. AV technologies represent a switch in driving responsibility from human to machine. AVs encompass a range of automated technologies from relatively simple driver assistance systems to fully autonomous or self-driving vehicles.

A *connected vehicle* has internal devices that enable it to communicate wirelessly with other vehicles, as in vehicle-to-vehicle (V2V) communication, or with an intelligent roadside unit, as in vehicle-to-infrastructure (V2I) communication. Such communications result in warnings or information for the driver of the vehicle.

AV trucks have the potential to reduce labor costs and increase efficiency. In the United States, there is a truck driver shortage that is estimated to grow in the future. A driverless truck can travel to its destination without breaks, therefore reducing operation costs and improving asset utilization. Even though autonomous trucks are not completely safe yet, several studies conclude that they will lead to a significant decrease in accidents compared to human-driven trucks (with as much as 90% decrease in traffic fatalities) (Bertoncello, 2015). Other advantage of autonomous trucks is that they can reduce traffic congestion as they can be programmed to take optimal routes.

The connected vehicle V2V and V2I interaction is based on wireless communication technologies. V2I is the wireless exchange of critical safety and operational data between vehicles and highway infrastructure, intended primarily to avoid or mitigate motor vehicle accidents but also to enable a wide range of other safety, mobility, and environmental benefits. V2I and V2V communication allows better driving safety or traffic efficiency and provide information to the driver (Péter et al., 2014). These capabilities make for a more efficient supply chain by reducing operation costs and better utilizing transportation and logistics infrastructure.

8.2.5 Ecommerce

The growth if ecommerce shipments is disrupting typical freight distribution patterns. During the 2019 Singles Day online event, Alibaba's gross merchandise volume was more than $38.3 billion. In addition to this new sales record, the total number of delivery orders also reached a new high: 1.292 billion, up 24% from 1.042 billion last year. Close to 300 brands were sold with products from many countries around the world using Alibaba's cross-border platforms (Alizila). According to a recent study, more than 100 billion packages will be sent in 2020, and that number could double by 2030 (McKinsey and Company).

The so-called Amazon effect has disrupted online and traditional retailers. Amazon and other online marketplaces now offer consumers low-cost/no-cost two-day, next-day, and even same-day delivery. Consumers now also have access to a large list of products, from appliances to books, electronic gadgets, and recently food.

Shippers and carriers, as well as other logistics companies that support these supply chains have had to rapidly adapt to serve these new demands. The implications of this strikes all aspects of the supply chain, from international shipping lines, warehouses, transportation companies, to last mile deliveries.

8.3 Impacts of disruptive technologies to trade and transportation infrastructure development

Disruptive technologies have positive and negative impacts on the trade and transportation infrastructure. On the positive side, all these technologies and the digitalization of the supply chains provide better, more reliable and detailed data for planning and operations.

Infrastructure planners now have a vast amount of information. This could be counterproductive if the infrastructure planning departments do not have the tools and systems to analyze and convert data into useful information. However, these technologies are already producing positive results. For example, some of the blockchain projects being tested could streamline operations at maritime ports by having an optimized process at ports, yards, and inspection spaces. When combined with IoT, containers at a port terminal can be easily located, and the inspection process can be more efficient and accurate. Customs inspectors could check remotely whether a container has been opened or has been subjected to temperature variations, revealing whether it has been tampered with. This could reduce or even eliminate space for container inspection.

3D printing will reduce the number of trips needed in the manufacturing industry. Some parts that currently are shipped from offshore will eventually be cost-effectively produced on-site, reducing the number of shipments and not only cutting transportation costs but also bringing other benefits like less traffic congestion and lowered greenhouse gases emissions. With 3D printing, warehousing and roadway infrastructure can be better utilized. German researchers have analyzed the impacts of 3D printing in the supply chain using a Facility Location-Allocation Model and have found that the total distance of travel and associated costs could decrease up to 30% in the factory-to-consumer trip, as well as in the trip between the raw material source and the factory (Barz et al., 2016).

The operation of CVs at land ports could increase throughput and security. CVs can communicate with customs inspectors providing information on the estimated time of arrival, exact GPS location, cargo contents, and driver identification. The customs information system could communicate back to the vehicle to move to a specific lane or inspection facility. AVs operating at land ports of entry would increase security, eliminating driver's risk and having the vehicle scanned in real time with gamma or X-ray machines.

AVs and CVs at maritime ports are already used at some terminals to handle containers inside the terminal premises. As these technologies are tested and become safer and more widely used, cargo movements can be automatized from the port to destinations in-land.

The common thread of positive impacts of disrupting technologies is that existing trade and transportation infrastructure could be utilized more efficiently. The development of new infrastructure should consider these technological developments.

- Roadways could have truck-only lanes where automated and connected commercial vehicles could drive safely on long-haul trips. Smart roadways would have the capability of communicating back to the vehicles of any incident or road conditions.
- Maritime and land ports of entry could be built with flexible layouts to accommodate smart containers and other equipment that could streamline inspection processes. AVs could transfer loads out of the port to external terminals, where land costs are lower and more available.

On the negative side of technology impacts on trade and transportation infrastructure development, the Amazon effect is impacting last mile deliveries and warehousing assets. Urban transportation infrastructure was not developed to support today's number and frequency of urban deliveries. There is no sufficient space for parking delivery trucks, creating congestion and safety hazards. The new delivery requirements require having products readily available and relatively near the customer. These require a completely different business model for the warehousing and transportation industries: more and smaller warehouses and more truck deliveries in smaller vehicles. Eventually the delivery issue would be streamlined with AVs.

8.4 Geopolitical developments

After a period of relative stability, the world is experiencing tensions that impact international trade. The US–China trade disputes, tariffs, along with modifications and renegotiation of tariffs and free trade agreements, are some of the major developments that affect international trade and transportation. The effect of these events brings distortion to existing supply chains and hence to the serving infrastructure.

Infrastructure planning and development takes years and trade patterns can change drastically due to these geopolitical events, with the related changes in global supply chains, such as oil and gas. Maritime ports and rail connection to the ports are developed based on long-term cargo volume forecasts. However, these forecasts could be impacted drastically. For example, a tariff imposed on grains and cereals could make the importer change the source of those commodities, so ports of call could change from one month to another due to the sourcing of some commodities. An example is natural gas. The US natural gas industry had a boom recently and in 2017, it became an annual net exporter for the first time since 1957. The US Energy Information Administration projected that net exports would grow to 4.6 billion cubic feet per day in 2019 (US Energy Information Administration, 2018). The impact of this shift on the infrastructure is important. Natural gas terminals were originally built to import natural gas at some locations, not to export. The Panama Canal expansion did not consider handling natural gas from the U.S. Gulf of Mexico going west, and that affects operations.

Global warming is melting ice-sheets in the Arctic, opening previously inaccessible shipping lanes. The Northern Sea Route (NSR) runs from the Barents Sea, near Russia's border with Norway, to the Bering Strait between Siberia and Alaska. Ships sailing through the NSR need the permission of Russian authorities, who collect transit fees and provide escorting ice-breakers. The NSR has been touted as a potential rival to the Suez Canal because it could dramatically slash some journey times between Asia and Europe. For example, a ship traveling from South Korea to Germany would take roughly 34 days via the Suez Canal and 23 via the NSR. However, the NSR has a short navigation season of only three to four months each year, unpredictable ice conditions, high insurance fees, costly specialized vessels, and a lack of search-and-rescue teams and support infrastructure. Some experts believe that the NSR will not become an economically feasible alternative before 2040 (L.G., 2018).

The implication of this important new potential shipping lane relates to the infrastructure that it will require to make it feasible. The new infrastructure will require special planning and maintenance given the changing weather conditions. Also important is which country will be responsible for the operation and maintenance of that infrastructure. Russia has the highest stake; however, Canada and Norway will also be impacted.

8.5 Conclusion

Disruptive technologies will not only modify current trade flow patterns, but will accelerate trade growth rate. In order to cope with these impacts, the way the transportation system is currently planned, funded, and built (hardware) and operated (software) needs to change radically.

Innovative transportation infrastructure development and operating funding sources need to be developed. Participation of private sector stakeholders is crucial, as traditional funding sources are lagging behind current needs. As previously discussed, 21st-century trade characteristics will add pressure to the transportation infrastructure, further increasing the funding gap. In the United States, a combination of state and federal excise taxes is used to sustain transportation funds. The federal gas tax, however, has not increased since 1993, and, without additional revenue, the Congressional Budget Office estimates anticipate that the Highway Trust Fund will be insolvent by 2021 (A-to-Be USA).

More agile transportation infrastructure planning development processes are required to match the pace of trade changes. At the national, regional and city levels, the transportation planning process needs to change to be able to expedite changes and the development of new transportation infrastructure. This issue is critical when binational infrastructure is developed.

At the operation level, processes need to change taking advantage of technologies to facilitate the movement of international and domestic trade. For example, new customs procedures can use electronic X-ray equipment, data sharing, and artificial intelligence to expedite trade and to maintain security and safety, reducing costs and energy consumption.

This book provides a description of how transportation infrastructure and trade interact in North America and Europe, but new technologies are changing the paradigm and we need to view the world differently, with no silos. The way transportation infrastructure is developed and operated must be transformed, so that the 21st-century economy may flourish.

References

Alizila. *News from Alibaba Group*. Retrieved from <https://www.alizila.com/alibabas-newest-11-11-gmv-record-us38-4b/>.

Annual 202 Session of the Parliamentary Conference of the Two. Back to basics: Connecting politics and trade. Geneva. (2012). Retrieved from <http://archive.ipu.org/splz-e/trade12/2-R2.pdf>.

A-to-Be USA. *America's Transportation Infrastructure: A funding crisis*. Retrieved from <https://www.prnewswire.com/news-releases/americas-transportation-infrastructure-a-funding-crisis-300940151.html>.

Barz, A., Buer, T., & Haasis, H.-D. (2016). *Quantifying the effects of and additive manufacturing on supply networks by means of a facility location-allocation model*. Retrieved from <https://link.springer.com/content/pdf/10.1007%2Fs12159-016-0140-0.pdf>.

Bertoncello, M. (2015). *Ten ways autonomous driving could redefine the automotive world*. McKinsey & Company. Retrieved from <http://www.mckinsey.com/industries/automotive-and-assembly/our-insights/ten-ways-autonomous-driving-could-redefine-the-automotive-world>.

Dupin, C. (2019). CMA CGM and MSC joining TradeLens. *American Shipper*. Retrieved from <https://www.americanshipper.com/magazine/daily/?year = 2019&month = 5&day = 28&-page_number = 2&via = asdaily>.

Ganne, E. (2019). *Can blockchain revolutionize international trade?* World Trade Organization. Retrieved from <https://www.wto.org/english/res_e/publications_e/blockchainrev18_e.html>.

L.G. (September 24, 2018). What is the Northern Sea Route? *The Economist*. Retrieved from <https://www.economist.com/the-economist-explains/2018/09/24/what-is-the-northern-sea-route>.

Marr, B. (August 22, 2018). 7 Amazing real-world examples of 3D printing. *Forbes*. Retrieved from <https://www.forbes.com/sites/bernardmarr/2018/08/22/7-amazing-real-world-examples-of-3d-printing-in-2018/#57285baa6585>.

McKinsey and Company. *The future of parcel delivery: Drones and disruption*. Retrieved from <https://www.mckinsey.com/featured-insights/the-next-normal/parcel-delivery?cid = other-eml-nxn-mip-mck&hlkid = 16cdee346fb94923aaa6aedb413ef77d&hctky = 2810470&hdpid = 1b7a 1675-65d9−476d-8095-3a21801dacd6>.

Péter, G., Zslot, Sz., & Szilárd, A. (2014). *Highly automated vehicle systems*. BME MOGI. ISBN: 978-963-313-173-2. Retrieved from <http://www.mckinsey.com/industries/automotive-and-assembly/our-insights/ten-ways-autonomous-driving-could-redefine-the-automotive-world>.

TradeLens. (2019). *The TradeLens Solution*. Retrieved from <https://www.tradelens.com/solution/>.

US Energy Information Administration. (January 25, 2018). *EIA expects 2018 and 2019 natural gas prices to remain relatively flat*.

Index

Printed in the United States
By Bookmasters